Challenge

2nd edition

> Eduardo Amos
> Elisabeth Prescher
> Ernesto Pasqualin

Richmond

Richmond

Diretoria: *Paul Berry*
Gerência editorial: *Sandra Possas*
Coordenação de edição de texto: *Gisele Aga*
Coordenação de arte: *Christiane Borin*
Coordenação de pesquisa iconográfica: *Ana Lucia Soares*
Coordenação de *bureau*: *Américo Jesus*
Coordenação de revisão: *Adriana C. Bairrada*
Gerência de produção gráfica: *André Monteiro*
Coordenação de produção gráfica: *Maria de Lourdes Rodrigues*
Gerência de produção industrial: *Wilson Aparecido Troque*

Coordenação do projeto: *Gisele Aga*

Edição de texto: *Izaura Valverde*
Preparação: *Maria Estela de Alcântara*
Revisão: *Camila Carmo da Silva, Katia Gouveia Vitale, Mariana Mininel de Almeida, Rafael Gustavo Spigel, Sheila Winckler S. da Silva, Vivian M. Viccino*
Projeto gráfico: *Raquel Buim*
Edição de arte: *Gláucia Koller*
Ilustração: *Erika Onodera, Leonardo Teixeira, Orlandeli, Zuba*
Criações: *Amanda Savoini, Gláucia Koller, Raquel Buim, Yara Campi*
Capa: *Andreza Moreira*
Pesquisa iconográfica: *Mariana Ferreira Veloso Lima*
Tratamento de imagens: *Arleth Rodrigues, Bureau São Paulo, Fabio N. Precendo, Rubens M. Rodrigues*
Cartografia: *Alessandro Passos da Costa, Anderson de Andrade Pimentel, Fernando José Ferreira*
Diagramação: *Grapho Editoração*
Pré-impressão: *Alexandre Petreca, Everton L. de Oliveira Silva, Helio P. de Souza Filho, Marcio H. Kamoto*
Impressão e acabamento: *Ricargraf*

Dados Internacionais de Catalogação na Publicação (CIP)
(Câmara Brasileira do Livro, SP, Brasil)

Amos, Eduardo
Challenge / Amos, Prescher, Pasqualin. – 2. ed. – São Paulo : Richmond Publishing, 2011.

ISBN 978-85-16-07017-5

1. Inglês (Ensino médio) I. Prescher, Elisabeth. II. Pasqualin, Ernesto. III. Título.

11-03976 CDD-420.7

Índices para catálogo sistemático:
1. Inglês : Ensino médio 420.7

ISBN 978-85-16-07017-5 (LA)
ISBN 978-85-16-07018-2 (LP)

Richmond Publishing
Editora Moderna Ltda.
Rua Padre Adelino, 758 – Belenzinho
São Paulo – SP – Brasil – CEP 03303-904
Central de atendimento ao usuário: 0800 771 8181
Fax +55 11 2790-1284
www.richmond.com.br
2014

Impresso no Brasil

Créditos das fotos:

Capa: © tan4ikk/Shutterstock; © Pincasso/Shutterstock; © Thinkstock/Getty Images; © kwest/Shutterstock; © kwest/Shutterstock; P.3: © Romulo Fialdini/Tarsila do Amaral Empreendimentos; © Carlos Luvizari/Olhar Imagem; © Everett/Keystock; © Dariush M./Shutterstock; © Yuri Arcurs/Shutterstock; © Tatik22/Shutterstock; © Bettmann/Corbis/Latinstock; © Wavebreakmedia ltd/Shutterstock; © Bonny Makarewicz/Epa/Corbis/Latinstock; © Photodisc/Getty Images; © Yuri Arcurs/Shutterstock; © Courtesy Everett Collection/Everett/Latinstock; P.16: © Micha Rosenwirth/Shutterstock; P.17: © Prism68/Shutterstock; © Victor de Schwanberg/Alamy/Other Images; P.20: © Romulo Fialdini/Tarsila do Amaral Empreendimentos; P.22: © WitthayaP/Shutterstock; P.24: © Supri Suharjoto/Shutterstock; © Jupiter Unlimited/Imageplus; P.26: © fotogiunta /Shutterstock; © SunnyS/Shutterstock; © Madlen/Shutterstock; © matin/Shutterstock; © marco mayer/Shutterstock; © Stockdisc/Getty Images; © kefiiir/Shutterstock; © Yellowj/Shutterstock; © Tatiana Popova/Shutterstock; © UniqueLight/Shutterstock; © Vinicius Tupinamba/Shutterstock; © SARYMSAKOV ANDREY/Shutterstock; © Viktar Malyshchyts/Shutterstock; © Yasonya/Shutterstock; © Viktar Malyshchyts/Shutterstock; © Viktar Malyshchyts/Shutterstock; © Leigh Prather/Shutterstock; © Yasonya/Shutterstock; © ZoneFatal/Shutterstock; © Gyorgy Barna/Shutterstock; © Argunova/Shutterstock; © Mircea BEZERGHEANU/Shutterstock; © dionisvera/Shutterstock; © Vitaly Korovin/Shutterstock; © LubaShi/Shutterstock; © Le Do/Shutterstock; © Zaneta Baranowska/Shutterstock; © optimarc/Shutterstock; © kontur-vid/Shutterstock; © Imageman/Shutterstock; © Leonid Shcheglov/Shutterstock; © Kitch Bain/Shutterstock; © zcw/Shutterstock P.31: © Ina Fassbender/Reuters/Latinstock; P.35: © Stockbroker/Glowimages; P.36: © Jupiter Unlimited/Imageplus; © EpicStock/Shutterstock; P.42: © 1000 Words/Shutterstock; © Vaclav Volrab/Shutterstock; © ekimizi/Shutterstock; © straga/Shutterstock; © Peter Wey/Shutterstock; © FWStupidio/Shutterstock; P.43: © Edson Sato/Pulsar Imagens; © Carlos Luvizari; © Carlos Luvizari/Olhar Imagem; P.47: © Jan Carroll/Alamy/Other Images; P.48: © Jan Carroll/Alamy/Other Images; P.53: © Thinkstock/Getty Images; P.57: © Nilton Fukuda/Agência Estado; P.62: © Jupiter Unlimited/Imageplus; P.66: © PhotosIndia.com LLC/Alamy/Other Images; P.69: © Reprodução/Cortesia de João Carlos Martins; P.73: © Stefano Rellandini/Reuters/Latinstock; P.78: © Marekuliasz/Shutterstock; © L.Watcharapol/Shutterstock; © Jeff Gynane/Shutterstock; © Wendy Kaveney Photography/Shutterstock; P.80: © Everett/Keystock; © London News the Illustrated – Ingram Publishing Limited 1996; © Reprodução/Louisa May Alcott Memorial Association, Massachusetts; © Pedro Lopez/CID - Biblioteca Nacional, Madrid; © Rex Features/Keystock; © Everett/Keystock; P.83: © Randy Glasbergen/Reprinted with permission from glasbergen.com; P.84: © Ivo Hugo Dohl/Agência RBS/Folhapress; P.88: © Blue Jean Images/Alamy/Other Images; P.90: © INC/Shutterstock; © Jupiter Unlimited/Imageplus; © Image Source/Getty Images; © Jupiter Unlimited/Imageplus; © Sandro Donda/Shutterstock; © Bernard Prost/StockFood Creative/Getty Images; © Theo Moye/Apex News and Pictures Agency/Alamy/Other Images; © Kavram/Shutterstock; © Ciapix/Shutterstock; P.91: © Design Pics/Diomedia; P.94: © djem/Shutterstock; © Nayashkova Olga/Shutterstock; © AGE RM/Other Images; © Basov Mikhail/Shutterstock; © Photodisc/Getty Images; © Juiceimages/Diomedia; P.97: © Deco/Alamy/Other Images; © Sebastian Kaulitzki/Shutterstock; © Argus/Shutterstock; © Jscreations/Shutterstock; P.99: © Peter Arnold/Other Images; P.101: © Reprodução/Museu Czartoryski, Polônia; P.104: © 2happy/Shutterstock; P.106: © Dariush M./Shutterstock; P.108: © Andresr/Shutterstock; © Monkey Business Images/Shutterstock; P.113: © Jupiter Unlimited/Imageplus; P.115: © AVAVA/Shutterstock; P.117: © Frank & Ernest 2010 United Media/Ipress; © Vgstudio/Shutterstock; P.132: © Thinkstock/Getty Images; P.133: © Justin Paget/Shutterstock; P.134: © Thinkstock/Getty Images; P.137: © Yuri Arcurs/Shutterstock; P.140: © Francesco Ridolfi/Shutterstock; © Alexkava/Shutterstock; P.143: © Plain Picture/Diomedia; © Hugh Threlfall/Alamy/Other Images; © Big Cheese/Diomedia; © Image Source/Getty Images; © Jupiter Unlimited/Imageplus; © Jupiter Unlimited/Imageplus; P.149: © Album/Akg-Images/Latinstock; © Reprodução P.162: © iQoncept/Shutterstock; © Johnnychaos/Shutterstock; P.163 © Peter Dazeley/Getty Images; P.168: © Tatik22/Shutterstock; © Login/Shutterstock; P.173: © Nasa; P.174: © Thinkstock/Getty Images; P.175: © Francesco Ridolfi/Shutterstock; P.182: © Bettmann/Corbis/Latinstock; P.187: © Thinkstock/Getty Images; © Edyta Pawlowska/Shutterstock; © Andrejs Pidjass/Shutterstock; © Hifashion/Shutterstock; © Fancy/Shutterstock; P.200: © Thinkstock/Getty Images; P.201: © Digital Vision/Getty Images; P.204: © Dmitriy Shironosov/Shutterstock; P.207: © Vacclav/Shutterstock; © Lightpoet/Shutterstock; P.208: © Thinkstock/Getty Images; © Thinkstock/Getty Images; © Thinkstock/Getty Images; © Thinkstock/Getty Images; © Wavebreakmedia ltd/Shutterstock; P.209: © Kurhan/Shutterstock; © Thinkstock/Getty Images; © Ben Weaver/The Image Bank/Getty Images; P.216: © Thinkstock/Getty Images; P.218: © Karen Kasmauski/Corbis/Latinstock; P.219: © Juca Martins/Olhar Imagem; © Dirk Ott/Shutterstock; P.227: © Christian Knepper/Opção Brasil Imagens; P.228: © Prism68/Shutterstock; © Masekesam/Shutterstock; P.229: © Jeff Greenberg/Alamy/Other Images; P.230: © Martha Holmes/Pix Inc./Time Life Pictures/Getty Images; P.237: © Thinkstock/Getty Images; P.239: © Italianestro/Shutterstock; © Tatniz/Shutterstock; © Yasna/Shutterstock; P.244: © Diego Azubel/Epa/Corbis/Latinstock; © Bob Daemmrich/Alamy/Other Images; © Tamas Kovacs/Epa/Corbis/Latinstock; © John Fryer/Alamy/Other Images; P.245: © Kieran McManus/Alamy/Other Images; © Bonny Makarewicz/Epa/Corbis/Latinstock; P.251: © konstantynov/Shutterstock; P.255: © Supri Suharjoto/Shutterstock; © Thinkstock/Getty Images; P.256: © Derek L. Miller/Shutterstock; © Stocksnapp/Shutterstock; © Robyn Mackenzie/Shutterstock; © Wiedzma/Shutterstock; © Yuri Arcurs/Shutterstock; © Thinkstock/Getty Images; © Anatol/Shutterstock; © Andrew Buckin/Shutterstock; © Alex Staroseltsev/Shutterstock; P.261: © D. Kusters/Shutterstock; © Artem Efimov/Shutterstock; P.264: © Thinkstock/Getty Images; P.266: © Worldpics/Shutterstock; P.268: © JustASC/Shutterstock; P.270: © Marco Simoni/Getty Images; P.271: © Photodisc/Getty Images; P.272: © Kotomiti/Shutterstock; © David Dohnal/Shutterstock; © Image Quest Marine/Alamy/Other Images; © J van der Wolf/Shutterstock; © Peter1977/Shutterstock P.275: © Roosevelt Cássio/Folhapress; P.277: © Thinkstock/Getty Images; P.280: © Thinkstock/Getty Images; P.281: © Thinkstock/Getty Images; P.286: © Soulgems/Shutterstock; © Thinkstock/Getty Images; P.292: © Yuri Arcurs/Shutterstock; P.297: © Fernanda Siwiec; © Thinkstock/Getty Images; © Thinkstock/Getty Images; © Tracy Whiteside/Shutterstock; © RoxyFer/Shutterstock; © Thinkstock/Getty Images; © Thinkstock/Getty Images; P.301: © Ryan Pyle/Corbis/Latinstock; P.302: © Eric Isselée/Shutterstock; P.305: © Iofoto/Shutterstock; P.307: © Lightpoet/Shutterstock; © suravid/Shutterstock; P.308: © Deklofenak/Shutterstock; P.312: © Courtesy Everett Collection/Everett/Latinstock; P.313: © Reprodução; P.314: © Everett Collection/Grupo Keystone; P.317: © Jonathan Lenz/Shutterstock; P.318: A40JGC; P.324: © DTO/Shutterstock; © K. Jakubowska/Shutterstock; P.328: © Reprodução; P.330: © Emiliya Docheva/Shutterstock; P.333: © Thinkstock/Getty Images; P.335: © Alexwhite/Shutterstock; P.338: © R. Gino Santa Maria/Shutterstock; P.344: © Megapress/Alamy/Other Images; © Mike Pease/ZUMA Press/Keystone; © Jeff Greenberg/Alamy/Other Images; P.346: © STILLFX/Shutterstock; P.348: © Satoshi Kawata/Osaka University/Reuters/Latinstock; P.350: © Hugo Correia/Camera Press/Other Images; P.352: © Thinkstock/Getty Images; P.358: © Heritage Images/Diomedia; © GAB Archive/Redferns/Getty Images; © Reprodução - www-irocknroll-com; P.360: © Rick Friedman/Corbis/Latinstock

SUMMARY

SUMMARY

In files 1 to 10, choose the correct alternative. If you need help, go to pages 10-11.

File 1 (To Be – Present Form)

1 It ________ summer, but it ________ hot.

a ☐ is – isn't
b ☐ am – is
c ☐ are – are

2 Paul and I ________ already late for school.

a ☐ am
b ☐ are
c ☐ is

3 His car ________ brand new.

a ☐ are
b ☐ aren't
c ☐ is

4 ________ we ready for the exam?

a ☐ Am
b ☐ Aren't
c ☐ Is

5 The doctor ________ worried because the patients ________ fine.

a ☐ isn't – are
b ☐ aren't – is
c ☐ are – aren't

6 ________ I a good student?

a ☐ Is
b ☐ Isn't
c ☐ Aren't

File 2 (To Be – Past Form)

1 Where ________ they yesterday?

a ☐ was
b ☐ wasn't
c ☐ were

2 In the fall of 1998 Mary and I ________ in Canada.

a ☐ was
b ☐ were
c ☐ are

3 My uncle ________ an architect. He ________ an engineer.

a ☐ wasn't – was
b ☐ were – was
c ☐ were not – isn't

4 ________ they at the party?

a ☐ Is
b ☐ Was
c ☐ Weren't

5 The dog ________ sick, only the cat ________.

a ☐ wasn't – was
b ☐ weren't – weren't
c ☐ aren't – was

6 Hi, kids. ________ you OK while Dad and I ________ at work?

a ☐ Were – were
b ☐ Was – wasn't
c ☐ Is – were

File 3 (There to Be – Present and Past Form)

1 **Mike:** Last night the movie was about a small city in the Midwest of the United States.
Paul: So?
Mike: _________ museums or art galleries, but this time the masked thief was there because _________ two unguarded banks.

a ☐ There is – there were
b ☐ There are – there weren't
c ☐ There weren't – there were

2 **Paul:** Two unguarded banks! _________ a masked thief in the movie you watched yesterday?
Mike: Sure! And _________ a hotel right in front of one of the banks.

a ☐ Was there – there was
b ☐ Is there – there isn't
c ☐ Was there – there were

3 **Paul:** _________ a police station?
Mike: No! And no squad car!

a ☐ Was there
b ☐ Aren't there
c ☐ Are there

4 **Paul:** Hey, let's go to Sit'n'Chat coffee shop.
Mike: Good idea! _________ a bus stop near here?

a ☐ Is there
b ☐ There is
c ☐ Aren't there

5 **Paul:** _________ one on the corner of Franklin and Madison.
Mike: Let's go!

a ☐ There was not
b ☐ There is
c ☐ There aren't

File 4 (Demonstrative Pronouns: *this, that, these, those*)

1 Take a look. _________ is my junior high school photo album.

a ☐ This
b ☐ These
c ☐ Those

2 _________ woman on the right wasn't a secretary. She was Ms. Windsor, the principal.

a ☐ That
b ☐ Those
c ☐ These

3 Look at _________ other four pictures.

a ☐ that
b ☐ these
c ☐ this

4 _________ three men were my teachers. _________ one on the left was my English teacher.

a ☐ These – This
b ☐ This – Those
c ☐ That – These

5 _________ are my parents. Mom was very happy and so was Dad.

a ☐ That
b ☐ This
c ☐ These

6 _________ little girl in the back is my sister. She was only three.

a ☐ These
b ☐ Those
c ☐ That

File 5 (Indefinite Articles: *a, an*)

1 ________ European bank is the best place to change your euros.

a ☐ An

b ☐ A

2 Troy is ________ front-desk manager and Kendra is ________ operator. They work in a hotel.

a ☐ a – an

b ☐ an – an

3 ________ human body was seen near the bridge and the police weren't there yet.

a ☐ A

b ☐ An

4 Is ________ American university in Europe or in the United States?

a ☐ an

b ☐ a

5 There was ________ job post on the internet about ________ hour ago. It was for ________ university professor. Call and see if it is OK.

a ☐ an – an – an

b ☐ a – an – a

c ☐ an – a – an

File 6 (Plural of Nouns)

1 This is my school. There are two ________.

a ☐ building

b ☐ buildings

c ☐ buildingis

2 We all have lockers and all our ________ are in ________ inside them.

a ☐ thing – box

b ☐ things – boxs

c ☐ things – boxes

3 Our ________ are excellent. Mrs. Barter teaches us how to play the ________.

a ☐ teacher – pianos

b ☐ teachers – piano

c ☐ teachers – pianoes

4 Mr. Jesterfield is the ________ and Sonia and Maggy are his ________.

a ☐ principal – secretaries

b ☐ principals – secretarys

c ☐ principal – secretares

5 The green building is where I study. There are twenty-five ________ in my classroom. Thirteen ________ and twelve ________.

a ☐ students – girls – boys

b ☐ student – girl – boy

c ☐ studentes – girls – boyes

File 7 (Genitive Case)

1 My ________ were lost. Dad was nervous because his laptop was in one of his ________. My uncle was very upset, too.

a ☐ suitcase's uncle – suitcase's brothers

b ☐ uncle suitcase's – brother suitcase's

c ☐ uncle's suitcases – brother's suitcases

2 My ________ was also very sad. She was sad and angry.

a ☐ brother's girlfriend

b ☐ brothers' girlfriends

c ☐ brothers's girlfriends

3 ________ was in the bag. She was sad because it was a gift from grandma.

a ☐ Dad' shoes

b ☐ Mom's necklace

c ☐ My brother's glasses

4 We lost our bags at JFK airport. My ________ were big and red, while my ________ was small and grey.

a ☐ parents' bags – sister's bag

b ☐ parents's bag – sisters's bag

c ☐ parents' bags – sister' bags

File 8 (Interrogative Words)

1 Can you tell me ________ the subway station is, please?

a ☐ which

b ☐ when

c ☐ where

2 ________ car is that one in front of the library?

a ☐ Whose

b ☐ Who's

c ☐ Who

3 Amanda is an art collector. ________ isn't she here for the auction?

a ☐ Why

b ☐ When

c ☐ Where

4 ________ are the sandwich and the fruit salad?

a ☐ How much

b ☐ How many

c ☐ What

5 ________ times do I have to repeat this order?

a ☐ How much

b ☐ How long

c ☐ How many

6 ________ one do you prefer? The green jacket or the blue one?

a ☐ Whose

b ☐ Who

c ☐ Which

File 9 (Personal Pronouns: Subject)

1 **Ann:** What is Sally doing?
David: _________ don't know what _________ is doing.

a ☐ She – you
b ☐ I – he
c ☐ I – she

2 **Ann:** Who was looking for me?
David: Cindy and I were.
Ann: Who was?
David: _________ were! Cindy and I were looking for you.

a ☐ They
b ☐ We
c ☐ You

3 **Ann:** Ask Sally where Tom is.
David: _________ doesn't know where _________ is.

a ☐ She – he
b ☐ He – she
c ☐ You – I

4 **Ann:** Where are the kids?
David: _________ are in the yard playing with Tom.
Ann: Oh, Tom is there, too!
David: Yes, _________ is.

a ☐ He – we
b ☐ They – he
c ☐ They – we

File 10 (Modal Verb: Can)

1 What can I _________ to protect myself from catching influenza A (H1N1)?

a ☐ say
b ☐ see
c ☐ do

2 You can _________ a mask when in close contact with the ill person.

a ☐ wear
b ☐ do
c ☐ say

3 You can rest and _________ plenty of fluids.

a ☐ take
b ☐ watch
c ☐ swim

4 **Patrick:** Can I _________?
Rose: If you have symptoms of influenza, you should not travel.

a ☐ study
b ☐ travel
c ☐ eat

5 You can _________ at home and keep away from work, school, or crowds.

a ☐ drink
b ☐ clean
c ☐ stay

File 1 – To Be (ser, estar) – Present Form

Afirmativa	Negativa	Interrogativa
I **am** (I**'m**)	I **am not** (I**'m not**)	**Am** I?
You **are** (You**'re**)	You **are not** (You **aren't**)	**Are** you?
He **is** (He**'s**)	He **is not** (He **isn't**)	**Is** he?
She **is** (She**'s**)	She **is not** (She **isn't**)	**Is** she?
It **is** (It**'s**)	It **is not** (It **isn't**)	**Is** it?
We **are** (We**'re**)	We **are not** (We **aren't**)	**Are** we?
You **are** (You**'re**)	You **are not** (You **aren't**)	**Are** you?
They **are** (They**'re**)	They **are not** (They **aren't**)	**Are** they?
I **am** a student.	She **is not** a teacher.	**Are** they here?

File 2 – To Be (ser, estar) – Past Form

Afirmativa	Negativa	Interrogativa
I **was**	I **was not** (I **wasn't**)	**Was** I?
You **were**	You **were not** (You **weren't**)	**Were** you?
He **was**	He **was not** (He **wasn't**)	**Was** he?
She **was**	She **was not** (She **wasn't**)	**Was** she?
It **was**	It **was not** (It **wasn't**)	**Was** it?
We **were**	We **were not** (We **weren't**)	**Were** we?
You **were**	You **were not** (You **weren't**)	**Were** you?
They **were**	They **were not** (They **weren't**)	**Were** they?
I **was** a student.	She **was not** a teacher.	**Were** they here?

File 3 – There to Be (haver, existir) – Present and Past Forms

Presente	Passado
› **There is** (há, existe) – **There is** a dog in the backyard. › **There are** (há, existem) – **There are** dogs in the backyard.	› **There was** (havia, existia) – **There was** a notebook here. › **There were** (havia, existiam) – **There were** notebooks here.

File 4 – Demonstrative Pronouns

Singular	Plural
› **This** (este, esta, isto) – **This** is my car.	› **These** (estes, estas) – **These** are my books.
› **That** (aquele, aquela, aquilo) – **That** is my father.	› **Those** (aqueles, aquelas) – **Those** are my sisters.

File 5 – Indefinite Articles

a (um, uma) – usado antes de palavras no singular iniciadas por:
- consoantes: **a** cat, **a** girl, **a** bus
- **h** aspirado: **a** horse, **a** house, **a** huge park
- som de **y** e **w**: **a** European, **a** uniform, **a** week, **a** year, **a** university

an (um, uma) – usado antes de palavras no singular iniciadas por:
- vogais: **an** egg, **an** eraser, **an** ugly picture
- **h** mudo: **an** hour, **an** honest person, **an** heir

Obs.: **a**/**an** não são usados antes de substantivos incontáveis: *some* bread, *some* coffee.

File 6

Plural of Nouns

Regra geral	Particularidades
O plural em inglês é formado acrescentando-se **s** ao substantivo. chair – chair**s** girl – girl**s**	› Substantivos terminados em **s, sh, ch, x, z** e **o** recebem **es** para formar o plural. kiss – kiss**es** peach – peach**es** topaz – topaz**es** brush – brush**es** fox – fox**es** potato – potato**es** › Substantivos terminados em **y** precedido de consoante fazem o plural com a substituição do **y** por **i** e o acréscimo de **es**. baby – bab**ies** / lady – lad**ies** / city – cit**ies**

File 7

Genitive Case

O **genitive case** é indicado por **'s** ou **'**, que se acrescenta ao substantivo para indicar posse.

› **'s** é usado quando o substantivo não termina em **s**: the man**'s** hat.

› **'** é usado quando o substantivo termina em **s**: the girls**'** dresses.

O **genitive case** geralmente é usado para pessoas ou animais.

File 8

Interrogative Words

› **What*** (O que, O qual) **What** do you need?	› **Why** (Por que) **Why** are they here?	› **Who*** (Quem) **Who** did you call?
› **Which**** (Que, Qual – usado para indicar uma escolha específica) **Which** color do you prefer?	› **When** (Quando) **When** did she arrive?	› **How** (Como) **How** are you?
› **Where** (Onde) **Where** do you live?	› **Whose** (De quem) **Whose** book is this?	› **How much/many** (Quanto/Quantos) **How much** is this book? **How many** girls are there?

*Quando a pergunta for sobre o sujeito do verbo, não se usa verbo auxiliar:

› **What** caused the accident? **Who** saw you?

**Usado em perguntas nas quais há um número fixo ou limitado de respostas ou possibilidades:

› **Which** bus do you take to school? / **Which** is more important: money or character?

File 9

Personal Pronouns: Subject

Os pronomes pessoais são usados como sujeito da oração.

I (Eu)	**I** am sorry.	It (Ele, Ela)	**It** runs fast.
You (Tu, Você)	**You** look tired.	We (Nós)	**We** like coffee.
He (Ele)	**He** dances well.	You (Vós, Vocês)	Kids, **you** are late.
She (Ela)	**She** loves me.	They (Eles, Elas)	**They** are at school.

File 10

Modal Verb: Can (poder)

Afirmativa	Negativa	Interrogativa
I **can**	I **cannot (can't)**	**Can** I?
You **can**	You **cannot**	**Can** you?
He **can**	He **cannot**	**Can** he?
She **can**	She **cannot**	**Can** she?
It **can**	It **cannot**	**Can** it?
We **can**	We **cannot**	**Can** we?
You **can**	You **cannot**	**Can** you?
They **can**	They **cannot**	**Can** they?

Can geralmente é seguido por um verbo no infinitivo, sem **to**:

› I **can** work. He **can** travel. They **can** stay here.

1 Recycling

Language in Context

A Complete the information. Then, read the cartoon and check your answers. 2

1 Number of people

____

2 Kids' names

____

3 Subject

____

B Give your opinion.

1 Why is the father proud of Tim?

2 Why does the mother sound surprised?

C Think about it. Read the sentences below and answer the questions.

Now, I'm making posters.
Alex is working on a recycling project.
We're collecting things for the campaign.

1 What do the sentences have in common?

2 Is it possible to know when the actions happen?

Vocabulary

proud: orgulhoso
recycling: reciclagem
What's going on?: O que está acontecendo?

Language Practice

Present Continuous

Presente do verbo **to be** + verbo terminado em **ing**		
I **am** You **are** He **is** She **is** It **is** We **are** You **are** They **are**	work**ing**.	**Afirmativa:** He **is working**. **Interrogativa: Is** he **working**? **Negativa:** He **is not working**. **Formas abreviadas: isn't** (is not) **aren't** (are not)

Uso

Expressa ações que estão ocorrendo na atualidade.

I **am working** on a project.

Expressa ações que estão ocorrendo no exato momento em que se fala. Pode ser usado com: **now, at this moment, at present** (*time adverbs*).

He **is making** posters **now**.

Pode expressar ações futuras. Geralmente usado com: **next week, tomorrow,** etc.

I **am going** to Maceió **next weekend**.

Ortografia

Alguns verbos não sofrem modificações ao receber a terminação **ing**.

try – try**ing** ski – ski**ing** agree – agree**ing**

Verbos terminados em um único **e** perdem o **e** ao receber **ing**.

love – lov**ing** have – hav**ing** Exceto: be – be**ing**

Verbos terminados em **ie** mudam o **ie** para **y** ao receber a terminação **ing**.

die – d**ying** tie – t**ying** lie – l**ying**

Se os verbos terminam em **consoante** + **vogal** + **consoante,** dobra-se a última consoante e acrescenta-se **ing** se a última sílaba for tônica.

swim – swim**ming** run – run**ning** begin – begin**ning**

A Write the verbs in the Present Continuous.

1 practice – He ~~he practice~~ he practice.
2 write – They They write.
3 do – You you do.
4 try – We We Try.
5 run – She She run.
6 swim – It It Swim.

B Underline the correct alternative.

1 The children (is have – are having) breakfast now.
2 We (are not studying – are studing) Portuguese at this moment.
3 I (are writing – am writing) a letter.
4 Jennifer (is try – is trying) to help you.
5 My sister (is running – is run) in the park.

C Complete the sentences with the correct form of the verb in parentheses.

1 Julie washing (wash) her hair now. She can't answer the phone.
2 I Begining (begin) a new course in March.
3 My friends Sking (ski) down the mountain.
4 We Tring (try) to help you.
5 Dad Working (work) in his office at this moment.

D Answer the questions. Give complete answers. Use the words in parentheses.

1 A: What are you doing now? (write)
B: Write Now

2 A: What are your friends studying now? (English)
B: English Now.

3 A: What is the teacher correcting? (an exercise)
B: What an exercise

4 A: Who is talking on the telephone? (Peter and Jim)
B: Who Peter and Jim

E **Unscramble the sentences.**

Example: crying – is – he

He is crying.

1 working – computer – is – my – not – at the moment

My computer is not working at the moment

2 cleaning – I – the – am – garage

I am cleaning the garage

3 not – they – visiting – are – Gisele – the – in – afternoon

Gisele is visiting are not afternoon

F **Answer the questions. Give complete answers.**

1 A: Is Peter lying to his father?

B: No, peter not lying to his father.

2 A: Are the girls helping their mother?

B: Yes, There isn't girls helping their mother.

3 A: Is he trying to make breakfast?

B: Yes, he trying to make breakfast.

4 A: Are we going to the movies tonight?

B: No, we not going to the movies tonight.

5 A: Is the man swimming in the river?

B: Yes, man swimming in the river.

6 A: Are the boys running?

B: No, the not boys running.

7 A: Are you starting the Math test?

B: Yes, you starting the math test.

8 A: Are they making a poster?

B: No, Are not they making a poster.

Go to page 32 for Extra Practice.

READING

Before Reading

Approaching the text

Discuss the questions below in Portuguese.

1 Do you know the 3 Rs (reduce, reuse, recycle)?

2 Do you recycle?

3 How many trees can we save if we recycle 1 ton of paper?

Vocabulary

A Find the meaning of the words below. Use the words in the boxes.

apresentar | ameaça | lixo | aumentar | embalagem | quantidade

1 increase ____________

2 pose ____________

3 packaging ____________

4 waste ____________

5 amount ____________

6 threat ____________

B Write the meaning of the words below. Use the glossary.

1 garbage ____________

2 caution ____________

3 change ____________

4 reuse ____________

5 cut down ____________

6 compost ____________

RECYCLING

3

The amount of garbage around the world is increasing dramatically. New packaging materials, lifestyle changes, and increasing population are some of the reasons. [...]

"The waste problem, in all types and forms, is definitely posing a serious threat to the environment," cautions Al Marashi [from the Emirates Environmental Group]. "Continuous dumping of waste in landfills is threatening our water tables, while more and more waste materials are finding their way into the sea and other water bodies," she says. [...]

"The only answer to the problem is to reduce, reuse, and recycle," says Al Marashi.

Extracted from <http://archive.gulfnews.com>.
Accessed on October 16, 2010.

% of Municipal waste recycled and composted EU10 (2007)

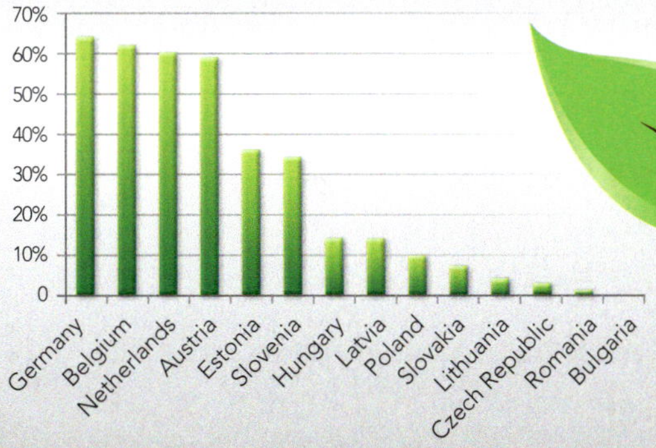

Source: Eurostat 2009. Extracted from <www.bankwatch.org>.
Accessed on October 17, 2010.

"We also encourage customers to reuse shopping bags," says a senior spokesperson from Spinneys.
Extracted from <http://archive.gulfnews.com>.
Accessed on August 16, 2009.

The UK government is trying to encourage more people to recycle their waste and reduce the UK's waste mountain.
Extracted from <http://news.bbc.co.uk>. Accessed on October 16, 2010.

Singapore, for example, which buys its water from Malaysia, is beginning to recycle water [...]
Extracted from <www.peopleandplanet.net>.
Accessed on October 16, 2010.

Recycling tops the list as the number one eco-action Canadians are taking [...]
Extracted from <www.greenlivingonline.com>.
Accessed on August 16, 2009.

After Reading

A Take a look at the first three paragraphs. Find cognates.

____

____

> **Cognatos**
> São as palavras em inglês parecidas em grafia e significado com suas correspondentes em português.
> *recycle, reduce*

B Match the columns.

1 reduce
2 reuse
3 recycle

a ( ) to turn used objects and materials into something new
b ( ) to cut down on the waste that we produce
c ( ) to find ways of using our unwanted items over again

C Write the meaning of the words in bold. Use the words in the boxes.

lençóis freáticos | clientes | reduzir | reservatórios | encabeça | aterros

1 **Landfills** are threatening our **water tables.** ______________________________

2 Waste materials are finding their way into the sea and other **water bodies.** ____________

3 The only answer to the problem is to **reduce** the use. ______________________________

4 We encourage **customers** to reuse shopping bags. ______________________________

5 Recycling **tops** the list as the number one eco-action Canadians are taking. ____________

D Check the correct information according to the graph on page 17.

1 The country that recycles and composts the most is ________.

a ( ) Germany
b ( ) Bulgaria
c ( ) Estonia

2 ________ and ________ recycle and compost the same quantity of waste.

a ( ) Lithuania – Romania
b ( ) Hungary – Latvia
c ( ) Austria – Belgium

3 More than 60% of waste is recycled and composted in ________.

a ( ) the Netherlands and Austria
b ( ) Belgium and the Netherlands
c ( ) Germany and Belgium

VOCABULARY EXPANSION

A Read the box and write new words.

1 to think ______

2 definition ______

3 to consider ______

4 construction ______

5 to organize ______

6 to create ______

Prefix re

O prefixo **re** é acrescentado a verbos e substantivos. Indica repetição.

B Rewrite the sentences. Add a prefix to replace the words in bold.

1 We are **starting** this lesson again.

______

2 I am not **constructing** the dog house again.

______

3 Are they **writing** the letter again?

______

4 They are **organizing** the groups again.

______

5 My company is **making** that old film again.

______

6 The festival is **creating** a 1960's atmosphere again.

______

C Match the columns.

1	Belgium	a ( )	Dutch
2	The Netherlands	b ( )	Czech
3	Poland	c ( )	Polish
4	Czech Republic	d ( )	German
5	Germany	e ( )	Belgian

D Read the box and complete the sentences.

about: sobre, a respeito de
around: ao redor
in: em, dentro de
on: sobre, em cima de

1 The boys are playing ______________ their mother's bed.

2 My dog is running ______________ the house.

3 Bob and Alice are playing ______________ the living room.

4 Billy is learning ______________ garbage and its impact ______________ our health.

5 The teachers are talking ______________ the new students.

Language in Use

A Read about the painting below. Then match the columns and talk to a classmate.

AMARAL, Tarsila do (1886-1973) – *Brazilian painter, sculptor, and art critic born in São Paulo [...]. She is regarded as one of the major figures in 20th-century Brazilian art, the creator of a style that combined nationalism with modernism. [...]*

Tarsila do Amaral. *A Família.* 79 cm x 101,5 cm, 1925.

The painting ***A Família*** shows a family with twelve people. There are five children, seven adults, a dog, and a cat. They may be poor because they are wearing no shoes. They don't look happy. One of the boys is playing with the cat. One of the girls is holding a doll. There are no other toys.

A mother is breastfeeding her baby. They are wearing white, pink, blue, and yellow clothes.

Extracted from <www.encyclopedia.com>. Accessed on August 11, 2009.

A	B
What	there to be
Who	smoke a pipe
How many	wear
	hold a stick

A: How many people are there?
B: There are twelve.
A: What is the mother wearing?
B: She's wearing a pink dress.

B NOW IT'S YOUR TURN!

Ask a classmate about his/her family. Look at the examples.

Where is your... now?
What is your... doing now?

WRITING

Write a paragraph describing your classroom and your classmates to a friend living abroad.

2 Healthy Colors

Language in Context

A Complete the information. Then, read the dialogue and check the answers.

4

1 Number of people: ____________

2 Gloria will probably get the job as a: ________________________________

Mr. Robins: What's your name, please?
Gloria: Gloria Elliot.
Mr. Robins: What do you do in the morning?
Gloria: I go to school.
Mr. Robins: Do you have the afternoons free?
Gloria: Yes, I do.
Mr. Robins: We have two afternoon positions: salad assistant and dish washer.
Gloria: I love salad!
Mr. Robins: What do you know about salad?
Gloria: A good salad is fresh and colorful.

B Give your opinion.

Do you think Gloria will get the job? Why/Why not?

Vocabulary
assistant: assistente
dish washer: lavador de pratos

C Think about it. Compare the sentences below with the ones in Mr. Robins's notebook and answer the questions.

I go to school in the morning.
I have the afternoons free.
I love salads.

1 What do the sentences in the notebook have in common?
2 What is the difference between the two groups of sentences?

Language Practice

Simple Present

Infinitivo sem **to** 3ª pessoa do singular recebe **s**	
I walk. You walk. He walk**s**. She walk**s**. It walk**s**. We walk. You walk. They walk.	I walk in the morning. He walk**s** in the morning. They walk in the morning.

Uso

Pode expressar verdades universais e ações futuras planejadas.

Dogs **bark.** Wood **floats.** Your bus **comes** at 4:15.

Expressa ações habituais ou que se repetem no presente.

Geralmente usado com **always, often, usually, frequently, sometimes, never, seldom, every day, on Mondays,** etc.

I always **arrive early.**

He **comes** home late **every day.**

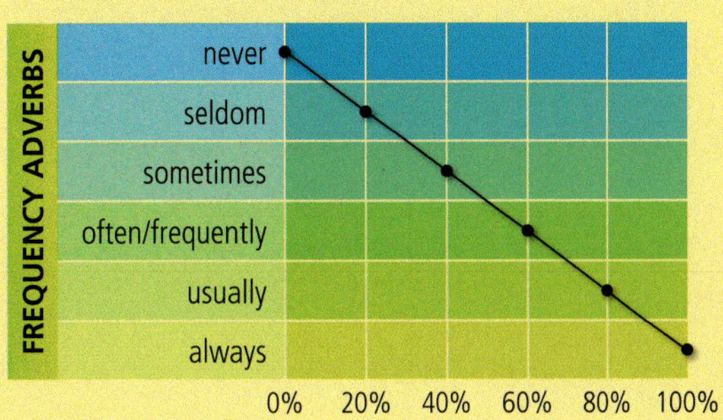

Ortografia

A maioria dos verbos forma a 3ª pessoa do singular com o acréscimo de **s**.

work – work**s** live – live**s** play – play**s**

Se o verbo termina em **ss, sh, ch, x, z** ou **o**, acrescenta-se **es**.

kiss – kiss**es** teach – teach**es** buzz – buzz**es**

wash – wash**es** fix – fix**es** do – do**es**

Se o verbo termina em **y** precedido de **consoante**, troca-se o **y** por **ies**.

try – tr**ies** study – stud**ies** hurry – hurr**ies**

A 3ª pessoa do singular do verbo **have** é **has**.

Verbos auxiliares

Do/Does		
Afirmativa:	You work.	He work**s**.
Interrogativa:	**Do** you work?	**Does** he work?
Negativa:	You **do not** work.	He **does not** work.
Formas abreviadas:	**don't** (do not)	**doesn't** (does not)

Nota

> **Do** e **does** não têm tradução quando possuem a função de auxiliares.

A Underline the verbs in the 3rd person singular.

I work in a bank and my friend John works there, too. I walk to work, but John goes by bus. We sometimes meet at the cafeteria and have a coffee together. After work, I go to night school and I study until late. John has more fun. He plays football with his friends or goes to the disco. But I want a better job, so while he plays, I learn.

B Underline the correct verb form.

1 They (speak – speaks) English fluently.

2 Do you (do – does) voluntary work?

3 Charles doesn't (know – knows) how to use the computer.

4 My friends (live – lives) in Dublin.

5 He (is – are) a doctor and (work – works) in a large hospital.

6 My brother (don't like – doesn't like) his job.

C Write the Simple Present of the verbs in parentheses.

1 My sister ______________________________ (hurry) to school every morning.

2 Janet ______________________________ (work) from 8:00 a.m. to 6:00 p.m.

3 In her free time she ______________________________ (play) rugby.

4 I often ______________________________ (have) to work on Saturdays.

5 What do you ______________________________ (do) in the morning?

6 We ______________________________ (wash – neg.) our dog every week.

D Complete the sentences.

Example: (apples/pears) He doesn't like apples. He likes pears.

1 (morning/afternoon)

They don't swim in the morning. They ______________________________.

2 (Chemistry/Physics)

She doesn't study Chemistry. She ______________________________.

3 (pub/restaurant)

We don't work in a pub. We ______________________________.

4 (French/English)

I ______________________________. I speak English.

5 (meat/sardines)

My cat ______________________________. It eats sardines.

E Check the correct questions.

1 Jimmy reads books after school.

a ☐ When does Jimmy read books?

b ☐ What does he read?

2 Yes, I do. I use the computer every day.

a ☐ What do you do every day?

b ☐ Do you use the computer every day?

3 Denise works at the hospital.

a ☐ When does she work at the hospital?

b ☐ Where does she work?

4 We go to school in the morning.

a ☐ Where do you go in the morning?

b ☐ Do you go to school in the morning?

5 No, he doesn't. He doesn't have coffee in the morning.

a ☐ Does he have coffee in the morning?

b ☐ When does he have coffee?

6 I live in Italy.

a ☐ Where do you live?

b ☐ Do you live in Italy?

Go to page 32 for Extra Practice.

Reading

Before Reading

Approaching the text

Number the words below. Use 1 for fruits, 2 for vegetables, and 3 for grains. Look at the glossary if necessary.

☐ corn	☐ banana	☐ carrot
☐ grapes	☐ beans	☐ lettuce
☐ broccoli	☐ tomato	☐ rice

Vocabulary

A Look at the text. Find the meaning of the food items below.

1 strawberry ____________ 3 cauliflower ____________

2 carrot ____________ 4 beet ____________

B Give the meaning of the words below. Use the glossary.

1 bone ____________ 4 heart ____________

2 muscle ____________ 5 bowel ____________

3 blood ____________

5 HEALTHY FOOD

Some people classify food according to the food pyramid: fats, sugars, proteins, fibers, and grains. Others classify them according to food types: fruit, meat, fish, and vegetables. Modern dieticians go back to the teachings of our great-grandmothers and say that food has to be colorful.

The color of food is determined by pigments. Pigments not only color fruit, vegetables, and other foods, but also protect our organism against diseases.

PURPLE FOOD

- Contains anthocyanin.
- Delays aging.

RED FOOD

- Contains lycopene, a potent antioxidant.
- Protects against some types of cancer.
- Stimulates blood circulation.

WHITE FOOD

- Contains calcium and potassium.
- Helps in the formation and maintenance of bones.
- Is basic for the functioning of nerves and muscles.

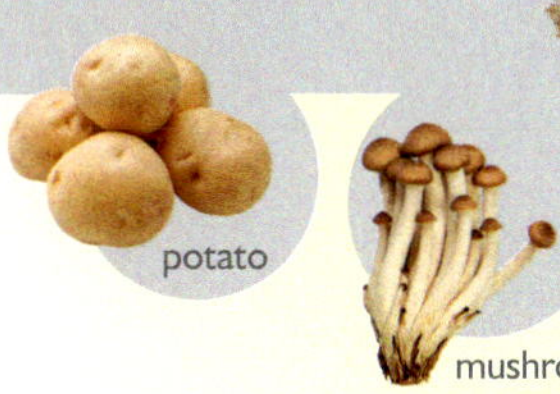

GREEN FOOD

- Contains chlorophyll and vitamin A.
- Detoxes cells.
- Inhibits free radicals.

BROWN FOOD

- Contains vitamins B and E.
- Prevents anxiety and depression.
- Reduces the risk of cancer and cardiovascular diseases.
- Provides for better bowel functioning.

ORANGE/ YELLOW FOOD

- Contains vitamin B3, vitamin C, and beta-carotene.
- Protects the heart, the eyes, and the nervous system.
- Reduces the risk of cancer.

Based on <www.ific.org>; <www.howdoesitfeel.com>; <www.arthritistoday.org>; <www.sciencenewsforkids.org>. Accessed on August 24, 2009.

Vocabulary

delay: retardar
detox: desintoxicar
functioning: funcionamento
inhibit: inibir
maintenance: manutenção
provide: proporcionar

After Reading

A **Read the magazine article on the previous page and find seven cognates.**

____

____

B **Match the words in the boxes with their equivalents in bold.**

envelhecimento | doenças | colorida | previne

1 Dieticians say that food has to be **colorful**. ____________

2 Pigments protect our organism against **diseases**. ____________

3 Purple food delays **aging**. ____________

4 Brown food **prevents** anxiety and depression. ____________

C **Read the text and complete the sentences. Look at the example.**

Example: White food helps the functioning of muscles.

1 ____________ inhibits free radicals.

2 ____________ stimulates blood circulation.

3 ____________ delays aging.

4 ____________ protects the heart, the eyes, and the nervous system.

5 ____________ reduces the risk of cardiovascular diseases.

D **Answer the questions according to the magazine article.**

1 A: What is lycopene?

B: ____________

2 A: Does white food contain lycopene?

B: ____________

3 A: What does orange/yellow food contain?

B: ____________

4 A: What types of food reduce the risk of cancer?

B: ____________

5 A: What type of food delay aging?

B: ____________

Vocabulary Expansion

A Read the information in the box and write new words.

Example: color colorful

1 peace ____________________

2 care ____________________

3 success ____________________

4 hope ____________________

5 help ____________________

6 power ____________________

7 beauty ____________________

Suffix ful

O sufixo **ful** é acrescentado a substantivos. Significa "cheio de".

B Use the new words in exercise A to complete the sentences.

1 Our neighborhood is ____________________.

2 That ball is ____________________.

3 He is a ____________________ person.

4 The teacher always says ____________________ words.

5 He is a ____________________ man.

6 Our country is ____________________.

7 This is glass. Be ____________________.

8 The surgeon is ____________________ of saving her eyes.

C Fill in the blanks with the prepositions from the box.

1 She is Italian. She is ____________ Rome.

2 Don't fight ____________ your destiny!

3 This type ____________ fruit is purple.

4 They go ____________ Santos to São Paulo every day.

5 This is important for the functioning ____________ the heart.

6 You can lean your bicycle ____________ that wall.

7 She married a dentist who comes ____________ London.

8 He's ____________ all forms of prejudice.

against: contra
from: de (origem)
of: de (posse, parte)

D Read the information in the box and complete the sentences.

Phrasal Verb	To go
Um **phrasal verb** é um verbo acrescido de uma partícula que lhe dá um significado diferente do seu significado original.	**go back** – return (voltar) **go by** – pass (passar – tempo) **go in** – enter (entrar) **go out** – leave (sair)

1 My grandma is 78 and still ______________________ a lot.

2 Mom asked the children to ______________________ the house because of the rain.

3 It's late. I have to ______________________ home.

4 A vacation always ______________________ quickly.

E Find opposites for the words in bold.

attack: atacar
careless: descuidado(a)
cause: causar
increase: aumentar
old-fashioned: antiquado

1 Brown food **reduces** the risk of cancer.

a ☐ equals
b ☐ increases
c ☐ diminishes

2 **Modern** dieticians know that food has to be colorful.

a ☐ recent
b ☐ fresh
c ☐ old-fashioned

3 Vegetables, fruits, and other foods **protect** our organism against diseases.

a ☐ look after
b ☐ take care
c ☐ attack

4 This procedure **prevents** risks.

a ☐ blocks
b ☐ causes
c ☐ stops

5 You must be **careful** with your health.

a ☐ careless
b ☐ carefully
c ☐ prudent

Language in Use

A **Read about Jade Barbosa. Then match the columns and talk to a classmate. See the examples.**

A BRAZILIAN PRECIOUS STONE

Jade Barbosa is one of the top Brazilian Olympic gymnasts. She lives in Curitiba. She rarely wakes up after 7 a.m. She always starts training at 8 a.m. She stops training at midday. Sometimes she has a typical Brazilian lunch: rice, beans, meat, and salad in moderate quantities. She goes to school at 1:15 p.m. Between 4:30 p.m. and 7 p.m. Jade works on her exercises. Then she goes home. Jade watches TV, takes a shower, and after dinner she chats with her friends on the internet. She usually goes to bed at 10 p.m. Sometimes she works in advertising campaigns.

Based on *Revista Varig – Revista de Bordo* (Issue 298, October 3, 2008, p. 42).

A	B
What time	have a typical Brazilian lunch
How often	live
Where	wake up
What	do in the morning
	go to school

A: What time does she wake up?
B: She rarely wakes up after 7 a.m.
A: How often does she have a typical Brazilian lunch?
B: Sometimes.

B **NOW IT'S YOUR TURN!**

Ask a classmate about his/her routine. Look at the example.

What time do you wake up?

Writing

In your notebook, write a short text about your classmate for the school magazine.

EXTRA PRACTICE 1

A **Answer the questions to describe the scene below.**

1 What are Gary and Janet doing?

____

2 What's Susan washing?

____

3 Who's making posters?

____

4 Where's Carla writing letters?

____

sweep the floor: varrer o chão
wash: lavar

B **Ask questions about the expressions in bold. Use the box for help.**

1 The baby is crying **at the entrance door**.

____

2 The dog is **running after** the cat.

____

3 Stella is eating **a sandwich**.

____

cry: chorar
eat: comer
run after: correr atrás de

C Complete the text. Use the verbs in parentheses in the Present Continuous.

From the top of the hill I can see the village in the valley: the houses, the streets, the school, everything. The children ____________________ (play) in the school yard.

Mr. Gardner ____________________ (to talk) to a friend. Some ladies ____________________ (walk) to the church. Some people ____________________ (run) around the lake.

The Taylors ____________________ (open) their store now and Mrs. Swanson ____________________ certainly ____________________ (buy) some bread for breakfast.

It is 8:00 now and the sun ____________________ (shine) brightly. I am here on the top of the hill.

I ____________________ (think) about my life.

Vocabulary

everything: tudo
shine: brilhar
top of the hill: topo da colina
yard: pátio

D Find synonyms for the words in bold.

1 Londoners are recycling their **waste**.

a ☐ campaign

b ☐ garbage

c ☐ project

2 Institutions are collecting great **quantities** of used paper.

a ☐ some

b ☐ ton

c ☐ amounts

3 The amount of garbage is **growing** around the world.

a ☐ increasing

b ☐ starting

c ☐ collecting

4 Governments are trying to **diminish** the quantity of garbage.

a ☐ learn

b ☐ launch

c ☐ reduce

5 The Pakistani campaign is **named** "Proud Pakistan Recycle".

a ☐ called

b ☐ massive

c ☐ thinking

6 Tarsila do Amaral is **regarded** as one of the major figures in 20th century.

a ☐ protect

b ☐ considered

c ☐ combined

7 My cousin works in a **large** and modern office downtown.

a ☐ near

b ☐ big

c ☐ select

8 Carol is **determined** that this semester things will be different.

a ☐ lazy

b ☐ quit

c ☐ insistent

E Write these sentences in the negative form.

1 White foods protect the bones.

____

2 Yellow and orange foods contain beta-carotene.

____

3 She prefers salad for dinner.

____

F Write these sentences in the interrogative form. Answer them using short forms. Number one is done for you.

1 He always eats potatoes.

Does he always eat potatoes?

Yes, he does.

2 You usually arrive late.

____

____

3 I rarely eat fish.

____

____

4 The kids frequently wash their hands.

____

____

5 Alice goes to school in the afternoon.

____

____

G Write the Simple Present or the Present Continuous of the verbs in parentheses.

1 This pigment ____________________ (reduce) the risk of cancer.

2 They ____________________ (go) to school by bus today.

3 Marian never ____________________ (eat) fish.

4 Alice ____________________ (read) the newspaper every morning.

5 Look! Sylvia ____________________ (cut) bread for the children.

H **Read the text about Janet. Then write a similar text about Chuck. Use the information in the chart.**

Janet lives in Dublin. She is a doctor and she works in a large hospital. She works from 8:00 a.m. to 6:00 p.m. She often has to work overtime. She loves her job. In her free time she plays rugby and rides her Harley Davidson motorcycle.

Name: Chuck Jones

Hometown: Honolulu

Job: checkout clerk

Place of work: supermarket

Working hours: 10:00 p.m. to 4:00 a.m.

Free time activities: go surfing, do volunteer work

I never/sometimes/frequently/always have to work overtime.

I love/like/don't like/hate my job.

JOB CORNER 1

CV

A CV or résumé is an important part of getting a job. It gives you an opportunity to sell yourself to potential employers.

Submit your résumé with a cover letter and one or more letters of reference.

GEORGE JAMES

Brazilian, single, 18 years old
(address)
(telephone number)
(e-mail address)

Objective

Seeking a position as a receptionist in a department that rewards hard work.

Education

- (name and address of the school)
  High school diploma, 2012

Work Experience

- (year and name of the company)
  Receptionist

Skills

- Receive phone calls and directed them to the appropriate departments.
- Arrange appointments between clients and employees.
- Receive and distributed mail and messages to appropriate departments and employees.

References

References and letters of recommendation available on request.

Based on <www.essortment.com>; <www.workjob-usa.info>. Accessed on October 20, 2010.

Vocabulary

appointment: compromisso
arrange: organizar
available: disponível
CV: *curriculum vitae*
employee: empregado
request: solicitação
résumé: *curriculum vitae*
reward: recompensar
seek: procurar

3 Chapada Diamantina

LANGUAGE IN CONTEXT

A Complete the information.
Then, read the cartoon. 6

1 Number of people

____

2 Conversation

☐ formal

☐ informal

B Give your opinion.

1 Are the girls going fishing together?

2 Why is one of the boys frightened?

C Think about it.
Read the sentences below and answer the questions.

What are you going to do today?
I'm going to get out of here.

1 What do the sentences have in common?

2 Do the sentences refer to the present, past, or future moment?

Vocabulary

get out: sair
go fishing: ir pescar
stay: ficar
you guys: turma, caras, pessoal

LANGUAGE PRACTICE

Future with *Going to*

Presente do verbo **to be** + **going to** + verbo		
I **am** You **are** He **is** She **is** It **is** We **are** You **are** They **are**	**going to** swim.	**Afirmativa:** He **is going to** swim. **Interrogativa: Is** he **going to** swim? **Negativa:** He **is not going to** swim. **Formas abreviadas: isn't** (is not) **aren't** (are not)

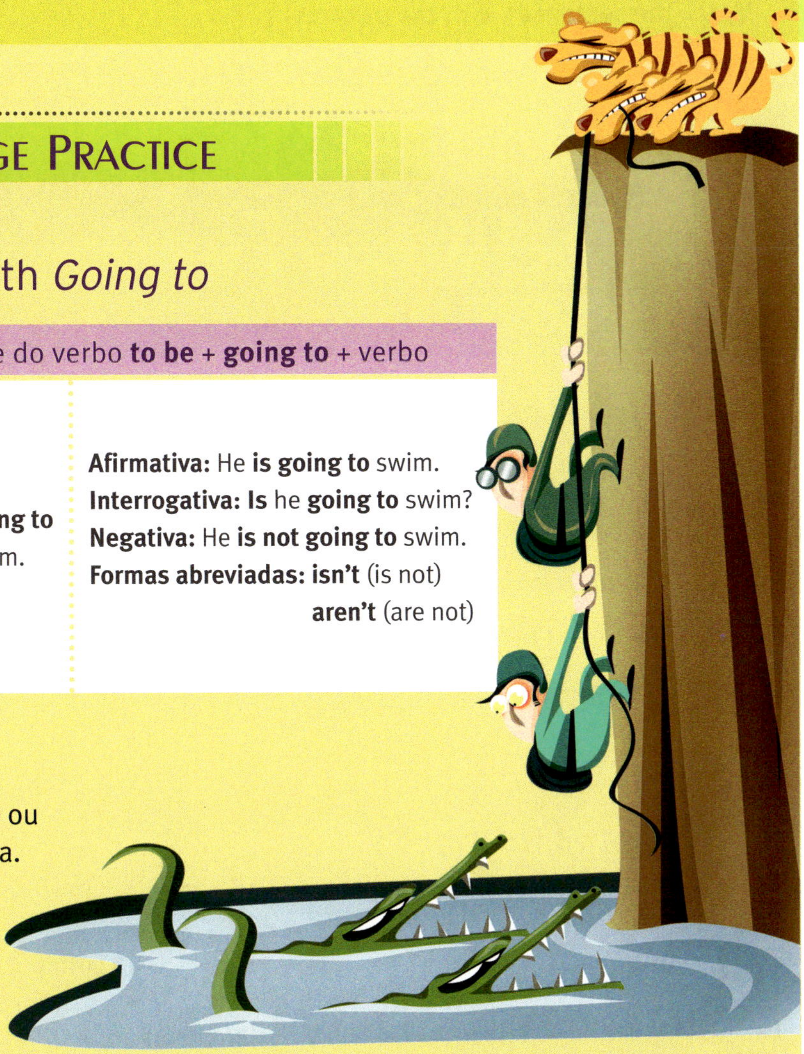

What is going to happen next?

Uso

Expressa ação ou intenção futura.

She is **going to travel** in two weeks.

They are **going to study** tomorrow.

I am **going to play** volleyball after class.

We are **going to meet** Paul tonight.

Geralmente vem acompanhado de advérbios de tempo: **tomorrow, next, in,** etc.

A Complete the sentences. Use *going to*.

1 I am not studying now. I ____________________ later.

2 She is not swimming now. She ____________________ tomorrow.

3 They are not working at this moment. They ____________________ after lunch.

4 We are not leaving now. We ____________________ in twenty minutes.

5 It is not raining now but it ____________________ in the afternoon.

B Match the sentences with the pictures.

1 [ ] He is going to buy some bread.

2 [ ] They are going to travel to Chapada Diamantina.

3 [ ] She is going to write a letter to her mother.

4 [ ] We are going to have a picnic at Blue Cave next weekend.

5 [ ] He's going to have dental implants.

6 [ ] I am going to study for the test.

Personal Pronouns

Subject	Object
I	me
you	you
he	him
she	her
it	it
we	us
you	you
they	them

Uso

Funcionam como objeto da oração. São usados após um verbo ou uma preposição.

I love **her**.

She always talks about **me**.

Quando o verbo tem dois objetos, usa-se uma destas construções:

Give the book to **her**.

Give **her** the book.

C Underline the correct alternative.

1 Leo wants to talk to (we – us) but we don't want to talk to (he – him).

2 She is waiting for (me – I).

3 Do you want to see (him – he)?

4 I meet (she – her) at the club every day.

5 The children are sick. Don't let (them – they) go to the park.

D Use the appropriate personal pronoun.

1 I want that book. Buy ______________________ for me.

2 I never visit the Johnsons. I don't like ______________________.

3 I really like Brenda. I always speak to ______________________ during the break.

4 Do you want Jason to help you? Then be nice to ______________________.

5 Wait a minute, Frank. I have to talk to ______________________.

Imperative

Infinitivo sem **to**
Afirmativo: Go out! **Negativo: Don't go** out!

Uso

Expressa ordem, comando, pedido.

Call me tonight.

Close the door, please.

Don't come late.

E Write sentences using the Imperative.

Example: Ask a friend to open the window.
Open the window, please.

1 Ask a friend to pass the salt.

____

2 Ask a friend to bring you the book.

____

3 Tell your friend not to smoke in your room.

____

4 Tell your friend not to close the door.

____

5 Tell your friend not to talk to you.

____

6 Ask your friend to call you tonight.

____

Go to page 58 for Extra Practice.

READING

Before Reading

Approaching the text

Discuss the questions below in Portuguese.

1 Do you like traveling?

2 What kind of place do you prefer to travel to?

3 Do you know Chapada Diamantina? Where is it?

Vocabulary

A Write the names of the places. Use the words given.

river **lake** **mountain** **cave** **valley** **waterfall**

1

2

3

4

5

6

B Read the words below.

best: o(a) melhor **highest:** o(a) mais alto(a) **newest:** o(a) mais novo(a)

C Look up the words below in the glossary.

1 climb ________________ 3 light ________________

2 late ________________ 4 trek ________________

Chapada Diamantina

You're gonna love it!

7 Try our exclusive tour packages to Chapada Diamantina, which is located at the heart of the state of Bahia.

You are going to climb mountains, swim under the waterfalls, and trek through the valleys.

How to Go

- By bus from Salvador (6 hours)
- By plane from Salvador (50 minutes)
- By car from Salvador (427 km)

What to See

Blue Cave – With a lake at the bottom, 40-minute trek.

Pai Inácio Mount – 1,120 meters, access by car, 20 minutes to walk last 300 meters, fabulous camping.

Mucugezinho River – Waterfalls, natural pools, beautiful views.

Smoke Waterfall – The highest in Brazil, 340 meters, 2-hour trek.

Where to Stay

Portal Lençóis – Excellent location, best for large families, swimming pool, sauna, 69 rooms with TV.

Cantos das Águas – The newest hotel in town, all 43 rooms with a view of the river, swimming pool, TV.

Pousada Lençóis – Near the church, 48 rooms, air-conditioning, swimming pool, TV.

Contact: Going Ecological (075) 9999-9090

Based on <www.terrachapada.com.br>. Accessed on October 26, 2010.

After Reading

A Take a look at the text and choose the best answer.

1 The text is ________.

a [ ] a tourism leaflet

b [ ] a Geography lesson

c [x] a tourist diary

2 The information in the text is appropriate for ________.

a [ ] teachers

b [x] people who want to travel

c [ ] students

B Check the correct statements according to the text.

In Chapada Diamantina ________.

1 [ ] there is a lake

2 [ ] there is a river

3 [ ] there is a theater

4 [x] there are waterfalls

5 [ ] there is a cave

6 [ ] there are schools of English

7 [ ] there is a camping site

8 [ ] there is a shopping mall

9 [ ] there are natural pools

10 [ ] there is a gas station

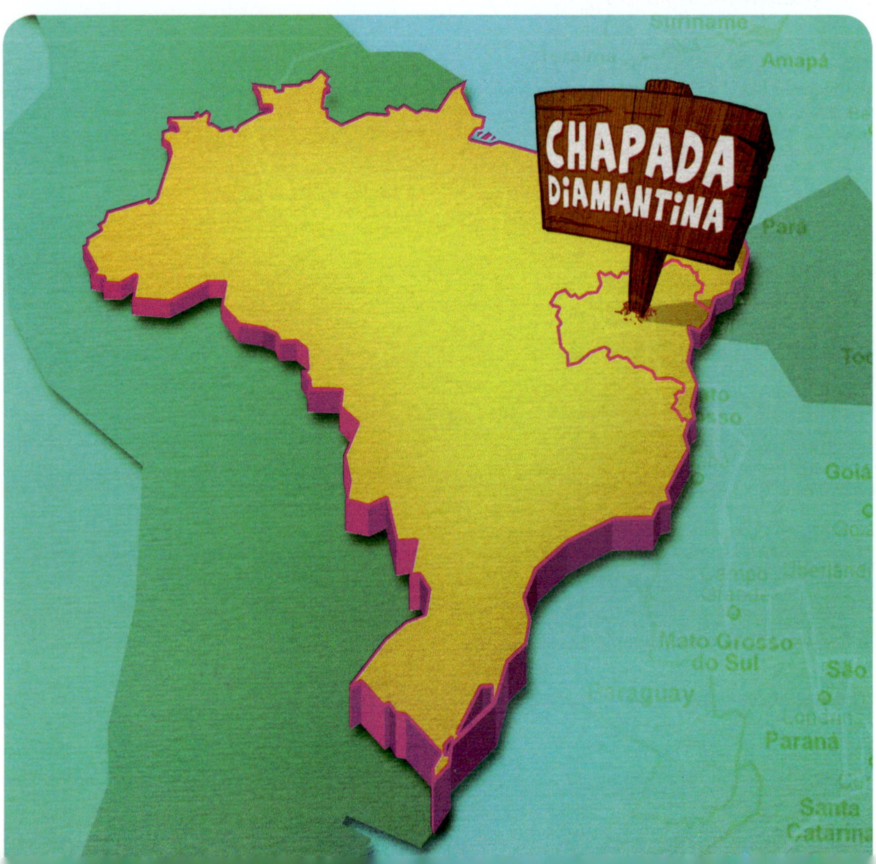

C Choose the correct alternative.

1 Chapada Diamantina is home to ________.

a ☐ the largest lake of the area

b ☐ the highest waterfall in Brazil

c ☐ the most fabulous camping in Brazil

2 A trip from Salvador to Chapada Diamantina ________.

a ☐ takes four days on foot

b ☐ takes six hours by boat

c ☐ takes fifty minutes by plane

3 Access to the Blue Cave is made ________.

a ☐ by bus

b ☐ by plane

c ☐ on foot

4 Access to Pai Inácio Mount is made ________.

a ☐ by car and on foot

b ☐ on foot and by plane

c ☐ by plane and by canoe

D Answer the questions according to the text.

1 Where is Chapada Diamantina located?

____

2 How do people get there?

____

3 Mention three things people are going to do there.

____

4 How far is Chapada Diamantina from Salvador by car?

____

5 Can people access Pai Inácio Mount only by car?

____

6 How do people get to Smoke Waterfall?

____

VOCABULARY EXPANSION

A Read the box and complete the sentences.

1 Paul is ________________ Lucy and John.

2 My school is ________________ the supermarket.

3 The cat is ________________ the car.

4 The umbrella is ________________ the door.

Prepositions of Place

behind: atrás
between: entre
near: perto de
under: embaixo de

B Complete the sentences. Use the words in the box.

1 She always travels ________________ car.

2 My sister is going to the beach ________________ bus.

3 The children usually go to school ________________ foot.

4 We are going to visit that island next week. We are going there ________________ boat.

5 He is afraid of traveling ________________ plane.

6 Kylie and her son go to the park ________________ foot every day.

Transportation

by boat: de barco
by bus: de ônibus
by car: de carro
by plane: de avião
on foot: a pé

C Use opposites to replace the words in bold. Use the box for help.

1 The hotel is **behind** the school. ________________

2 There are clothes **on** the chair. ________________

3 They are going to live **near** the library. ________________

4 The papers are **on** her desk. ________________

5 There is a river **near** the camping site. ________________

far from: longe de
in front of: na frente de
under: embaixo de

LANGUAGE IN USE

A Read the leaflet about a hotel in the Amazon. Then match the columns and talk to a classmate. See the examples.

Ariau Amazon Towers

This hotel in the jungle is built on suspended towers that are interconnected by 8 km of walkways. It is located 60 km northwest of Manaus, Brazil, on the bank of the Negro River. There are two observation towers. Each one is 41 meters high.

Two restaurants offer local dishes and many types of meat, fish, chicken, pasta, rice, beans, soup, salad, a selection of exotic fruits, and regional desserts.

Transportation
by regional boat = 2 hours;
by helicopter = 15 minutes;
by speedboat = 50 minutes.

Accommodations
288 single rooms and special suites with a private bathroom and verandas.

Rainy season
from January till June.

Excursions canoe ride, trek on jungle trails, piranha fishing, visit to a *caboclo*'s house, night tour through the jungle, alligator-spotting tour, sunrise tour, and bird-watching.

Based on <www.amazonastravel.com.br>. Accessed on October 27, 2010.

A	B
Where	be
When	get
What	there be
How	stay
	see
	do
	eat

A: Where is the hotel?
B: It is in the jungle.
A: How do people get there?
B: By boat.

B NOW IT'S YOUR TURN!

Ask a classmate about his/her plans for a trip. Look at the examples.

Where are you going next holiday?
How are you going?

WRITING

In your notebook, write a message to a friend. Invite him/her for a trip to Chapada Diamantina or to the Amazon. Mention: (a) when and how you are going; (b) where you are going to stay; (c) what you are going to do.

Example:
Dear Josh,
I'm going to the Amazon next month. Do you want to come with me?
I'm going to stay in... I'm going to fish.

4 School Dropouts

Language in Context

A Complete the information. Then, read the dialogue and check your answers.

8

1 Names: Mrs. Morgan, ____________________

2 Tone of conversation: ☐ serious ☐ funny

3 Subject: ____________________

Mrs. Morgan: Jennifer, you missed classes last week, didn't you?

Jennifer: Yeah!

Mrs. Morgan: Did you fail Math last month?

Jennifer: Yeah.

Mrs. Morgan: Did you fail Literature, too?

Jennifer: Yeah, Mrs. Morgan.

Mrs. Morgan: Then, why did you miss classes? Did you tell your parents about it?

Jennifer: I didn't.

Mrs. Morgan: Listen, this is your last year. Don't give up. You don't want to drop out, do you?

Gary: Mrs. Morgan…

Mrs. Morgan: I'm busy now, Gary. Wait a moment, please.

B Give your opinion.

1 What is Mrs. Morgan's occupation?

2 What is the academic situation of that student?

Vocabulary

fail: falhar

miss: faltar

C Think about it.
Answer the question below.

When did Jennifer miss classes?

Language Practice

Simple Past – Regular verbs: **verbo + d/ed**

To work		
I You He She It We You They	work**ed**.	**Afirmativa:** He work**ed**. **Negativa:** He **did not work**. **Interrogativa: Did** he **work**? **Forma abreviada: didn't** (did not)

Uso

Expressa hábitos passados.

I **walked** to school when I was a child.

Expressa ações terminadas ou ações ocorridas em um momento definido.

É geralmente usado com **yesterday, last..., ago, in...**, etc.

She **arrived** late **yesterday**.

Ortografia

Acrescenta-se **d/ed** ao verbo.

love – lov**ed** agree – agree**d** play – play**ed** want – want**ed**

Verbos terminados em **y** precedido de **consoante** trocam o **y** por **ied**.

study – stud**ied** carry – carr**ied** cry – cr**ied** try – tr**ied**

Verbos terminados em **consoante** + **vogal** + **consoante**, cuja sílaba tônica é a última, **dobram a consoante** antes do acréscimo de **ed**.

permit – permi**tted** occur – occu**rred** stop – sto**pped** drop – dro**pped**

A Write the Simple Past form of the verbs below.

1 dance ______
2 miss ______
3 hop ______
4 try ______
5 flash ______
6 check ______
7 dress ______
8 share ______
9 act ______
10 fail ______
11 ban ______
12 identify ______
13 compose ______
14 watch ______
15 ignore ______

B Write the Simple Past of the verbs in parentheses.

1 Yesterday we ______ (dance) from 1 to 4 in the morning.
2 The government ______ (ban) arms sales in the country last year.
3 The girl ______ (ignore) me after the show.
4 She ______ (dress) in her new clothes to go to the party.
5 Last Saturday we ______ (wait) for Linda but she didn't show up.
6 The kids ______ (watch) TV and ______ (play) video games last night.
7 I ______ (clean) the kitchen before going to sleep.

C Write the sentences in the negative form.

1 Martha showed up to see me.

______

2 She waited for me in the dressing room.

______

3 I played all night long.

______

4 He composed a song for his girlfriend.

______

5 The girls listened to his songs.

______

D Choose the correct question for each answer.

1 Baron de Coubertin organized the modern Olympic Games.

a ☐ What did Baron de Coubertin organize?

b ☐ When did he organize the games?

2 No, they didn't identify the criminal.

a ☐ Who did they identify?

b ☐ Did they identify the criminal?

3 We studied Geography in the park yesterday.

a ☐ Did you study yesterday?

b ☐ Where did you study Geography yesterday?

4 Yes, they did.

a ☐ Did the children wash their hands before dinner?

b ☐ When did they wash their hands?

5 Brenda arrived home after lunch.

a ☐ Did Brenda arrive home after lunch?

b ☐ When did Brenda arrive home?

Go to page 62 for Extra Practice.

E Change the verbs in the following sentences to the Simple Past.

1 My mother and I love Japanese food.

____

2 The waitress asks us about reservations.

____

3 My boyfriend drops food on my new dress.

____

4 We slowly walk back to the car.

____

5 He stops at the grocery store and asks for some sandwiches.

____

6 The kids watch TV in the morning.

____

Before Reading

Approaching the text

Discuss the questions below in Portuguese.

1 What is a "school dropout"?

2 In your opinion, is it important to get a high school diploma? Why/Why not?

3 In your community, what usually happens to the kids who abandon school?

Vocabulary

A Check the cognates.

How many cognates can you find?

☐ 5 ☐ 10 ☐ 15 or more

American	☐	explain	☐	persuade	☐
chance	☐	fail	☐	poverty	☐
consider	☐	graduate	☐	public	☐
decision	☐	graduation	☐	recent	☐
department	☐	important	☐	school	☐
diploma	☐	inmate	☐	stay	☐
district	☐	jail	☐	student	☐
dropout	☐	mind	☐	study	☐
education	☐	only	☐	system	☐
epidemic	☐	percent	☐	tired	☐

B Take a look at the text on page 53.

The text is about...

1 ☐ the good students of Berrien County.

2 ☐ students who abandon high school.

3 ☐ an epidemic in a high school.

(Nov. 20, 2006)

STUDENTS DROPPING OUT OF HIGH SCHOOL

9 Half of the students are dropping out in several of the largest school systems in the USA. A recent study made across the nation by the Department of Education found that 31 percent of American students are failing to graduate or dropping out of the nation's largest public schools.

Eli Thomasson, 16, from Berrien High School, Georgia, explained he wanted to drop out of school because he was just tired of school.

And, at his school, he wasn't the only one to consider walking away without a diploma. More than 40 percent of students at Berrien High School do not graduate.

Their graduation coach, Sheila Hendley, has the daunting job of trying to stop this epidemic. She literally begs the students "not to do this".

It is estimated that about 2,500 students drop out of U.S. high schools every day. The individual implications are enormous.

High school dropouts have a life span that is nine years shorter than people who graduate. They are more likely to face poverty, and their chances of running afoul of the law increase.

The Sheriff of Berrien County said that 81.2 percent of the inmates of the local jailhouse are high school dropouts.

Anthony White, a 17-year-old inmate, was arrested just three days after he quit school, the Sheriff explained. ■

Based on <http://abcnews.go.com>. Accessed on October 14, 2010.

(May 12, 2009)

Nationwide, 7,000 students drop out every day and only about 70 percent of students graduate from high school with a regular high school diploma.

Extracted from <http://edlabor.house.gov>. Accessed on October 14, 2010.

After Reading

A Check the correct alternative for the words in bold.

1 I was **just** tired of school.

a ☐ right

b ☐ simply

c ☐ justice

2 "[...] 81.2 percent of the **inmates** of the local jailhouse are high school dropouts."

a ☐ visitors

b ☐ companions

c ☐ prisoners

3 He was arrested just three days after he **quit** school.

a ☐ left

b ☐ lived

c ☐ calmed

B Choose the alternative that has the same meaning as the sentence given.

1 Dropouts are more likely to face poverty.

a ☐ Dropouts will certainly be poor.

b ☐ Dropouts may be poor.

2 If you drop out of high school, your chances of running afoul of the law increase.

a ☐ If you drop out of high school, you will be arrested.

b ☐ If you drop out of high school, you can easily get into trouble with the law.

3 Sheila Hendley has the daunting job of trying to stop this epidemic.

a ☐ Sheila Hendley has a stimulating job.

b ☐ Sheila Hendley's job is discouraging.

C Find the statements that are not true.

1 ☐ Eli Thomasson liked school.

2 ☐ Sheila Hendley tried to orient Thomasson.

3 ☐ High school dropouts get rich.

4 ☐ Most students of public schools want to graduate.

5 ☐ Most jail inmates are dropouts.

D Answer the questions.

1 How old is Eli Thomasson?

____

2 How many students drop out of U.S. high schools every day?

____

3 How many students at Berrien High School do not graduate?

____

4 How many Berrien County jail inmates are high school dropouts?

____

VOCABULARY EXPANSION

A Read the information in the box and write new words.

Suffixes ion, ation

Formam substantivos, indicando "ato" ou "estado de".
Ex.: irritate – irrita**tion**; graduate – gradu**ation**

1 act ______________
2 attract ______________
3 explode ______________
4 operate ______________
5 infect ______________
6 select ______________
7 protect ______________
8 invent ______________

B Read the information in the box. Then guess the meaning of *just* in the sentences below.

1 **Just** a moment, please. ______________
2 You didn't pay a **just** price for this book. ______________
3 I **just** want to see you. ______________
4 He is not angry. He is **just** tired. ______________
5 The coach is a **just** person. ______________
6 I have **just** enough money to buy a car. ______________

just

fair: He is a **just** man.
only: We are **just** friends.
simply: It's **just** beautiful.

C Read the information in the box. Then guess the meaning of *like* in the sentences below.

1 [ ] They acted **like** babies.

2 [ ] He **liked** his girlfriend a lot.

3 [ ] She is a teacher but she sings **like** a professional singer.

4 [ ] Did you **like** the show last night?

5 [ ] I cried **like** a child yesterday.

6 [ ] You drive **like** me: badly.

7 [ ] My sister **likes** fruit and vegetables. She doesn't eat meat.

like

a gostar

b como se fosse

D Match the words with the appropriate definitions according to the text.

1 sheriff

2 epidemic

3 high school

4 coach

5 to estimate

6 inmate

a [ ] a secondary school

b [ ] a tutor who prepares students for examinations

c [ ] a person confined to an institution

d [ ] the chief law enforcement officer in a county

e [ ] to calculate approximately

f [ ] an outbreak of a disease that spreads rapidly

E Complete the sentences with the words below.

make up | walk away | like | arrested | quit

1 I felt ______________ I was in prison.

2 You have to ______________ your mind and choose a career.

3 He was ______________ three days after he fired a gun in the air.

4 One of my classmates wants to ______________ without a diploma.

5 The young man ______________ school before graduation.

Language in Use

A Read about Roberto Carlos Ramos, a story-teller. Then match the columns and talk to a classmate. See the examples.

ROBERTO CARLOS RAMOS

Roberto Carlos Ramos was born in a slum in Belo Horizonte. When he was 6 his mother took him to FEBEM (Fundação Estadual do Bem-Estar do Menor).

He escaped from FEBEM more than a hundred times. He was illiterate and considered "hopeless". He learned to rob, to do drugs and to live on the streets. When he was 13 he met Marguerit Duvas, a French woman who was visiting Brazil.

Duvas adopted him. She took him to France where he learned the art of story-telling. He was back to Brazil at the age of 19. Here, he graduated in Pedagogy and took a Master's Degree in Education. In 2001, in San Diego, he was elected one of the greatest story-tellers in the world.

He has already adopted 14 teenagers and is very proud of them.

"When I was 9, my FEBEM record had a stamp on it: 'HOPELESS'. When I was 13 I was wandering on the streets, smoking and, every now and then, pickpocketing."

Based on <http://cinema.cineclick.uol.com.br>. Accessed on September 15, 2009.

A	B
Where	happen (happened)
What	be born (was born)
Who	take (took)
	learn (learned)
	live (lived)
	adopt (adopted)

A: Where was he born?
B: He was born in Belo Horizonte.
A: Where did his mother take him to at the age of six?
B: She took him to FEBEM.

B NOW IT'S YOUR TURN!

Ask a classmate about his/her life history. Look at the examples.

When were you born?

Where did you live when you were 10 years old?

Writing

In your notebook, write a paragraph about your life for the school magazine.

Extra Practice 2

A Rewrite the sentences in the negative form.

1 Give this letter to her, please.

____

2 Write it in your notebook.

____

3 Talk to him.

____

4 Buy her a new dress.

____

5 Call me after dinner.

____

6 Close the window now.

____

7 Study more for the Math test.

____

8 Come and stay with me.

____

B Complete the sentences.

Example: I hear them but they don't hear me.

1 They smile at me but _______________.

2 We talk to you but _______________.

3 She likes him but _______________.

4 They can see us but _______________.

5 I look for them but _______________.

6 You love her but _______________.

7 He listens to her but _______________.

8 The kids help you but _______________.

C Rewrite the sentences in the negative and interrogative forms.

Example: He is going to have dinner at home.
He is not going to have dinner at home.
Is he going to have dinner at home?

1 He is going to visit his friends in Italy.

____

____

2 She is going to buy a new dress next Saturday.

____

____

3 They are going to study for the test tomorrow.

____

____

4 He is going to talk to the teacher next class.

____

____

5 She is going to live in Paris next year.

____

____

6 I am going to live with my grandma in Curitiba.

____

____

D Read about Jane, Peter, and Raphael. What are their New Year's resolutions?

Example: Peter is 22 years old. He wants to run the São Silvestre marathon in December but he smokes one pack of cigarettes a day.
(quit/smoke) He is going to quit smoking.

1 Jane is 18 years old. She eats fast food and is getting fat.

(eat/healthy food) ______________________________

2 Raphael is 17 years old. He wants to study in England but he speaks little English.

(study/hard) ______________________________

E Write questions. Use the words in parentheses.

1 I am going to travel next week.

(When) ____________________

2 They are going to study in the library.

(Where) ____________________

3 Linda is going to help me.

(Who) ____________________

4 He is going to clean the garage on Sunday.

(What) ____________________

5 We are going to visit grandma next week.

(What) ____________________

6 She is going to stay in her cousin's house.

(Where) ____________________

7 My parents are going to come back tonight.

(When) ____________________

F Rewrite the sentences below using *going to*. Don't forget to use the time adverbs.

Example: He usually works in the morning.

He is going to work tomorrow morning.

1 She always travels to Bahia in January.

____

2 They often go camping with friends in the summer.

____

3 He always sleeps after lunch.

____

4 They play ball in the park on Sundays.

____

5 She listens to the radio every day.

____

6 We do our homework in the afternoon.

____

G Rewrite the sentences in the Simple Past.

1 The car crashes into the lamp post and almost kills a cat.

____

2 Somebody calls the police.

____

3 My father never agrees with me.

____

4 The local community complains when the factory closes.

____

5 The slaves in colonial Brazil develop a martial art called *capoeira*.

____

6 My sister cries every time I stop talking to her.

____

H Rewrite the sentences in the interrogative form. Follow the example.

Example: The police stopped us on our way to the concert.
Did the police stop you on your way to the concert?

1 The U.S. military created the internet.

____

2 The flood destroyed many houses in the city.

____

3 The success of the album permitted tours abroad.

____

4 The photographers started taking pictures when the car door opened.

____

5 Raphael wanted to study abroad at that time.

____

6 The principal talked to the students in the morning.

____

I Write sentences in the Simple Past. Follow the example.

Example: my friend / work / as a DJ / last year
My friend worked as a DJ last year.

1 What / you / study / last night / ?

____

____

2 Vicky / walk / to work / yesterday

____

3 Why / the baby / cry / five minutes ago / ?

____

J Match the bubbles and form dialogues.

1 When did the fire destroy the city?

2 Who invited you to the party?

3 What did you all do on Saturday morning?

4 Where did you do your homework then?

5 What time did your uncle arrive there?

☐ In the library.

☐ At around five in the morning.

☐ Two days ago.

☐ We played soccer and watched TV.

☐ My best friend Joana did.

Job Corner 2

Cover Letter

A cover letter accompanies your résumé and introduces you to the employer. Explain why you are interested in the job and include information on how you can be contacted.

George James
(Address)
(Telephone number)

March 17, 2012

Paul Strain
Personnel Manager

(Name of the company)
(Address of the company)

Dear Mr. Strain,

I would like to join your organization as a receptionist because I am good at this job. Enclosed is a résumé showing my educational background and work experience.

As a receptionist for (name of the present company), I am responsible for answering the telephone, directing calls, and booking appointments. I am certain that my work experience would be an immediate contribution to (name of the company you are writing to).

I would love to be part of your team. I am available to meet with you at your earliest convenience. You can contact me at the address and phone number above, or at (e-mail address).

Thank you for your consideration.
Sincerely,
George James

Résumé enclosed

Based on <http://jobsearchtech.about.com>; <www.essortment.com>. Accessed on October 1, 2010.

Vocabulary

accompany: acompanhar
appointment: compromisso
available: disponível
background: formação
book: agendar
cover letter: carta de apresentação
directing calls: transferir ligações
earliest: mais próximo
employer: empregador
enclosed: anexo
introduce: apresentar
join: ingressar
Personnel Manager: Gerente de Recursos Humanos

5 João Carlos Martins

Language in Context

A **Complete the information. Then, read the dialogue and check your answers.** 10

1 Names: Gloria, ______________

2 An occupation: ______________

B **Give your opinion.**

1 What is Carol's occupation?

2 Do Carol and Gloria know each other?

Gloria: Hi, Carol! What's up?
Carol: Not much, but I got that job at the pet shop.
Gloria: Great. When did you start?
Carol: Last week.
Gloria: I got that job as a salad assistant.
Carol: Cool. How are you doing?
Gloria: I cut my finger two days ago. But, it's OK.
Carol: And I lost a dog yesterday, but then I found it.
Gloria: Do the dogs like you?
Carol: Yeah. The problem is... there are too many.

Vocabulary

How are you doing?: Como vai você?
What's up?: E aí?

C **Think about it. Compare the sentences and answer the questions.**

A	She missed classes last week. She failed Math last month.

B	I cut my finger two days ago. I lost a dog yesterday.

1 What is the difference between the verbs in groups A and B?

2 Is it possible to know when the actions happened?

Language Practice

Simple Past – Irregular verbs (ver p. 396)

To go		
I You He She It We You They	went.	**Afirmativa:** He **went** to the club yesterday. **Negativa:** He **did not go** to the club yesterday. **Interrogativa: Did** he **go** to the club yesterday? **Forma abreviada: didn't** (did not)

Notas

- Nas formas em que se usa o auxiliar **did**, o verbo principal fica no infinitivo sem **to**.
- O auxiliar **did** não tem tradução.

Alguns verbos irregulares

Infinitive	Past	Infinitive	Past
to be*	was/were	to have	had
to become	became	to know	knew
to break	broke	to make	made
to buy	bought	to meet	met
to come	came	to see	saw
to cut	cut	to take	took
to do	did	to think	thought
to go	went	to write	wrote

* *To be* é um verbo auxiliar; faz as próprias formas interrogativas e negativas.

A Underline all irregular verbs in the Simple Past.

He was my best friend when I was ten. We went to school together. Sometimes we walked. Sometimes Mom took us by car. We did our homework and we watched TV. We met our friends at the club and played soccer. We bought popcorn and made kites. Then, my best friend moved to another country. Today I am fourteen and I have many friends but no best friend.

B Write the Simple Past of the verbs in parentheses.

1 We ________________ (enjoy) the show last night.

2 Grandpa ________________ (be) a salesperson when he ________________ (be) young.

3 Later, he ________________ (become) a businessman.

4 I ________________ (try) to talk to her, but she ________________ (ignore) me.

5 The car ________________ (stop) near the children.

6 I ________________ (think) about you last week.

C Put the sentences below in the interrogative form.

Example: She broke her foot.

Did she break her foot?

1 He wrote a letter last night.

____

____

2 They met him at the theater.

____

____

3 She saw him at the shopping mall.

____

4 They took a lot of pictures at the show.

____

D Complete the sentences.

1 A: What did you buy last week?

B: ________________________ a magazine.

2 A: How did you come to school today?

B: ________________________ by car.

3 A: When did you do your homework?

B: ________________________ my homework yesterday.

4 A: Where did you go last Sunday?

B: ________________________ to the movies.

Possessive Adjectives and Pronouns

Possessive adjectives	Possessive pronouns
my	mine
your	yours
his	his
her	hers
its	its
our	ours
your	yours
their	theirs
This is **my** book.	This book is **mine**. (**my** book)

Nota

- **Of + pronome possessivo** = "um dos", "uma das":
  She is a friend **of mine**. (She is one of my friends.)
- **Pronome indefinido** como possuidor:
  Everyone must bring **his** *or* **her** *slide projector.*
  Everyone must bring **their** *slide projector.*

Uso

Os adjetivos possessivos vêm antes de substantivos.

Os pronomes possessivos substituem os substantivos.

Adjetivos e pronomes possessivos concordam com o possuidor.

We are doing **our** homework. Are you doing **yours**?

E Circle all possessives.

I am mad at my friend Janice. I showed my composition to her and she simply copied it. Mr. Swanson, our teacher, thought that the composition was hers and not mine. I told him what had happened and he said that it was not his problem.

Some of my friends tried to help me and talked to Mr. Swanson, but he said that it was not their problem. Finally, Janice confessed that the composition was mine.

F Use the appropriate possessives.

1 Sheila, I didn't bring __________ umbrella. Can I get __________?

2 The boys ate __________ sandwiches, but the girls didn't eat __________ this morning.

3 Glenda is going to take __________ kids to the park. Why don't you take __________, too?

4 Whose book is this? It isn't __________.

5 Last year my parents lost __________ luggage at the airport.

6 Rick likes __________ new job, but Alan and David don't like __________.

7 I did __________ homework. Did you do __________?

Go to page 86 for Extra Practice.

READING

Before Reading

Approaching the text

Discuss the questions below in Portuguese.

1 Do you know João Carlos Martins, the Brazilian pianist?

2 What is the importance of the hands to a pianist?

Vocabulary

A Write the meaning of each word below. Use the words in the boxes.

pressionado | acontecimento | proporcionar | seguir | contador de histórias | fixar

1 story-teller ____________________

2 hard-pressed ____________________

3 set ____________________

4 trace ____________________

5 event ____________________

6 provide ____________________

B Give the meaning of the words below. Use the glossary.

1 fate ____________________

2 already ____________________

3 inconceivable ____________________

4 remain ____________________

5 true ____________________

6 surgery ____________________

C Take a look at the text on page 69. Check the type of text.

The text is...

1 ☐ a synopsis of a documentary.

2 ☐ a synopsis of a book.

3 ☐ a synopsis of an article.

MARTINS' PASSION

11

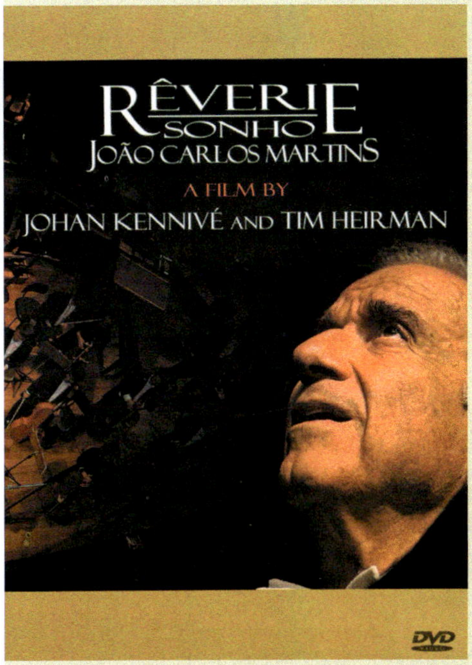

International title: MARTINS' PASSION

Original title: DIE MARTINS PASSION

Country: GERMANY

Year: 2003 – **Genre:** FICTION

Directed by: IRENE LANGEMANN

Film run: 96'

[...]

Extracted from <http://cineuropa.org>.
Accessed on October 16, 2010.

SYNOPSIS

Any story-teller would be hard-pressed to invent a biography as incredible as the life of Brazil's celebrated star pianist, João Carlos Martins. Success and personal tragedies, traumatic injuries and triumphant comebacks mark his fate. In the early sixties, this temperamental Brazilian [...] is celebrated as the greatest interpreter of the music of Bach next to Glenn Gould. But a disastrous injury throws his life off-balance. [...] In the late nineties, Martins' career seems finally over, when he has to undergo a surgery to sever the nerves of his right hand. The one-armed pianist decides to attempt a comeback with his left hand only. With fanatic fervor he makes his left hand work for two. The date for a concert with a renowned orchestra is already set – and yet again, the inconceivable happens. [...] His dream to create something great on the piano seems finally buried.

The film accompanies João Carlos Martins during his darkest hours, traces the early triumphs and dramatic events of his life. [...] Martins' encounters with his friend, the soccer genius Pelé, and the legendary jazz pianist Dave Brubeck, provide moments of bliss. And in the end, once again a small miracle occurs.

A film about a man who never gives up and remains true to his passion – music.

Extracted from <www.lichtfilm.com>.
Accessed on October 16, 2010.

1940	1969	1995	2002	2003	2004
João Carlos Martins, pianist and conductor, is born in São Paulo.	He severely hurt his right arm during a soccer match.	He lost part of his hand movement due to injuries received during an assault in Sofia, Bulgaria.	A tumor was discovered in his left hand.	He started preparing to be a conductor.	He founded the Bachiana Chamber Orchestra and initiated social programs for young people in São Paulo.

Based on <www.bach-cantatas.com>; <www.eunanet.net>.
Accessed on October 16, 2010.

Vocabulary

attempt: tentar
balance: equilíbrio
buried: enterrado
comeback: retorno
injury: lesão, ferimento
sever: cortar
throw his life off-balance: abalar sua vida
undergo: submeter-se a

After Reading

A Take a look at the text. Look for the following information.

1 Date of birth: ______________________

2 Original title of the documentary: ______________________

3 Country where it was produced: ______________________

4 Name of a friend: ______________________

B Check the meaning of the words in bold.

1 In the **early** sixties he is celebrated as the greatest interpreter of the music of Bach.

a ☐ início

b ☐ apenas

c ☐ cedo

2 A date for a concert with a **renowned** orchestra is already set.

a ☐ contemporânea

b ☐ famosa

c ☐ próxima

3 His encounters with his friend Pelé provide moments of **bliss**.

a ☐ tormento

b ☐ tristeza

c ☐ alegria

C Check the meaning of the sentences.

1 "In the late nineties, Martins' career seems finally over..."

a ☐ His career seems to be at an end.

b ☐ Martins started his career in 1990.

2 "The one-armed pianist decides to attempt a comeback with his left hand only."

a ☐ He can't play the piano with his left hand only.

b ☐ He intended to play with just one hand.

3 "His dream to create something great on the piano seems finally buried."

a ☐ He was successful.

b ☐ He probably had to give up.

D Check the statements that are true.

João Carlos Martins is...

a [ ] a man who never gives up.
b [ ] a celebrated pianist.
c [ ] a man who makes documentaries.
d [ ] a man who remains true to music.
e [ ] an interpreter of the music of Bach.

E Answer the questions.

1 What happened in 2002? ____________________
2 When did he start preparing to be a conductor? ____________________
3 Did he succeed? ____________________

Vocabulary Expansion

A Read the information in the box and write new words.

1 race ________
2 dance ________
3 sing ________
4 rap ________
5 paint ________
6 work ________
7 teach ________
8 swim ________

Suffix er

Quando acrescentado a verbos, indica "quem pratica a ação".

write – writ**er**

run – runn**er**

B Write opposites/synonyms for the words in bold. Use words from the text.

Opposites

1 In the **late** sixties, Martins is celebrated as a great interpreter. ____________
2 The film traces the **failure** and dramatic events of his life. ____________

Synonyms

1 His **fantasy** to create something great on the piano seems buried. ____________
2 But a **terrible** injury throws his life off-balance. ____________
3 The pianist decides to attempt a **return** with his left hand only. ____________
4 He is celebrated as the greatest interpreter of the music of Bach **alongside** Glenn Gould. ____________

C Read the information in the box and complete the chart.

Prefixes in, un

Significam "não", "o oposto de", quando acrescentados a adjetivos.

active – **in**active   able – **un**able

		in
1	conceivable	inconceivable
2	correct	incorrect
3	credible	incredible
4	definite	indefinite

		un
1	happy	unhappy
2	known	unknown
3	important	unimportant
4	natural	unnatural

D Check the best alternatives to complete the sentences.

1 She said she is going ________ at that job.

a [x] insolvable b [ ] insane c [ ] inoffensive

2 This song is so famous that many people consider it ________.

a [x] unbelievable b [ ] unforgettable c [ ] unknown

3 I didn't buy that chair because it was very ________.

a [ ] unknown b [x] uncomfortable c [ ] improbable

4 He is ________ to her suffering.

a [ ] indefinite b [ ] incredible c [x] indifferent

5 Jack doesn't have a job. He is ________.

a [ ] unnatural b [ ] uninteresting c [x] unemployed

6 Ted was ________ yesterday at the party because Ann didn't show up.

a [x] unhappy b [ ] uninterested c [ ] unconscious

Visto 06/05/2014

LANGUAGE IN USE

A Read about Cesar Cielo. Then match the columns and talk to a classmate. See the examples.

Cesar Augusto Cielo Filho (born on January 10, 1987, in Santa Bárbara d'Oeste, São Paulo, Brazil) is the most successful Brazilian swimmer in history.

He has obtained two Olympic medals, two World Aquatics Championships gold medals, and has broken a world record. His gold medal at the 2008 Olympics, in the 50 m freestyle competition, is Brazil's sole Olympic gold in swimming to date.

Cielo began his career at small swimming clubs in his native town. At the age of 16, he transferred to Esporte Clube Pinheiros, in São Paulo.

In 2006, he received a scholarship from Auburn University, in the United States, where he competed for the Swimming and Diving team. Cielo is sponsored by Clube de Regatas Flamengo, Avanço, Embratel, and Correios. He represents Flamengo in Brazilian competitions.

Based on <www.facebook.com>; <http://auburntigers.cstv.com>. Accessed on October 26, 2010.

A	B
Where	be born
When	swim at the age of 16
What	win gold medals
How many	spend childhood
	go in 2006
	go to the USA
	do in 2008

A: When was he born?
B: He was born in 1987.
A: Where did he spend his childhood?
B: He spent his childhood in Santa Bárbara d'Oeste.

B NOW IT'S YOUR TURN!

Ask a classmate about his or her life history. Look at the examples.

When were you born?
What did you do...?

WRITING

In your notebook, write a paragraph for the school magazine about one famous personality.

6 Misjudging

Language in Context

A **Complete the information. Then, read the cartoon and check your answers.** 12

1 Dialogue between: ____________________

2 A verb: ____________________

B **Give your opinion.**

1 Classify the boy's attitude the day before.

2 Do you agree with the girl's decision? Why/Why not?

C **Think about it.**
Observe the two groups of sentences below and answer the questions.

A	B
What were you doing yesterday at 5 o'clock?	I was sleeping.

A	B
What did you do yesterday at 5:00?	I slept.

1 What do the two groups of sentences have in common?

2 Is there a difference in meaning between the two groups?

Vocabulary

What about me?: E eu?
while: enquanto

Language Practice

Past Continuous

Passado do verbo **to be** + verbo terminado em **ing**		
I **was** You **were** He **was** She **was** It **was** We **were** You **were** They **were**	sleep**ing**.	**Afirmativa:** He **was** sleep**ing**. **Interrogativa: Was** he sleep**ing**? **Negativa:** He **was not** sleep**ing**. **Formas abreviadas: wasn't** (was not) **weren't** (were not)

Uso

Expressa ações em andamento em um determinado momento do passado.

It **was raining** hard 5 minutes ago.

É frequentemente usado com **when** e **while**.

When (quando): He **was sleeping** when she arrived.

While (enquanto): He **was sleeping** while his sister was cleaning the garage.

A Rewrite the sentences in the Past Continuous.

1 He slept in his bedroom.

____

2 Your sister cleaned the garage.

____

3 Your mother and I washed the car.

____

4 I didn't talk to the teacher in the classroom.

____

5 The kids watched a funny movie yesterday afternoon.

____

B **Write the Past Continuous of the verbs in parentheses.**

1 Yesterday, Sally ______________ (read) a book while I ______________ (make) dinner.

2 Jessica ______________ (watch) TV when I got home last night.

3 It ______________ (rain) hard when I left this morning.

4 ______________ you ______________ (have) dinner when I called you last night?

5 While the children ______________ (sleep), we cleaned the house.

6 What ______________ she ______________ (do) when I arrived?

7 Why ______________ they ______________ (cry) yesterday?

8 They ______________ (help – neg.) me, they ______________ (ask) me a question.

9 My dad ______________ (cancel) his flight when I called him.

10 While I was packing the bags, my parents ______________ (look for) our passports.

Go to page 87 for Extra Practice.

Modal Verbs (I)

Os verbos modais – **can, could, must** – são verbos auxiliares que dão um significado específico ao verbo principal.

You **should** go now. (conselho)

It **may** rain. (possibilidade)

She **must** arrive on time. (obrigação)

Características

Os verbos modais:

- não têm infinitivo;
- não têm conjugação regular;
- têm a mesma forma para todas as pessoas;
- são seguidos pelo verbo principal no infinitivo sem **to**;
- fazem as próprias formas interrogativas e negativas.

	Can	Could	Must
Afirmativa	I **can** read.	I **could** read.	You **must** read.
Interrogativa	**Can** he read?	**Could** he read?	**Must** she read?
Negativa	We **cannot** read.	They **could not** read.	He **must not** read.
Forma abreviada	**can't**	**couldn't**	**mustn't**
Substituível por	to be able to	to be able to	to have to

Can/could (pode, podia, poderia)

Expressam:

› capacidade e habilidade

He **can** read fast. I **could** swim well years ago.

› possibilidade, permissão, pedido

They **can** go now. **Could** you open the door, please?

Be able to pode substituir **can/could**.

I **am able** to swim. He **was able** to read that letter.

Must (deve)

Expressa:

› obrigação, dedução

We **must** visit her. You **must** help me. She **must** be sick.

› proibição (forma negativa e abreviada)

You **must not** use your cell phone in the classroom. You **mustn't** smoke here.

Have to pode substituir **must**.

I **have to** go now. He **had to** work yesterday.

C **Read the sentences below. Choose their correct meanings.**

a obligation b deduction c prohibition

1 [ ] Look at Fred! He must be sad.

2 [ ] We must study because we have a test next week.

3 [ ] You mustn't enter this room. It's for employees only.

4 [ ] Everybody is in the classroom. The teacher must be there.

5 [ ] The children mustn't go out now. It's raining.

D **Complete the sentences using *can, could, can't, couldn't*.**

1 ____________ he cook? I guess he ____________.

2 I'm sorry but I ____________ talk to you right now.

3 He's an excellent athlete. He ____________ do it.

4 We ____________ see that he was very happy.

5 Picasso ____________ paint when he was five. He started painting when he was 10.

E Rewrite the sentences. Follow the example.

Example: I must go now.
I have to go now.

1 We must talk after dinner.

____

2 You must deliver your compositions after class.

____

3 They must come back before lunch time.

____

4 She must visit her grandpa because he is seriously ill.

____

F Rewrite the sentences. Follow the example.

Example: I can read this. I am able to read this.

1 She can walk fast. _______________

2 We can run five miles. _______________

3 They can solve this problem. _______________

4 Jerry can fix your car. _______________

Go to page 89 for Extra Practice.

G Look at the pictures and complete the sentences using *can*, *mustn't* and *have to*.

1

You _______________ turn left.

3

You _______________ smoke here.

2

You _______________ ride a bicycle.

4

You _______________ take photos.

READING

Before Reading

Approaching the text

Discuss the questions below in Portuguese.

1 Do you criticize the people around you?

2 Do the people around you criticize you?

Vocabulary

A Write the verbs next to their definitions.

to judge | to flunk | to be fired

1 ____________________: to be forced to leave your job

2 ____________________: to form an opinion

3 ____________________: to fail a test

B Look these verbs up in the glossary.

1 belong ____________________

2 succeed ____________________

3 criticize ____________________

4 misjudge ____________________

C Match.

1	poet	a	☐ cineasta
2	composer	b	☐ físico
3	scientist	c	☐ cientista
4	physicist	d	☐ cartunista
5	novelist	e	☐ romancista
6	filmmaker	f	☐ compositor
7	cartoonist	g	☐ cantor
8	singer	h	☐ poeta

MISJUDGING

13 Albert Einstein, Walt Disney, Elvis Presley, and many other famous people were criticized when young. People told them things like:

"You're good for nothing! You're hopeless! You're not going to make it!"

Did people misjudge them? Make your own conclusions.

Walt Disney – filmmaker; cartoonist

Once, when Walt Disney was working at a newspaper, the publisher told him that he didn't have good ideas and fired him.

Beethoven – composer

One day, when Beethoven was playing one of his compositions on the piano, his music teacher told him, "You're hopeless as a composer."

Albert Einstein – physicist

When Einstein was in elementary school, the director told his parents, "He'll never succeed in life." He, later, created the Theory of Relativity.

Charles Darwin – scientist

Darwin couldn't finish medical school. However, he wrote *The Origin of Species* and changed the history of science.

Louisa May Alcott – novelist; poet

An editor told Louisa that she couldn't write anything good. In 1868 she wrote *Little Women*, a best-seller all over the world.

Elvis Presley – singer

He flunked the audition for a popular TV show called *Talent Scouts*, in the 1950's.

Based on <www.crazyabouttv.com>; <http://famguytoday.blogspot.com>. Accessed on October 25, 2010.

Vocabulary

anything: nada
hopeless: sem esperança
You are good for nothing.: Você não serve para nada.
You are not going to make it.: Você não vai conseguir.

After Reading

A **Take a look at the text and find the following information.**

1 Occupations ending in **er**: ______________________

2 Occupations ending in **ist**: ______________________

3 Name of a composer: ______________________

4 Name of a writer: ______________________

B **Read and complete the sentences.**

1 Se *hope* significa "esperança" e *hopeless* significa sem esperança, o sufixo **less** significa ______________________.

2 Se *to judge* significa "julgar" e o prefixo **mis** indica "erro", *to misjudge* significa ______________________.

C **Answer the questions according to the text.**

Example: What did Louisa May Alcott write?
She wrote *Little Women*.

1 Could Darwin finish medical school?

____

2 Where was Disney working when he was fired?

____

3 What was a famous TV show in the 50's?

____

4 Who was Beethoven?

____

5 Who created the Theory of Relativity?

____

D **Think about it.**

1 In your opinion, were Disney, Einstein, etc. misjudged?

2 Have you ever been misjudged?

VOCABULARY EXPANSION

A Read the information in the box and complete the definitions. Use the words in bold.

Prefix mis

O prefixo **mis** indica falta de, erro.

1 **place** things in the wrong place: ____________________

2 not **behave** adequately: ____________________

3 **hear** things incorrectly: ____________________

4 **treat** badly (people, animals, or plants): ____________________

5 **understand** things wrongly: ____________________

6 not **pronounce** words correctly: ____________________

B Complete the sentences. Use the words in the box.

and: e
because: porque
but: mas
however: entretanto

1 Walt Disney was a genius. ____________________, the publisher fired him.

2 Albert Einstein ____________________ Charles Darwin were scientists.

3 Darwin changed the history of science, ____________________ he never finished medical school.

4 Elvis flunked the audition for a show ____________________ the director didn't like his voice.

C Read the information in the box. Then substitute the words in bold.

accomplish: realizar
actually: de fato, realmente
bookstore: livraria
false cognates: falsos cognatos (palavras semelhantes na forma, mas diferentes em significado)
library: biblioteca
nowadays: atualmente, hoje em dia
parents: pais
realize: perceber, ter consciência de
relatives: parentes

1 When Ross arrived there, he **noticed** that it was too late. ____________________

2 Is there a **place that sells books** nearby? ____________________

3 I live in that house with my **father and my mother**. ____________________

4 The politician was not able to **perform** his plans. ____________________

5 That school has a big **place where you can read books**. ____________________

6 She loves her new house. **In fact,** it's a nice place to live. ____________________

7 Be careful. The streets are dangerous **at the present time**. ____________________

D Read the information in the box. Then write new words and translate them.

Example: luck luckless azarado

1 speech ____________ ____________

2 use ____________ ____________

3 care ____________ ____________

4 home ____________ ____________

5 power ____________ ____________

6 end ____________ ____________

Suffix less
O sufixo **less** indica sem, falta de.

E Choose the correct alternative to complete the sentences.

1 Jorge Amado ________ Clarice Lispector were great writers.

a [ ] but b [x] and c [ ] however

2 He completely ________ the exercise. It was so difficult.

a [ ] misunderstand b [ ] misunderstood c [ ] understand

3 The kids saved a lot of money. ________ it wasn't enough to buy the new video game.

a [ ] However b [ ] Because c [ ] And

4 Last weekend I went to a ________ and bought an excellent book about global warming.

a [ ] library b [ ] shoe store c [ ] bookstore

5 Lots of people travel abroad ________.

a [ ] accomplish b [ ] nowadays c [ ] actually

6 He couldn't call me ________ he didn't have my number.

a [ ] because b [ ] however c [x] but

F Read the cartoon below. Choose the correct alternative.

"I'm trying to be a good listener, but you keep breaking my concentration by talking!"

The word **but** can be substituted with:

a [ ] and

b [ ] however

c [ ] because

Taken from: <www.glasbergen.com>. Accessed on November 27, 2010.

LANGUAGE IN USE

A Read the narrative about flying objects over the city of Ipuaçu. Then match the columns and talk to a classmate. See the examples.

LIGHTS & CIRCLES OVER IPUAÇU, BRAZIL

The appearance of big circles in the crops of Ipuaçu, Santa Catarina, attracts the world's attention.

According to a local woman, it was Monday, November 10, at about 15 minutes after nine p.m. The witness was at home, looking through the window, when she saw the flying objects. They were large with triangles on top and green and red neon lights. They turned around slowly.

The woman thought the objects were trying to land, but they did not. She believes they left marks because they were close to the ground. She called some neighbors and they saw the same thing.

The president of the Brazilian Center for Flying Saucer Research is convinced the circles have an extraterrestrial origin.

Based on: *Could the Crop Circles of Brazil be Extraterrestrial?* By Billy Booth, posted at <http://ufos.about.com>. *"Sinais" em plantações suscitam boatos de visitas extraterrestres em Ipuaçu (SC)*, 14/11/2008, by Elisa Estronioli, posted at <http://noticias.uol.com.br>. Accessed on October 30, 2010.

A	B
What	happen
When	appear
Where	see
How many	do
What time	be

A: When did it happen?
B: On November 10.

A: Where did the circles appear?
B: In Ipuaçu, Santa Catarina.

B NOW IT'S YOUR TURN!

Ask a classmate about a strange, funny situation he or she has experienced or witnessed. Look at the examples.

What happened?
Where were you?

WRITING

Write a narrative for a magazine about a scary, strange, or bizarre situation in your life.

EXTRA PRACTICE 3

A Read the information in the box. Then match the opposites.

1	hot	a	[ ]	nervous
2	nightmare	b	[ ]	married
3	calm	c	[ ]	cold
4	outside	d	[ ]	dream
5	single	e	[ ]	attic
6	big	f	[ ]	inside
7	basement	g	[ ]	small

basement: porão
big: grande
calm: calmo(a)
hot: quente
nightmare: pesadelo
outside: fora
single: solteiro(a)

B Read the information in the box. Then complete the sentences.

1 She's going ________________ school now.

2 The teacher went ________________ California last vacation.

3 My sister's arriving ________________ Japan this afternoon.

4 Helen came ________________ her house last night.

5 The milk we drink comes ________________ his farm.

6 I'm not traveling ________________ a foreign country this month.

Prepositions

from: de
to: para
The girl went **from** Cleveland **to** New York.

C Substitute the words in bold. Use possessive pronouns.

Example: This is **my book**.
This book is mine.

1 This is my favorite color. What is **your favorite color**?
This is my favorite color. What is ______________________?

2 Paul brought his book. Did Sheila bring **her book**?
Paul brought his book. Did Sheila bring ______________________?

3 Louise is writing her composition and Richard is writing **his composition**.
Louise is writing her composition and Richard is writing ______________________.

4 I couldn't finish my exercise. Could they finish **their exercise**?
I couldn't finish my exercise. Could they finish ______________________?

5 They invited their friends. We can invite **our friends**.
They invited their friends. We can invite ______________________.

D **Choose the correct alternative to complete the sentences.**

1 João Carlos Martins ________ his left hand work for two.

a ☐ made b ☐ sees c ☐ make

2 In 1969 he ________ his right arm severely.

a ☐ saw b ☐ brought c ☐ hurt

3 He ________ the Bachiana Chamber Orchestra in 2004.

a ☐ learns b ☐ found c ☐ founded

E **Answer the questions. Use the box for help.**

bring: brought **take:** took
destroy: destroyed **try:** tried
find: found

Example: A: Did you bring the blue box? (the red box)
B: No, I didn't bring the blue box. I brought the red box.

1 A: Did the dogs destroy the vase? (the flowers)

B: No, ____.

2 A: Did you find your watch? (my keys)

B: No, ____.

3 A: Did he take the bus to school? (a taxi)

B: No, ____.

4 A: Did she try to play tennis? (soccer)

B: No, ____.

F **Circle the verbs in the Past Continuous.**

I love Sunday afternoons because everything is calm and peaceful.

Last Sunday, around 4:00 p.m., everybody was at home. My brother was reading a book in his bedroom, Mom was painting in the garden, Grandma was baking a cake, Dad was washing the car, the cats were sleeping, and I was talking on the phone.

Suddenly, my sister Glenda arrived with her two kids and a dog.

In a few minutes, the house turned into chaos. The dog ran after the cats, and the children ran after the dog. When Glenda left, at 9:00 p.m., one of the kids was crying and the other was sleeping.

And Sunday was over.

G Complete the sentences about the text on page 87.

Example: My brother was not reading a magazine.
He was reading a book.

1 Mom wasn't cooking. She ______________________________.

2 Dad wasn't fixing the car. He ______________________________.

3 Grandma ______________________________.

4 The cats ______________________________.

5 I wasn't sleeping. I ______________________________.

H Answer the questions according to the text.

1 What time did Glenda arrive?

____

2 What did the kids do in the house?

____

3 What time did she leave?

____

4 What were the kids doing when they left?

____

I Make sentences with the prompts given. Use the Simple Past or the Past Continuous.

1 My father / hurt / his foot / while he / play / basketball.

____

2 I / have / a nightmare / when the alarm clock / go off.

____

3 My family / see / amazing animals / when they / travel to / the Amazon.

____

4 Carla / chat / on the computer / while her parents / watch TV.

____

5 It / rain / when I / leave the gym.

____

J **Ask questions about the words in bold.**

Example: They were running **in the park at 5 o'clock.**
(Where) Where were they running at 5 o'clock?
(What time) What time were they running in the park?

1 He was buying **a magazine this morning**.

(What) ______________________________

(When) ______________________________

2 Mom **was sleeping because she was tired**.

(What) ______________________________

(Why) ______________________________

3 **The children** were eating **sandwiches in the kitchen** 5 minutes ago.

(Who) ______________________________

(What) ______________________________

(Where) ______________________________

K **Write sentences about your abilities. Use *can* or *can't* and the expressions given.**

ride a bicycle | use a computer | swim | play the guitar | play volleyball
dance | drive a car | play soccer | run fast | sing in English

Examples: I can play tennis.
I can't play volleyball.

____

____

____

____

L **In your notebook, write about the things you could do when you were a child.**

ride a bike

drive a car

watch TV all day

work in an office

play soccer

eat hot dogs

read magazines

swim

go to the park

JOB INTERVIEW TIPS

THERE ARE TWO SIMPLE RULES TO MAKE YOUR JOB INTERVIEW GO WELL:

BE PREPARED

Learn about the company you will have the interview with – where they are from, what they do/offer, etc.

Practice the interview with a friend. You can try these questions:

- Why are you interested in this job?
- Why are you interested in this company?
- What are your strengths and weaknesses?
- Why are you leaving your current job?
- Where do you see yourself in five years?

Get ready for the interview ahead of time: decide what you're going to wear and how you're going to get to the interview location.

Get together anything you must bring with you.

Wear comfortable, clean clothes. Do not chew gum or smoke. Make a good first impression.

BE RELAXED

People don't believe you can be relaxed at an interview, but you can. Listen to the questions attentively and answer them thoughtfully. Speak in a normal conversational tone.

When you're done, thank the interviewer for taking the time to meet with you.

Based on <www.bls.gov>; <http://jobsearch.about.com>. Accessed on October 17, 2010.

Vocabulary

ahead of time: com antecedência
attentively: atentamente
chew: mascar
clothes: roupas
current: atual
done: terminado
get ready: apronte-se
get together: junte
interview: entrevista
location: local
rule: regra
strengths: pontos positivos/fortes
thoughtfully: refletidamente
tone: tom
weaknesses: pontos negativos/fracos
wear: vestir

7 Stem Cells

Language in Context

A **Complete the information. Then, read the dialogue and check your answers.** 14

1 Number of people: ____________________

2 Relationship: ____________________

Mr. Stanley: How much did you spend at the mall, Josie?

Josie: Not much, Dad.

Mr. Stanley: Is that so? Those things look expensive!

Josie: Don't worry. I spent little money.

Billy: How much is "little" money, Dad?

Mr. Stanley: It depends on the person. For me, it's about $20 or $30 dollars.

Josie: Then, I spent a few dollars, Dad.

Billy: How much is "a few" dollars, Dad?

Mr. Stanley: I think it's $40 to $50 dollars.

Josie: In that case, I spent many dollars, Dad.

B **Give your opinion.**

1 Does Billy know much about money?

2 Do Josie and her father share the same opinion about money?

Vocabulary

look: parecer
mall: *shopping center*

C **Think about it.**
Observe the words in bold and answer the questions.

a I spent **few** dollars. b I spent **a few** dollars. c I spent **many** dollars.

1 Which sentence indicates the greatest amount of money?

2 Which sentence indicates the smallest amount of money?

Language Practice

Quantifiers: Much, Many, Few...

Substantivos

Os substantivos podem ser contáveis ou incontáveis.

Os substantivos contáveis (*countable nouns*) referem-se a coisas que podemos contar.

Examples: dollars, bottles, liters, kilos, packs, slices, apples, boys, etc.

Os substantivos incontáveis (*uncountable nouns*) referem-se a coisas que não podemos contar.

Examples: money, milk, sugar, bread, meat, liberty, happiness, etc.

Uso

Antes de substantivos contáveis, usa-se:

- **many:** muitos(as)

  I bought **many** bottles of milk.
- **few:** poucos(as) / **a few:** alguns(mas)

  I have **few** cents; I can't take a bus. We have **a few** minutes to talk.
- **fewer:** menos

  You have **fewer** friends than I do.

Antes de substantivos incontáveis, usa-se:

- **much:** muito(a)

  There wasn't **much** milk in the bottle.
- **little:** pouco(a) / **a little:** algum(a)

  He has **little** money; he can't buy a car. We have **a little** time to rest.
- **less:** menos

  I have **less** time than you.
- **a lot of, lots of, plenty of** podem substituir **much** e **many** em frases afirmativas.

  We have **a lot of** books.

  There is **lots of** meat.

  I have **plenty of** money.

Nota

- **Very** significa "muito" e é usado antes de adjetivos e advérbios com a função de enfatizar.

  She's **very** tired.

  My father speaks Spanish **very** well.

A Check what you need for a party.

1

invitations

- [ ] much
- [ ] many

2

balloons

- [ ] little
- [ ] a few

3

sandwiches

- [ ] a lot of
- [ ] a little

4

soda

- [ ] many
- [ ] much

5

money

- [ ] a little
- [ ] a few

6

friends

- [ ] many
- [ ] much

B Complete the sentences. Use *few* or *little*.

1 There is ______________________ money in the drawer.

2 There was ______________________ sugar in the sugar pot.

3 There are ______________________ children in the park.

4 There were ______________________ people at the party yesterday.

5 She needs ______________________ time to get ready.

6 I bought ______________________ bottles of soda for lunch.

7 There is ______________________ juice for dinner.

C Complete the sentences. Use *much* or *many*.

1 There are ______________ Brazilians in the USA.

2 There are ______________ animals at the zoo.

3 There isn't ______________ water in the refrigerator.

4 There isn't ______________ work today.

5 We don't need ______________ time to finish this exercise.

6 They aren't going to bring ______________ CDs.

7 She invited ______________ friends for her birthday party.

D Find the mistakes. Correct them. Some sentences may be correct.

1 Give fewer food to the animals. ______________

2 Invite a little children to the game. ______________

3 I have lots of friends to invite to the party. ______________

4 She knows less songs than me. ______________

5 I don't spend much money at the mall. ______________

6 He has few money because he is jobless. ______________

7 The omelet tastes good. Add just a few salt. ______________

8 She doesn't like me very much. ______________

Go to page 113 for Extra Practice.

E Choose the correct alternative.

1 I received ______ presents on my 15th birthday.

a ☐ a little b ☐ many c ☐ much

2 My mother was ______ tired yesterday.

a ☐ very b ☐ many c ☐ few

3 We spent a ______ dollars shopping. It was a big sale.

a ☐ much b ☐ many c ☐ few

4 He has ______ time; he's working a lot.

a ☐ little b ☐ a few c ☐ less

5 My brother has ______ friends now than when he was a teen.

a ☐ less b ☐ a little c ☐ fewer

6 They didn't receive ______ love when they were children.

a ☐ many b ☐ much c ☐ very

Reading

Before Reading

Approaching the text

Discuss the questions below in Portuguese.

1 Have you heard about stem cells?

2 What are they? What are they used for?

Vocabulary

Write a synonym for each word below. Use the words given.

consequently | illnesses | presently | replace | restoration | turn into

1 diseases (l. 3) ____________________

2 become (l. 7) ____________________

3 replenish (l. 9) ____________________

4 therefore (l. 9) ____________________

5 repair (l. 10) ____________________

6 currently (l. 13) ____________________

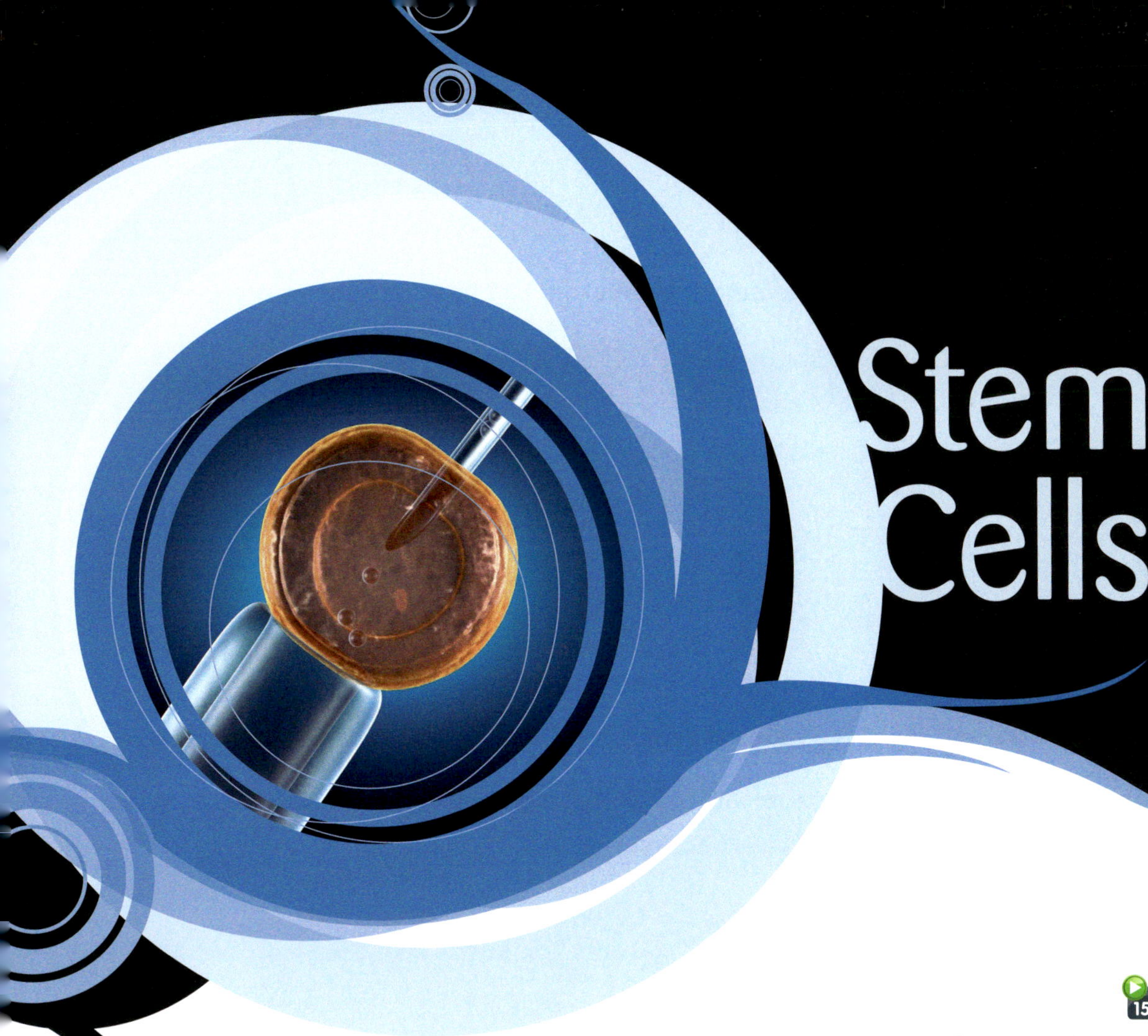

Stem Cells

Background on Stem Cells

Stem cells, which can transform themselves into many other tissue types, give rise to all the cells in the human body and hold the key to finding cures for many diseases, such as Parkinson's, Alzheimer's, heart disease, and diabetes. These master cells are found in the body at any age, acting as the root of all the cells that make up the body's tissues.

When a stem cell divides, each new cell has the potential to either remain a stem cell or become a specialized cell, such as a muscle cell, a red blood cell, or a brain cell. Stem cells can theoretically divide without limit to replenish other cells [...]. Scientists believe, therefore, that it should be possible to turn stem cells into a "repair kit" for the body.

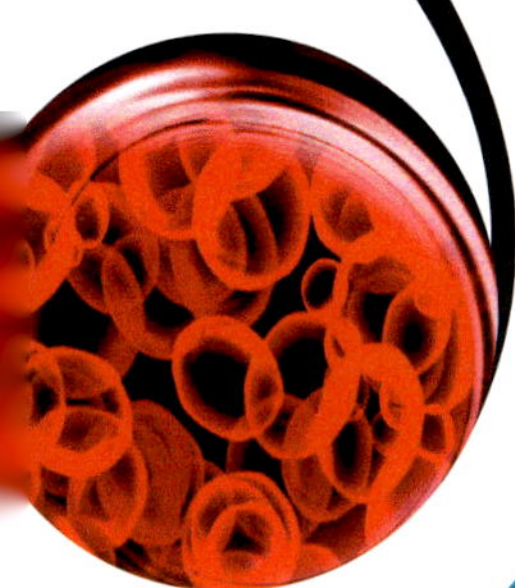

Human fetal tissue provides the best source of stem cells (embryonic stem cells). Stem cells are also found within adult organs (adult stem cells), but currently their potential to become other types of cells is limited. [...]

Extracted from <www.sciencedaily.com>.
Accessed on October 31, 2010.

Vocabulary

blood: sangue
brain: cérebro
heart: coração
muscle: músculo
stem cell: célula-tronco

After Reading

A Circle the cognates in the paragraph below.

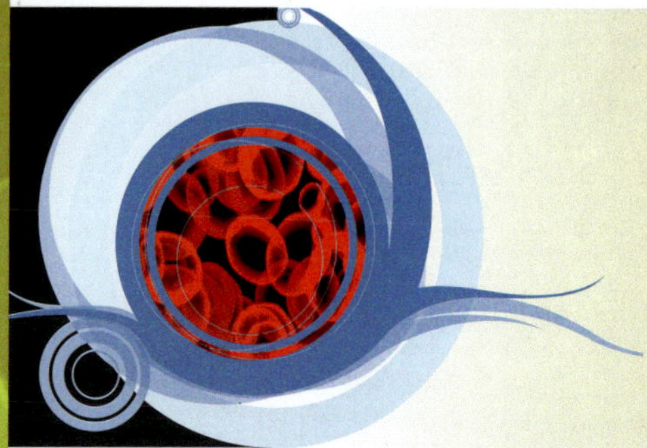

When a stem cell divides, each new cell has the potential to either remain a stem cell or become a specialized cell, such as a muscle cell, a red blood cell, or a brain cell. Stem cells can theoretically divide without limit to replenish other cells [...]. Scientists believe, therefore, that it should be possible to turn stem cells into a "repair kit" for the body.

B Check the meaning of the words in bold.

1 (l. 1) "Stem cells [...] can transform themselves into many other **tissue** types [...]"

a ☐ lenço

b ☐ tecido

c ☐ textura

2 (l. 2) "[...] **give rise** to all the cells in the human body [...]"

a ☐ causar

b ☐ crescer

c ☐ dar origem

3 (l. 6-7) "[...] each new cell has the potential to either **remain** a stem cell or become a specialized cell [...]"

a ☐ permanecer

b ☐ remanejar

c ☐ favorecer

4 (l. 9-10) "Scientists believe, **therefore**, that it should be possible to turn stem cells into a 'repair kit' for the body."

a ☐ entretanto

b ☐ ainda

c ☐ portanto

5 (l. 11) "Human fetal tissue provides the best **source** of stem cells [...]"

a ☐ fonte

b ☐ conteúdo

c ☐ recurso

C Check the correct alternative according to the text.

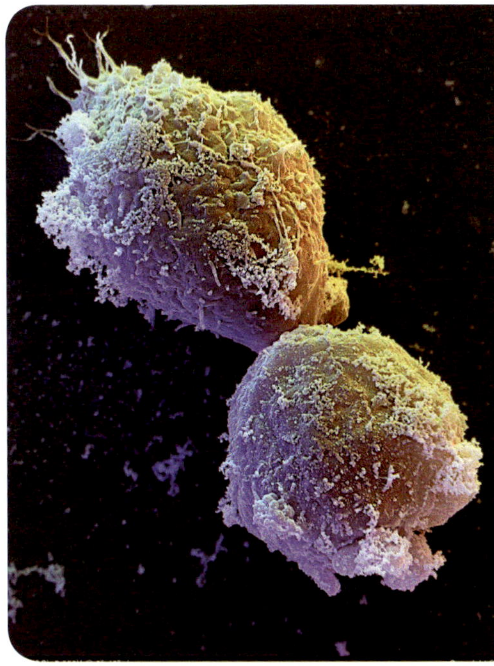

1 Stem cells...
   a [ ] can become different types of cells in a body.
   b [ ] do not divide.
   c [ ] are special muscle cells.

2 According to scientists, stem cells...
   a [ ] can cause diseases.
   b [ ] can repair damages caused by illnesses.
   c [ ] can cause heart diseases.

3 Stem cells can be obtained from...
   a [ ] blood and brain cells.
   b [ ] embryonic or adult cells.
   c [ ] Alzheimer cells.

4 Stem cells...
   a [ ] cannot divide in people with heart disease.
   b [ ] theoretically divide adult cells.
   c [ ] can replenish other cells.

5 According to scientists...
   a [ ] embryonic cells are the best source of stem cells.
   b [ ] adult cells are better than embryonic cells.
   c [ ] embryonic stem cells are as good as adult stem cells.

VOCABULARY EXPANSION

A Read the information in the box and write new words.

1 current ______________________
2 present ______________________
3 theoretical ______________________
4 special ______________________
5 immediate ______________________
6 dramatic ______________________

Suffix ly

Acrescentado a adjetivos, forma advérbios.

Indica circunstância de modo, tempo, etc.

Jim works slow**ly**.

B **Complete the sentences. Use *ly* and the words in parentheses.**

1 (extreme) That boy arrived home ______________________ sick.

2 (repeated) Jessica makes the same mistake ______________________.

3 (lazy) Bob is not a lazy boy. But today he is doing things ______________________.

4 (weak) He held her hands ______________________ last night.

C **Complete the sentences with the words in the box.**

either... or: ou... ou
like: como, do mesmo modo
such as: tal/tais como

1 He can't do that. He must ______________________ be mad ______________________ drunk.

2 She sings just ______________________ her mother.

3 I like colors ______________________ these you are wearing.

4 Frank can ______________________ remain here ______________________ go to another room.

D **Write synonyms and opposites. Use the words in the boxes for help.**

heal | separate | permitted | multiply | impossible | retain | continue | ordinary

Synonyms

1 divide ______________________

2 cure ______________________

3 remain ______________________

4 hold ______________________

Opposites

1 special ______________________

2 divide ______________________

3 possible ______________________

4 prohibited ______________________

LANGUAGE IN USE

A **Read the medical information about ADD (attention deficit disorder). Then match the columns and talk to a classmate. See the examples.**

Leonardo da Vinci

Leonardo da Vinci (1452-1519) was one of the greatest painters of the Italian Renaissance, yet he completed only seventeen paintings in sixty-seven years. His interests were so diverse that he usually failed to finish what he started. He liked to spend time studying science and contemplating nature.

Attention Deficit Disorder

ADD/ADHD or attention deficit/hyperactivity disorder is a mental disorder that commonly develops in children. It is a biological, brain-based condition whose characteristics are poor attention, hyperactivity and impulsive behaviors.

When untreated, ADHD can lead to low self-esteem, poor school performance, and poor social relationships.

Learn more about this disorder at the **National Resource Center on AD/HD**. The NRC provides answers to frequently asked questions about ADD.

Based on *Museum of Science: Renaissance Men*. Posted at <www.mos.org>. Accessed on November 3, 2010.

Based on *Understanding AD/DH at CHADD: Children and Adults with Attention Deficit Hyperactivity Disorder*. Posted at <www.chadd.org>. Accessed on November 3, 2010. *Learn More About Attention Deficit Disorder*, by Keath Low (About.com). Posted at <http://add.about.com>. Accessed on November 3, 2010.

A	B
What	be
When	develop
How many	make
How	like
Why	spend
	fail

A: What is ADD?
B: It's attention deficit disorder.
A: What is one characteristic of ADD?
B: Poor attention.

B **NOW IT'S YOUR TURN!**

Ask a classmate about his/her concentration.

Can you concentrate in the classroom/at home/listening to music?
When can't you concentrate?

WRITING

In your notebook, write an e-mail to a local magazine. Say you know a person with ADD. Ask...

1 what ADD is;
2 when people develop it;
3 what the symptoms are;
4 if you can help the person.

8 Physical Exercise

Language in Context

A Complete the information. Then, read the dialogue and check your answers.

16

1 Names: ______________________

2 Sports: ______________________

3 Period of the day: ______________________

4 Adjectives: ______________________

Naomi: Hi, Kenny. What's up? You look bored this morning!

Kenny: I am bored! I think I'm going to play volleyball from now on.

Naomi: Are you going to quit tennis?

Kenny: Yeah, I guess I will.

Naomi: Why? You're a good tennis player.

Kenny: I don't know, Naomi. Volleyball is more exciting than tennis.

Naomi: Well, if you want excitement, you can practice kitesurfing.

Kenny: In fact, I want to be a sport professional in the future. I want to work professionally with sports. Maybe as a coach.

Naomi: Then, choose a sport you like. Do you like volleyball?

Kenny: Good point...

B Give your opinion.

1 What is the boy bored about?

2 Does he like tennis?

Vocabulary

from now on: daqui em diante
maybe: talvez
quit: abandonar

C Think about it. Read the sentences below and answer the questions.

Volleyball is more exciting than tennis.
Kitesurfing is more dangerous than volleyball.

1 Find the adjectives in the sentences.

2 What do the sentences have in common?

Language Practice

Comparison (I)

Em inglês, a maioria dos adjetivos e alguns advérbios podem aparecer nos graus absoluto, comparativo e superlativo.

Nota

› **More** e **most** são usados com adjetivos longos ou com mais de duas sílabas, como *comfortable, expensive, intelligent, dangerous*, etc.

***more** comfortable than / the **most** expensive*

Absoluto

She is **pretty**. He speaks **slowly**.

Comparativo

É usado quando comparamos dois itens.

as... as (tão... quanto)	I run **as fast as** you.
not as... as (não tão... quanto)	Ann is **not as smart as** Paul.
less... than (menos... do que)	Today is **less cold than** yesterday.
more... than (mais... do que)	Jane is **more beautiful than** Sally.

Superlativo

É usado quando comparamos mais de dois itens.

the least... (o/a menos...)	He is **the least strong** of the boys.
the most... (o/a mais...)	His is **the most expensive** car in town.

A Read the sentences and answer the questions.

1 Julian is not as successful as Charles. But Gill is.

Who is as successful as Gill? ______

2 Tom is as tall as Barry. But neither of them is as tall as Helen.

Is Tom as tall as Helen? ______

3 **Eve:** I'm going to buy this motorbike.
Carol: Why? It's uncomfortable!
Eve: I only have money to buy a motorbike.
Carol: That red car is as expensive as the motorbike.
Eve: Really?

Can Eve afford the red car? ______

4 If Math is as difficult as Physics and Physics is as difficult as Biology, is Math as difficult as Biology? ______

B Complete the sentences with the words in parentheses. Use *more... than* or *the most...*

1 Brenda is ______________________ ______________ (energetic) her brother.

2 Uranium is ______________________ ______________ (radioactive) radium.

3 You are ______________________ ______________ (nervous) person that I know.

4 Physics is ______________________ ______________ (complicated) subject that I study.

5 In my opinion, cars are ______________________ ______________ (comfortable) buses.

6 Skydiving is ______________________ ______________ (dangerous) sport that I know.

C There are mistakes in some of the sentences below. Find and correct them.

1 John is the least popular than Peter.

____

2 Mary and I are less curious than my cousin.

____

3 My car is the least expensive than yours.

____

4 The new football team is the least popular team in our school.

____

5 Chris is less intelligent girl in my class.

____

6 These books are less difficult than those.

____

7 Your jacket is least durable than your sister's.

____

8 The new dictionary is the least complete in our library.

____

Verb Tense Review		
Simple Present	**Forma**	Infinitivo sem **to** 3ª pessoa do singular + **s/es** Auxiliar: **do/does**
	Advérbios	often, always, every day, sometimes, never, etc.
	Exemplos	I often **drink** tea. / He **likes** tea.
	Indica	hábitos, verdades universais
Present Continuous	**Forma**	To be (Present) + verbo + **ing**
	Advérbios	now, at present, at this moment, etc.
	Exemplo	The kids **are sleeping** now.
	Indica	ação em andamento
Future with Going to	**Forma**	To be (Present) + **going to** + verbo
	Advérbios	tomorrow, next..., in..., etc.
	Exemplo	I **am going to visit** you next month.
	Indica	ação futura
Imperative	**Forma**	Infinitivo sem **to**
	Advérbios	now, right now
	Exemplos	**Get** out now! / **Don't come** back!
	Indica	ordem, pedido
Simple Past	**Forma**	Regulares: verbo + **d/ed** Irregulares: ver pág. 396 Auxiliar: **did**
	Advérbios	yesterday, last..., in..., etc.
	Exemplos	I **danced** last night. / He **swam** last week.
	Indica	ação passada em determinado tempo
Past Continuous	**Forma**	To be (Past) + verbo + **ing**
	Advérbios	yesterday, last..., in..., when, while, etc.
	Exemplo	She **was sleeping** two minutes ago.
	Indica	ação passada em andamento

D Underline the verbs in the text and list them below.

[...]

Street dance is a term for a whole load of dance styles. The reason it's called "street" is because these styles developed outside of professional dance studios, inspired instead by people dancing in streets, schools and also nightclubs. Usually street dancing involves quite a lot of improvisation, contact with other dancers, and also interaction with the audience. New street dances are developing all the time.

[...]

Extracted from <www.need2know.co.uk>. Accessed on September 17, 2010.

Simple Present ____________________

Present Continuous ____________________

Going to ____________________

Imperative ____________________

Simple Past ____________________

Past Continuous ____________________

Go to page 115 for Extra Practice.

READING

Before Reading

Approaching the text

Discuss the questions below in Portuguese.

1 What is "intelligence"?

2 Does exercise have any effect on intelligence over time?

Vocabulary

A Write synonyms for the words below. Use the words in the boxes.

can | in the same way | to mend | to adjust | to maintain

1 fix ____________________

2 keep ____________________

3 adapt ____________________

4 like ____________________

5 be able to ____________________

B Look up the words below in the glossary.

1 stay ____________________

2 mind ____________________

3 sharp ____________________

4 brain ____________________

C Fill in the blanks with words from the text on page 108. The first letter is given.

1 Sunbathing **i**______________ the risk of getting skin cancer.

2 His eyes were **u**______________ for that job.

3 The doctor will **s**______________ him before he can go home.

4 We had a very **a**______________ vacation.

5 The police officer made an **e**______________ to check all the cars.

Physical Exercise and Intelligence

Intelligence is not a simple quality. It involves:

- **> the ability to learn;**
- **> the ability to solve problems;**
- **> the ability to think quickly.**

Different people use these abilities in different ways in dealing with ideas and symbols, solving practical problems (fixing the washing machine, for example), and relating with other people.

One of the most effective ways to stay mentally sharp is to keep the mind active – especially as we grow older.

Intelligence increases until the age of 26. It stabilizes until the age of 40, and then declines slowly.

A well-exercised mind uses less energy than an untrained one. One reason for this is that the brain adapts to mental training just like our muscles respond to physical training.

A trained brain uses fewer neurons, just like fit muscles use less fibers to perform a task. As a result, less fuel (carbohydrates) is consumed and more efficiency is achieved.

And the mind, like the body, is able to do more with less effort. In short, although the combination of physical and mental activity is not the Fountain of Youth, it certainly is the best thing we can do to keep our intelligence sharp.

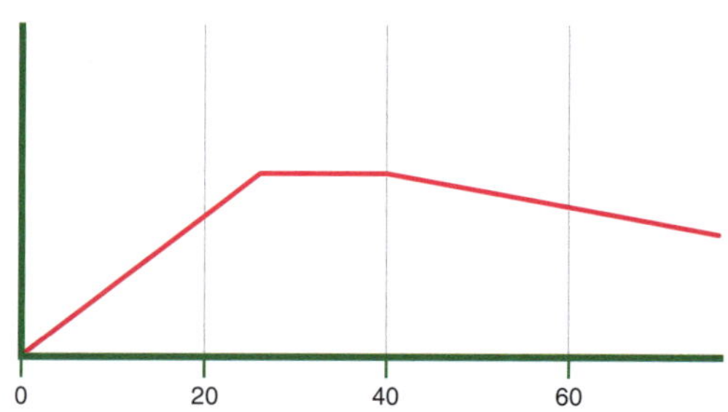

Intelligence increases until the age of 26. It stabilizes until the age of 40, and then declines slowly.

Based on <www.earthden.org>. Accessed on May 2, 2010.

Vocabulary

deal: lidar com
fit muscle: músculo exercitado
grow older: envelhecer
like: como
perform: executar

After Reading

A Take a look at the text page. Identify the type of text.

a ☐ anúncio
b ☐ crônica
c ☐ texto informativo
d ☐ conto

B Take a look at the text. Find 10 cognates.

____

____

C Find out what the words in bold refer to.

1 (1st paragraph)

"Intelligence is not a simple quality. **It** involves the ability to learn." ____________

2 (5th paragraph)

"A well-exercised mind uses less energy than an untrained **one**." ____________

D Find in the text the extracts that say...

1 [...] especialmente enquanto envelhecemos.

____

2 [...] a mente, como o corpo, é capaz de fazer mais com menos esforço.

____

E Answer the questions about the text.

1 What does intelligence involve?

____

2 What is one of the most effective ways to stay mentally sharp?

____

3 Which uses more energy: an untrained or a trained mind?

____

4 What fuel do our body and our mind use?

____

5 Do you keep your mind active?

____

VOCABULARY EXPANSION

A Complete the sentences. Use the appropriate form of the verbs given.

eat | spend | finish | work | pay | leave

Preposition + verb + ing

Example: The kids can play after eating something.

1 You can't leave without ______________________ your debts.
2 I'd like to thank you for ______________________ a lot of money on me.
3 Please call me before ______________________ to school.
4 I'm tired of ______________________ for him.
5 He left the office after ______________________ his work.

B Find out the meaning of the words below.

1 well-defined	a	[ ]	bem conhecido
2 well-done	b	[ ]	bem-intencionado
3 well-known	c	[ ]	bem passado / benfeito
4 well-intentioned	d	[ ]	bem definido

Well + adjective
well-exercised: bem exercitado

C Complete the sentences. Use the words from exercise B.

1 Cielo is a ______________________ swimmer. Everybody knows him.
2 Tom wanted his steak ______________________.
3 Mary is the most ______________________ girl in the school. She helps everyone.
4 All of John's projects are ______________________. They are very precise.

D Give the correct meaning for the word *as*. Use the box for help.

as

enquanto/quando	uma vez que
tão... quanto	como (na função de)

1 My uncle's friend worked as a personal trainer. ______________________
2 Last week I talked to Mary as we were jogging. ______________________
3 My father is as intelligent as my mother. ______________________
4 As a child, Pelé lived in Bauru. ______________________
5 As you aren't reading the book, I will give it back to Peter. ______________________

LANGUAGE IN USE

A **Complete the health evaluation form below.**

Health Evaluation Form

Name: ______________________

Age: ______

Would you like your weight to be different?	( ) Yes	( ) No
Do you sleep well?	( ) Yes	( ) No
Do you wake up at night?	( ) Yes	( ) No
Do you take any vitamins/medications?	( ) Yes	( ) No
What role does exercise play in your life?	( ) Big	( ) Small
Do you drink coffee?	( ) Yes	( ) No
Do you get enough rest?	( ) Yes	( ) No
How is the health of your father/mother?	( ) Good	( ) Not very good
What's your diet like these days?	( ) Good	( ) Not very good

B **NOW IT'S YOUR TURN!**

Interview a classmate and write down the answers. Look at the examples.

A: What is your name?
B: My name's Joe.

A: How old are you?
B: I'm seventeen.

A: Would you like your weight to be different?
B: ☐ Yes. ☑ No.

WRITING

In your notebook, write a report describing your classmate's health habits based on his/her answers to the form.

Joe is 17. He wouldn't like his weight to be different.

EXTRA PRACTICE 4

A Check the meaning of the words and expressions in bold.

1 **Few people** are aware that children are harvesting cocoa.

a ☐ Muitas pessoas

b ☐ Várias pessoas

c ☐ Poucas pessoas

2 The man promised to help the boy **get** to the Ivory Coast.

a ☐ chegar

b ☐ voltar

c ☐ ficar

3 Sally is in poor **health**.

a ☐ doença

b ☐ saúde

c ☐ mal-estar

4 Waves **beat** against the cliffs for hours this morning.

a ☐ presentearam

b ☐ bateram

c ☐ lembraram

5 The traffickers tried **to avoid** the official border checks.

a ☐ evitar

b ☐ encontrar

c ☐ enganar

B Remove the suffixes. Find the original words.

a production ______________________

b dangerous ______________________

c immediately ______________________

d trafficker ______________________

e owner ______________________

f doer ______________________

g honorary ______________________

h repeatedly ______________________

i Malian ______________________

j Consulate ______________________

k extremely ______________________

l slowly ______________________

m comfortable ______________________

n monthly ______________________

C Check the correct alternative.

1 I don't have ________ time to talk to you because I am ________ late.

a ☐ very – very
b ☐ many – very
c ☐ much – very
d ☐ much – many

2 ________ people know that there are ________ children working on cocoa plantations.

a ☐ Many – less
b ☐ Few – many
c ☐ Less – little
d ☐ Fewer – much

3 There isn't ________ bread in the house. Please, buy ________ loaves.

a ☐ many – less
b ☐ little – much
c ☐ much – a few
d ☐ much – much

4 We don't have ________ eggs either, buy ________.

a ☐ many – a few
b ☐ fewer – less
c ☐ much – a little
d ☐ many – a fewer

5 I ordered ________ gallons of lemonade this month because the children aren't home.

a ☐ fewer
b ☐ very
c ☐ less
d ☐ much

6 I want to ask you ________ questions. It won't take ________ time.

a ☐ a lot of – many
b ☐ a few – much
c ☐ many – very
d ☐ much – many

7 ________ work brings ________ money.

a ☐ Little – little
b ☐ Much – very
c ☐ Little – few
d ☐ Less – fewer

8 Nowadays we spend ________ money to buy ________ things.

a ☐ less – less
b ☐ much – less
c ☐ few – few
d ☐ more – fewer

9 My brother is a ________ curious person.

a ☐ many
b ☐ a few
c ☐ few
d ☐ very

10 She drinks ________ coffee because she has ________ problems.

a ☐ many – much
b ☐ few – little
c ☐ a lot of – lots of
d ☐ very – a little

D Complete the sentences. Use *less... than* or *the least...*

1 Douglas is ____________________ (popular) Charles.

2 Harold is ____________________ (intelligent) boy in my class.

3 A bicycle is ____________________ (expensive) a car.

4 This is ____________________ (important) aspect of the problem.

5 You are sitting on ____________________ (comfortable) chair in the room.

E Complete the sentences. Use *more... than* or *the most...*

1 My project was ____________________ (successful) of all.

2 Our experiment is ____________________ (difficult) theirs.

3 Your car is ____________________ (economical) mine.

4 This dictionary is ____________________ (complete) in the library.

5 Apple pies are ____________________ (delicious) strawberry pies.

6 English is ____________________ (interesting) Geography.

F Complete the sentences. Use *as... as* and the words given.

1 The red blouse is (cheap/skirt) ____________________.

2 I am (hungry/the children) ____________________.

3 Grace is (beautiful/Sally) ____________________.

4 Your apartment is (big/my house) ____________________.

5 Aren't you going to help me? I am (tired/you) ____________________.

G Ask questions. Use the Simple Present.

1 We like coffee.

What ____________________?

2 She goes to school in the afternoon.

When ____________________?

3 He lives nearby.

Where ____________________?

4 They study English in the morning.

What ____________________?

H Complete the sentences. Use the verbs in parentheses.

1 Rivers ______________________ (flow) to the sea.
2 Jimmie never ______________________ (worry) about his examinations.
3 That cat always ______________________ (destroy) the flowers in my garden.
4 The kids never ______________________ (help) me when I need something.
5 Does your brother ______________________ (study) in the morning?

I Answer the questions. Use the Present Continuous and the words given.

1 What is she doing now? (read a magazine)

____

____

2 Where are the boys swimming? (lake)

____

____

3 What are the kids doing? (watch TV)

____

4 What is Sally eating? (a sandwich)

____

5 Where are the girls studying? (their room)

____

6 What is he doing? (fix the car)

____

7 Where are the teens playing soccer? (on the field)

____

J Complete the sentences. Use the words given.

1 She isn't swimming now. She ______________________ (dance).
2 They aren't working now. They ______________________ (play) the guitar.
3 I ______________________ (not / read) now. I am writing letters.
4 We ______________________ (not / leave) now. We are just talking.
5 They ______________________ (not / help) me. They are doing their homework.

K Rewrite the sentences. Use the future with *going to* and the words given.

1 She types her homework every day. (tomorrow)

____

2 I eat fish every week. (next week)

____

3 They tell stories to the children every day. (in the afternoon)

____

4 The weather is fine today. (the day after tomorrow)

____

5 I work from Monday to Friday. (next year)

____

L Underline the correct alternative.

1 Hip-hop is (the most / more) modern dancing.

2 There aren't (much / many) things to do in this city.

3 We can't go out tonight. I have (little / few) money.

4 Best friends (doesn't / don't) lie to each other.

5 Chico Mendes (was fighting / fought) for human rights.

6 When I (was coming / came) to school yesterday, I (see / saw) a big accident.

7 We (destroy / are destroying) our forests faster and faster.

8 My mom (starts / is starting) a new course next week. She (is going to study / studies) Mandarin.

M Complete the sentences with the appropriate verb tense. Use the Simple Past and Past Continuous.

1 It ______________ (rain) this morning when I got up.

2 I ______________ (sleep) while he was writing me a message.

3 When you called, she ______________ (take) a shower.

4 I ______________ (cut) my finger while I was cutting some bread.

5 You ______________ (cross) the street when I saw you.

6 The light went out while we ______________ (have) dinner.

7 He was talking to his friend when he ______________ (hear) a strange noise.

Things Never to Do during a Job Interview

There are many things that you should **NEVER** do during an interview. Some are listed below.

- Talk about how much you need the job.
- Impose conditions.
- Emphasize your weaknesses. If asked questions like "What is your greatest weakness?" say you don't like to waste time on small talks and are working on being more friendly where you work. This is a positive "weakness."
- Use careless language.
- Criticize a former employer.
- Ask about how much the job pays.
- When asked if you have any questions, don't say "No." Ask questions about the company's plans for the future, for example.
- Tell them your life story. If asked to talk about yourself, tell them where you went to school, or where you have worked.

Based on <http://hubpages.com>; <http://subtlefortitude.wordpress.com>. Accessed on November 1, 2010.

Vocabulary

careless: desleixada	**employer:** empregador	**impose:** impor	**need:** precisar
criticize: criticar	**former:** anterior	**looking forward:** esperando ansiosamente	**should:** deveria
emphasize: enfatizar	**friendly:** amigável		**waste:** desperdiçar

9 The Happiest People in the World

Language in Context

A Complete the information. Then, read the dialogue and check your answers. 18

1 Subject

____

2 Adjectives

____

Boy 1: My dad is strong. He can lift 50 kilos.

Boy 2: My dad can lift 70 kilos. He is stronger than your dad.

Boy 1: My dad is big and tall.

Boy 2: My dad is bigger and taller than yours.

Boy 1: My dad is good.

Boy 2: My dad is better.

Boy 1: My dad is old.

Boy 2: Yeah! That's right.

B Give your opinion.

1 Do you think children usually make this kind of comparison?

2 Why do you think one of the boys finally agrees with the other?

Vocabulary

better: melhor
lift: erguer

C Think about it.
Compare the sentences and answer the questions.

My dad is stronger than yours.
My dad is bigger and taller than yours.

1 Two people are being compared. Who are they?

2 When the comparisons were made, the word **more** was not used. Why?

Language Practice

Comparison

Ortografia

Geralmente, formam-se o comparativo e o superlativo de adjetivos e advérbios de **uma** ou **duas** sílabas acrescentando-se **er**/**est**:

strong – strong**er** – strong**est**

Roy is strong**er** than me.

young – young**er** – young**est**

Roy is the young**est** person I know.

Adjetivos com **duas ou mais** sílabas recebem **more**/**most**:

more hopeful	**most** obscure	**most** curious
more charming	**more** surprised	**most** comfortable

She is **more** charming than her sister.

He is the **most** curious boy I know.

Observe as alterações de grafia:

e: larg**e** – larg**er** – larg**est**; wid**e** – wid**er** – wid**est**

y: happ**y** – happ**ier** – happ**iest**; sh**y** – sh**ier** – sh**iest**

consoante/vogal/consoante: hot – hott**er** – hott**est**; big – bigg**er** – bigg**est**

This room is larg**er** than the kitchen.

She is the happ**iest** girl in our group.

Today is hott**er** than yesterday.

Formas irregulares:

good – better – best

far – farther/further – farthest/furthest

bad – worse – worst

much/many – more – most

That was the **worst** day of my life.

You threw the ball far but I threw it **farther**.

Yesterday was the **best** day of my life.

Uso

Construções especiais:

It is getting colder and colder. (Está ficando cada vez mais frio.)

She is getting more and more beautiful. (Ela está ficando cada vez mais bonita.)

The hotter, the better. (Quanto mais quente, melhor.)

The more difficult, the more fascinating. (Quanto mais difícil, mais fascinante.)

A Write the comparative and superlative forms of the words below.

		Comparative	Superlative
1	heavy	____________	____________
2	lucky	____________	____________
3	fat	____________	____________
4	thin	____________	____________
5	good	____________	____________
6	light	____________	____________
7	furious	____________	____________
8	tall	____________	____________
9	sweet	____________	____________
10	old	____________	____________
11	bad	____________	____________

B Complete the sentences. Use the words in parentheses in the comparative form.

er

1 I am ____________ (young) than you.

2 Cars are ____________ (safe) than buses.

3 Your brother is ____________ (thin) than mine.

4 My backpack is ____________ (light) than yours.

5 This book is ____________ (bad) than that.

6 My son is ____________ (tall) than yours.

7 Planes are ____________ (fast) than cars.

C Complete the sentences. Use the words in parentheses in the superlative form.

est

1 My dad is ____________ (strong) man in my family.

2 Your grandpa is ____________ (old) man in the neighborhood.

3 Peter is ____________ (fat) boy among the students.

4 Our uncle is ____________ (lucky) person in the world.

5 This car is ____________ (large) one in Brazil.

6 Gloria is ____________ (short) girl among my friends.

7 English is ____________ (easy) subject at school.

D Write the sentences in English.

1 Quanto mais fácil, melhor.

____

2 Quanto mais difícil, pior.

____

3 Eu estou ficando cada vez mais curiosa.

____

Go to page 138 for Extra Practice.

E Read the sentences below. Then, answer the questions.

Example: I am 17, Joan is 19, and Fred is 21 years old.
Who is the oldest of the three?
Fred is the oldest of the three.

1 My mother was born in 1961. Dave's mother was born in 1957. Lionel's mother was born in 1974.
Who is the oldest of the three?

____

2 Your teacher is 170 cm tall. Your brother's teacher is 180 cm tall.
Who is the tallest of them?

____

3 The blue book costs 10 dollars, the red book costs 15 dollars, and the white one costs 50 dollars.
Which is the cheapest of the three?

____

4 The temperature in São Paulo is 25° C, the temperature in Rio de Janeiro is 31° C, and the temperature in Santa Catarina is 28° C.
Which temperature is the hottest of the three?

____

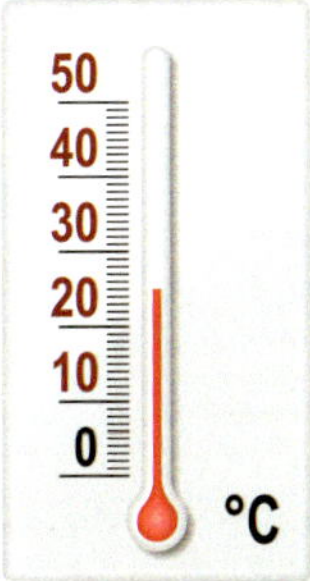

São Paulo 25° C

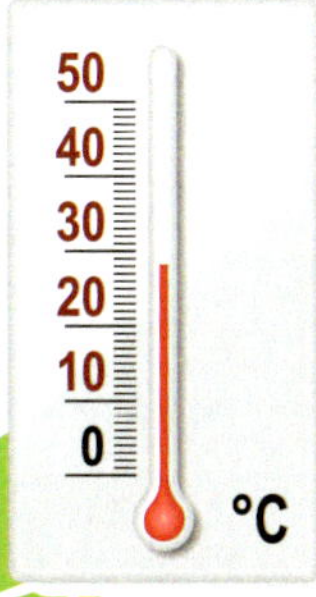

Santa Catarina 28° C

Rio de Janeiro 31° C

READING

Before Reading

Approaching the text

Discuss the questions below in Portuguese.

1 What do people need in order to feel happy?

2 Do you think money can bring happiness? Why?/Why not?

3 Do you think love can bring happiness? Why?/Why not?

Vocabulary

Look up the words below in the glossary.

1 interchangeably ______________________________

2 well-being ______________________________

3 enjoy ______________________________

4 disguise ______________________________

5 database ______________________________

6 sense ______________________________

Group task

Take a quick look at the text on page 123. Then answer the questions.

1 What is the text about?

____

2 Why do you think there is a list of countries in a table?

____

3 Where can you find this text?

____

4 Can anyone access this text?

____

5 Who are the probable readers?

____

http://worlddatabaseofhappiness.eur.nl

World Database of Happiness

19

Continuous Register of Scientific Research on Subjective Appreciation of Life
Directed by: Ruut Veenhoven, Erasmus University Rotterdam

2008 REPORT – The Happiest People in the World

The word "happiness" is used in various ways. In the widest sense it is an umbrella term for all that is good. In this meaning it is often used interchangeably with terms like "well-being" or "quality of life" and denotes both individual and social welfare. This use of words suggests that there is one ultimate good and disguises differences in interest between individuals and society. Here the word happiness is used in the more limited sense of subjective enjoyment of life.

[...]

Overall happiness is the degree to which an individual judges the overall quality of his/her own life-as-a-whole favorably. In other words: how much one likes the life one leads.

[...]

We do not use the word "happiness" to characterize satisfaction with specific aspects of life, such as marriage or work. "Happiness" refers to satisfaction with life-as-a-whole. It covers past, present and anticipated experiences.

[...]

Extracted from <http://worlddatabaseofhappiness.eur.nl>. Accessed on November 5, 2010.

Average Happiness in Some Nations

How much people enjoy their life-as-a-whole on scale 0 to 10:

Top > 7.9		Middle Range ± 6.0	
Iceland	8.5	Philippines	6.3
Denmark	8.4	China	6.3
Colombia	8.1	Iran	6.0
Switzerland	8.1	India	5.9
Mexico	8.0	South Korea	5.9

Bottom < 4.3	
Chad	4.2
Togo	4.1
Angola	4.0
Zimbabwe	3.3
Tanzania	3.2

Brazil	
2002	7.0
2008	7.4

Extracted from <http://worlddatabaseofhappiness.eur.nl>. Accessed on November 5, 2010.

These Do Not Always Bring Happiness

Love – There's no guarantee that finding a great love makes you happier, at least it does not for a long time.

Money – The richest people are not necessarily the happiest people in the world. A survey of 100 American millionaires showed that they were as happy as middle-class people.

Vocabulary

lead: levar, conduzir
ultimate: maior, máximo
whole: todo
survey: pesquisa
umbrella term: expressão guarda-chuva

After Reading

A Take a look at the text again. What kind of text is it? ____________

B Look for the numbers below in the text. What do they refer to?

1	0 to 10	a ☐	bottom grade of life enjoyment
2	3.2	b ☐	top grade of life enjoyment
3	2008	c ☐	scale of life enjoyment
4	8.5	d ☐	year of the report

C Find out what the words in bold refer to.

1 "In the widest sense **it** is an umbrella term for all that is good." ____________

2 "[...] **they** were as happy as middle-class people." ____________

D Write the meaning of the words in bold in the sentences below.

1 (box) "There's no guarantee that **finding** a great love makes you happier [...]" ____________

2 (2nd paragraph) "**Overall** happiness is the degree to which an individual judges the **overall** quality of his/her own life-as-a-whole favorably." ____________

E Check the sentences that are true according to the text.

1 ☐ The survey involved countries from only two continents.

2 ☐ Brazilian people felt happier in 2008 compared to 2002.

3 ☐ Many people understand happiness as well-being or quality of life.

4 ☐ In 2008 Brazil ranked at the top of the list of countries.

F Answer these questions according to the text.

1 Is money a guarantee of happiness?

____

2 According to the report, what does happiness refer to?

____

G Group discussion.
Discuss the sentence below with your friends.

"Probably, conditions for happiness have not been the same at all times and at all places."

VOCABULARY EXPANSION

A Complete the sentences. Use the box for help.

Adverbs

also (também)**:** Chris is **also** going to London.
too (também, em frases afirmativas)**:** Chris is going to London, **too**.
either (também, em frases negativas)**:** Chris isn't going to London, **either**.

1 Carla plays the piano very well, and she sings, ________________.

2 I didn't know the answer to the question, but he didn't know it, ________________.

3 Frank was ________________ in the room and saw everything.

4 Harry is not living in Canada. Susan is not living there, ________________.

5 We are studying for the test. They are ________________ studying.

B Read the box. Circle the best alternative.

False Cognates

attend: frequentar, comparecer	**pretend:** fingir	**policy:** política
atender (ao telefone, à porta)**:** answer	**pretender:** intend	**polícia:** police

1 She never **answers** – **attends** the phone when she is having dinner.

2 My friend is a medical student. He **pretends** – **intends** to be a doctor.

3 The party was so noisy last night that my neighbor called the **policy** – **police**.

4 Alice is not hurt. She is just **intending** – **pretending**.

5 My father **attended** – **answered** high school in London.

6 The thief **intended** – **pretended** to be innocent.

7 The Brazilian president is expected to pursue an environmental **policy** – **police**.

C Read the box. Write new words.

1 responsible ________________

2 personal ________________

3 real ________________

4 complex ________________

5 able ________________

6 national ________________

Suffix ity

O sufixo **ity** forma substantivos e indica o estado ou a qualidade descrito pelo adjetivo.

***Adjective*:** *probable*
Noun*:** *probabil**ity

D Complete the sentences. Use *ity* and the words given.

personal | responsible | probable | national

1 Where are you from? What's your ____________________?

2 What I admire in him is his strong ____________________.

3 These boys are under my ____________________.

4 There is a high ____________________ of rain tonight.

Language in Use

A Read the text. Then read the conversation and talk to a friend.

Extracted from <http://houstonclownschool.myweb.net>. Accessed on November 13, 2010.

A: What subject would you like to study?

B: History and Tradition of Clowning, I think. What about you?

A: I'd rather study Make-up.

B NOW IT'S YOUR TURN!

Talk to a friend using new words from the text.

WRITING

Write an e-mail to the clown school. Ask about:

- the price of the course;
- when you can start a course;
- the meaning of "hospital clowning".

From:

To:

Subject:

Links

Send

10 Relationships

Language in Context

A Complete the information. Then, read the cartoon and check your answers. 20

1 People

____

2 Relationship

____

3 Subject

____

____

B Give your opinion.

1 Why is the boy speaking so cautiously with his father?

2 Have you ever done something like that? What happened?

C Think about it. Compare the sentences and answer the questions.

You love me, don't you?
It's not my problem, is it?

1 Are the sentences above interrogative, negative or affirmative?

2 What is the purpose of "don't you?" and "is it?" in the sentences above?

Vocabulary

I've kicked too far: Chutei longe demais.

Language Practice

Tag Questions

Verbo Auxiliar/Modal + Pronome	
Oração afirmativa	*tag question* negativa (verbo na forma abreviada)
Oração negativa	*tag question* afirmativa

Uso

As *tag questions* são usadas para pedir uma confirmação do que foi dito.

***Tag question* negativa:** Cindy works hard, **doesn't she**?
The girls ate the cake, **didn't they**?
You can read, **can't you**?

***Tag question* afirmativa:** That boy doesn't work, **does he**?
Your mom wasn't happy, **was she**?
The babies won't cry, **will they**?

Exceções: I am late, **aren't I**?
Let's dance, **shall we**?
Don't open the door, **will you**?
I may go, **may I not**?
Open the door, **will you**?

A Choose appropriate tag questions.

a will you
b aren't they
c were they
d hasn't she
e will he
f shall we
g doesn't she
h did he
i must we

1 The students are tired, ___?
2 Your sister has seen the accident, ___?
3 Your brother won't come for dinner, ___?
4 That girl plays the piano, ___?
5 Let's talk, ___?
6 He didn't help you, ___?
7 We mustn't stay here, ___?
8 They weren't sleeping, ___?
9 Don't step on the grass, ___?

B Complete the sentences with appropriate tag questions.

1 I am crazy, ______________________________?

2 Mary doesn't like hot coffee, ______________________________?

3 The boys are going to school on foot, ______________________________?

4 You ate my sandwich last night, ______________________________?

5 Paul didn't work yesterday, ______________________________?

The Simple Future

Will + verbo		
I You He She It We You They	**will work**.	**Afirmativa:** He **will work** on Sunday. **Interrogativa: Will** he **work** on Sunday? **Negativa:** He **will not work** on Sunday. **Formas abreviadas: 'll** (will); **won't** (will not)

Uso

Para expressar ação ou previsão quanto ao futuro.

É usado com advérbios ou expressões que indicam tempo futuro: **tomorrow, next summer, in July, on Monday**, etc.

We **will study** hard next year.

Para dar ideia de pedido.

Will you **open** the door, please?

Nota

> Com **I** e **we**, é possível substituir **will** por **shall**, mas esse uso é considerado formal. É mais comum em perguntas ou quando se oferece, sugere ou convida.

Shall I help you?

Shall we go?

The Future Continuous

Will be + verbo terminado em **ing**
Afirmativa: He **will be** work**ing** tonight. **Interrogativa: Will** he **be** work**ing** tonight? **Negativa:** He **will not be** work**ing** tonight.

Uso

Para expressar uma ação que ocorrerá num determinado tempo no futuro.

Tomorrow at 4 o'clock **I'll be talking** to him.

C Write the following sentences in the negative and interrogative forms.

Example: They will study Math tomorrow.
They will not (won't) study Math tomorrow.
Will they study Math tomorrow?

1 She will come home after 10 o'clock.

____

____

2 We will meet them in the cafeteria.

____

____

3 My brother will run in the park after school.

____

____

D Complete the sentences. Use the Future Continuous and the information in parentheses.

1 (leave for London) At 4 o'clock tomorrow, they ______________________.
2 (paint my house) Next year, in July, I ______________________.
3 (swim) Saturday, at this time, we ______________________.
4 (arrive from Canada) Tomorrow evening, grandma ______________________.

Go to page 141 for Extra Practice.

E Unscramble the sentences.

1 people / will be eating / salad / a few / at lunchtime

____

2 bus / his / tonight / we / for / will be waiting / him / arrives / when

____

3 tomorrow / come back / will / she / probably

____

4 meet / won't / next / my / weekend / friends

____

5 my sister / library / this / afternoon / will be studying / at the

____

READING

Before Reading

Approaching the text

Discuss the questions below in Portuguese.

1 What do you understand by "abusive relationship"?

2 Do you think this is a problem in your community?

Vocabulary

A Read the definitions below.

alike: in a very similar way; equally
batter: strike heavily and repetitively
harm: physical or mental damage
partner: a person with whom we share an intimate relationship

B Look up the words below in the glossary.

1 married ________________

2 among ________________

3 reluctant ________________

4 husband ________________

Group task

Take a look at the text on page 133. What do you think the main idea of the text is?

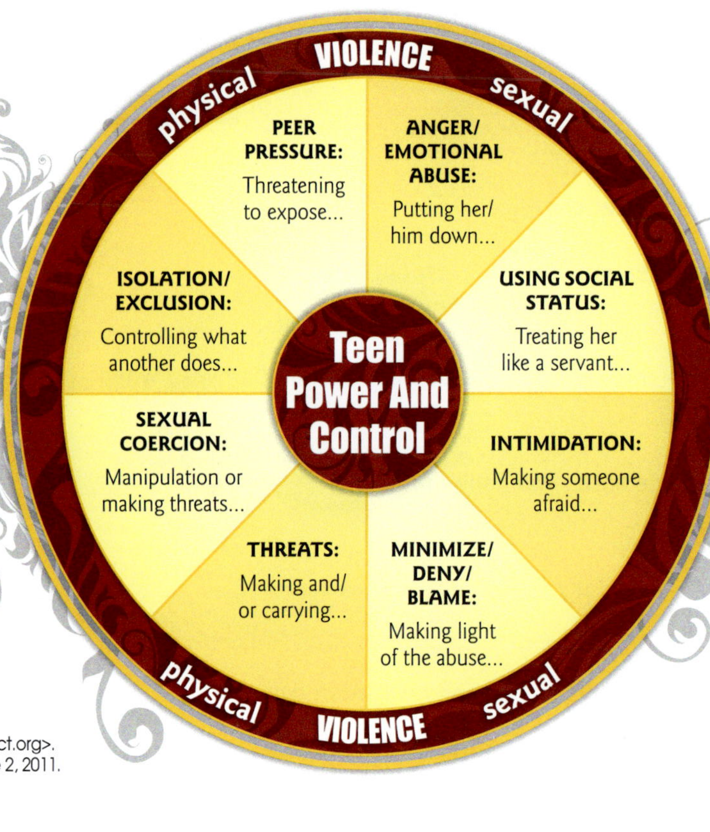

Extracted from <www.loveisrespect.org>. Accessed on June 2, 2011.

ADOLESCENT RELATIONSHIP VIOLENCE

Teen Dating Violence Statistics

21 Women do not have to be married or living with a partner to be victims of domestic violence. In fact, battering among young people who are "dating" – also called teen dating violence or relationship violence – is all too common. Some of the staggering statistics regarding teens and relationship violence include:

- Approximately one-third of young people experience violence in their relationship [...].
- A study among pregnant teens revealed that one in five, or 20%, experience physical or sexual violence during pregnancy.
- A recent study of high school students determined that 59% had experienced at least one dating violence incident over the course of the year.
- For adolescent girls between the ages of 13-18 who have dated, 36% reported that they have experienced physical violence in a dating relationship.
- When questioned about their worst experiences of dating violence, 47.8% of girls reported serious harm and physical injury in 33.6% of the incidents.
- A study of 8th and 9th grade male and female students indicated that 25% had been victims of non-sexual dating violence and 8% had been victims of sexual dating violence.

Sadly, intimate partner violence among teens has been largely ignored by the adults around them, most likely because adolescents and their relationships are not taken seriously. Adults tend to believe that teen relationships are transient and less significant than adult relationships.

Also, adults and youth alike are often reluctant to talk about violence within relationships. These two factors may serve to isolate young women from the support they need when they are confronted with a violent date or boyfriend.

The consequences of violence are significant in the lives of young women. According to the FBI, 30% of the women murdered each year in the U.S. were killed by a husband or boyfriend. Of these women, 20% are between 15 and 24 years old. These numbers reflect only the crimes that are reported.

Extracted from <www.fvlc.org>.
Accessed on November 17, 2010.

Vocabulary

date: namorar
injury: ferimento
pregnancy: gravidez
report: informar
support: apoio
transient: passageiro

After Reading

A Are the statements T (true) or F (false)?

1 ☐ 36% of the girls between 13 and 18 who have dated reported that they have been victims of physical violence while dating.

2 ☐ 8% is the percentage of girls and boys in the 8th and 9th grades who have reported that they have experienced sexual dating violence.

3 ☐ 30% is the percentage of students who have been victims of dating violence in the period of one year.

4 ☐ 59% is the percentage of women killed by a husband or boyfriend in the United States.

B Find synonyms. Match the columns.

1	also	a ☐	frequently
2	likely	b ☐	concerning
3	often	c ☐	too
4	regarding	d ☐	probably
5	sadly	e ☐	lamentably

C Answer the questions according to the text.

1 Why are most cases of dating violence among adolescents ignored by adults?

____

2 How many pregnant teens have been victims of physical or sexual violence during pregnancy?

____

3 In the United States, 30% of the women murdered each year were killed by a husband or boyfriend. Of these women, 20% are between 15 and 24 years old. Do these figures represent the total number of cases?

____

D **Complete the questionnaire below.**

How's Your RELATIONSHIP?

See if there are signs of abuse in your relationship. Answer the questions below. Write **YES** or **NO**.

How is your partner treating you?

- ◯ Does your partner call you names or embarrass you?
- ◯ Are you afraid of your partner?
- ◯ Is your partner nice sometimes and really mean at other times?
- ◯ When there are fights, does your partner always blame you?
- ◯ Does your partner promise to change only to repeat the same behavior later?

How are you treating your partner?

- ◯ Do you give your partner ultimatums (make him or her choose between you and other things he or she wants)?
- ◯ Do you believe women are inferior to men? Do you believe a woman is a man's property?
- ◯ Do you want your partner to spend time only with you?
- ◯ Do you feel you have the right to tell your partner what to do, where to go, etc.?
- ◯ Do you break or throw things when you are angry with your partner?

If you have answered **yes** to some of the questions, you may be in an abusive relationship.

VOCABULARY EXPANSION

A Read the box and write new words. Translate the new words.

Example: friend friendship amizade

1 author ______ ______

2 leader ______ ______

3 champion ______ ______

4 member ______ ______

Suffix ship
Forma substantivos e indica condição, *status*, arte ou funcionamento (de).

B Find out the meaning of the words below.

1 citizenship
2 dictatorship
3 relationship
4 partnership
5 companionship

a [ ] relacionamento
b [ ] parceria
c [ ] cidadania
d [ ] companheirismo
e [ ] ditadura

C Complete the sentences. Use the words given.

Too (demais)
É usado antes de adjetivos.

against | too | always | only | too

1 I'm not going to the game today. I'm ______ tired.

2 ______ teachers can come into this room.

3 He is very mean. Everybody is ______ him.

4 Jack never goes out on Sundays. He is ______ at home.

5 She will not buy that house because it is ______ expensive.

D Add suffixes or prefixes to form new words.

less | ion | ing | al | un | ive | ship

1 safe ______
2 abuse ______
3 relation ______
4 regard ______
5 intimidate ______
6 possess ______
7 sex ______
8 emotion ______
9 finance ______
10 hit ______
11 control ______

Language in Use

A **Read the manifesto below. Then talk to a classmate. See the example.**

Coalition for Young People

Putting Young People First

A Manifesto for Young People

Young people are a number one priority. They are our present and our future.

[...]

The Coalition for Young People's manifesto lists out a set of demands for all political parties:

1. We want great places for young people to go and great things to do.
2. We want young people to be able to make the most of facilities on offer.
3. We want young people to flourish – to get the most from their education and wider learning – in school, in their youth centre and at home.
4. We want young people to get the help and support they need when they need it.
5. We want more young people involved in decision making.
6. We want great people to work with young people to inspire, motivate, support, and help them gain new skills.
7. We want to prevent vulnerable young people from getting involved in crime.
8. We want to ensure that all government policies work for young people, not against.

Working Together – Putting Young People First
For more information please contact:

The National Youth Agency
Viv McKee – Director of Policy and Research
Telephone: 0116 242 7391
E-mail: vivm@nya.org.uk

4Children
Anne Longfeld OBE – Chief Executive
Telephone: 020 7522 6913
E-mail: anne.longfeld@4children.org.uk

Extracted from <www.makespace.org.uk>. Accessed on October 20, 2010.

A: Do you agree with demand number one?
B: Sure. I agree with it one hundred percent.
Only to a certain extent.
Not really. As a matter of fact, I totally disagree with it.

B **NOW IT'S YOUR TURN!**
Think about a class or school manifesto. Ask a classmate about his or her demand to be included in the manifesto. Look at the example.

A: What demand would you like to include in our manifesto?
B: I'd like to include one that says: "We want good and free transportation to school.".

Writing

Write a manifesto to be sent to all political parties in your country. Include 8 demands from your group of friends.

EXTRA PRACTICE 5

A Choose the correct alternative.

1 The rich man said, "________"

a ☐ The more interesting, the better.
b ☐ The most interesting, the best.
c ☐ The interesting, the better.
d ☐ The more interesting, the good.

2 His financial situation was getting ________.

a ☐ worse and worst
b ☐ worser and worser
c ☐ worse and worse
d ☐ bad and badder

3 This dog is ________ dangerous ________ a lion.

a ☐ more – as
b ☐ as – as
c ☐ as – most
d ☐ as – more

4 Sandra is thin. Josie is ________ Sandra. Anne is ________.

a ☐ as thin – the most thin of all
b ☐ thinner than – the thin of all
c ☐ thinner than – the thinnest of all
d ☐ thinner as – the thinnest of all

5 I think I have ________ car in town.

a ☐ the slow
b ☐ slower
c ☐ the more slow
d ☐ the slowest

6 Which was the ________ day of your life?

a ☐ bad
b ☐ baddest
c ☐ the worse
d ☐ worst

B **There are mistakes in some of the sentences below. Circle the mistakes and rewrite the wrong sentences.**

1 Their car is more new than ours.

2 I bought the cheapest skateboard in the store.

3 The basin of the Amazon river is the longer in the world.

4 Small cities are most safest than big cities.

5 Apples are sweeter than lemons.

6 Metal is heaviest than cotton.

7 Giraffes are thinnest than elephants.

8 John looks younger than his brother Peter.

9 Sports cars are faster than trucks.

10 Lions are the smarter of all animals.

11 Brazil isn't larger than Canada.

12 I read his latest novel.

13 This coffee is hoter than the milk.

14 My brother is the luckiest person in our family.

C Choose the appropriate tag question.

1 The doctor didn't give you any medicine, ________?

a ☐ did he
b ☐ did she
c ☐ didn't they
d ☐ *a* and *b*

2 You will travel next month, ________?

a ☐ will you
b ☐ are you
c ☐ won't you
d ☐ *a* and *c*

3 Drink your milk, ________?

a ☐ shall we
b ☐ won't you
c ☐ do you
d ☐ will you

4 Kate can sleep here tonight, ________?

a ☐ can't she
b ☐ can she
c ☐ doesn't she
d ☐ *a* and *c*

5 Those men work hard, ________?

a ☐ don't he
b ☐ don't they
c ☐ doesn't he
d ☐ do they

6 Your friend couldn't come today, ________?

a ☐ did he
b ☐ could he
c ☐ could she
d ☐ *b* and *c*

D Write the Simple Future of the verbs in parentheses.

1 (arrive – neg.) I ______________ before 2 o'clock.

2 (work) ______________ Paul ______________ next weekend?

3 (be) Cars ______________ lighter in the future.

4 (move) The Browns ______________ to the mountains in November.

5 (catch – neg.) They ______________ the midnight train to Amsterdam.

6 (begin) ______________ the new project ______________ in March?

7 (help – neg.) I ______________ her later.

8 (make) Dad ______________ dinner for us next Monday.

E Rewrite the sentences in the Future Continuous.

1 Tomorrow at 7 o'clock I will play tennis.

____

2 Will you travel by the end of next week?

____

3 They will fly to Japan at this time tomorrow.

____

4 We will meet Linda in the afternoon.

____

5 She will study when I get home.

____

6 In half an hour I will sit in front of my TV.

____

7 Charlie will come to the party on Friday.

____

8 They will eat pizza soon.

____

9 I will do a test tomorrow afternoon.

____

F Write the correct tag questions.

1 Susan isn't studying, ______________________________?
2 The babies are crying, ______________________________?
3 I am late, ______________________________?
4 You don't speak Russian, ______________________________?
5 You were working two hours ago, ______________________________?
6 Your sister will come for dinner, ______________________________?
7 That boy plays the violin, ______________________________?
8 The kids aren't making a cake, ______________________________?
9 You weren't in the park yesterday, ______________________________?
10 Tom didn't help you, ______________________________?
11 The teacher corrected all the mistakes, ______________________________?
12 The dogs won't escape, ______________________________?
13 We are going to leave, ______________________________?
14 Let's talk for a minute, ______________________________?
15 Don't open the door, ______________________________?
16 Mother bought some fresh eggs, ______________________________?
17 Your parents are upset this morning, ______________________________?

G Unscramble the sentences.

1 meet – will – I – Janet – cafeteria – at the – next week

____

2 at this time – to London – in February – she – be flying – will

____

3 they – will – us – visit – when – come – they – to São Paulo – ?

____

4 they – won't – no – ,

____

5 call – him – he – be sleeping – will – when – you

____

6 be – raining – Manaus – will – it – probably – we – reach – when

____

www.quintcareers.com

Job Ideas for Teens: beyond Babysitting and Lemonade Stands

Okay, you're somewhere between having your own neighborhood lemonade stand and working at a real job, so what should a young teen do? Many states have laws that limit when teens can get a job and how long they are allowed to work per week, so how are you expected to make the money you need for clothes, dates, cars, etc.? The answer: go into business for yourself!

[...]

So, what are some ideas for a business beyond a lemonade stand or babysitting? Here goes:

A car-detailing business With so many people working multiple jobs and having such busy lifestyles, very few people have the time to really take care of their cars and you could offer a weekly or monthly service of washing, waxing, vacuuming, etc.

A cleaning service Maybe you hate doing your chores at home, but getting paid for doing them is completely different! You could offer complete housecleaning services, or specialize in one or more areas, such as attic/basement/garage cleanups.

An online Web business If you are a master at creating Web pages, perhaps what you need to do is brainstorm a concept for an online business – where your potential customers can come from anywhere in the world, not just in your local neighborhood.

A PC tutor/Website development service Are you a whiz with computers and the Web? Well, many adults are not, and you could make a good business helping people learn to use PCs and develop Websites for their families – or for their businesses.

A pet sitting service Typically more of a summer business when people tend to go on vacation, but you might be able to have a year-round business by offering pet walking, bathing, cleaning, etc. services.

An errand, messenger, or delivery service This idea works best in larger cities where there are more people and public transportation, but these are busy times and people need help with all sorts of errands.

Extracted from <www.quintcareers.com>. Accessed on November 22, 2010.

11 Animal Farm

Language in Context

A Complete the information. Read the dialogue and check your answers. 22

1 Names

____

2 Subject

____

____

Dr. Costello: Dr. Costello speaking.

Sophie: Dad? Where did you put the first-aid kit?

Dr. Costello: Second drawer of the desk in my bedroom. What's the matter, Sophie?

Sophie: I need a bandage. Josie cut herself with a piece of broken glass. Her finger is bleeding a lot.

Dr. Costello: Wash it in running water.

Sophie: I did, but it is still bleeding. It's a bad cut.

Dr. Costello: Bring her to the hospital.

Sophie: I can't. Mom is out with the car.

Dr. Costello: Wait, then. I'm coming home. I want to see that finger myself.

B Give your opinion.

1 How do you think Sophie is feeling about the situation?

2 What would you do if you had an emergency like that?

Vocabulary

bleed: sangrar
drawer: gaveta
running water: água corrente

C Think about it. Read the sentences and answer the questions.

1 Josie cut the apple in three pieces.

a Who did the action?

____

b What received the action?

____

2 Josie cut herself with a piece of broken glass.

a Who did the action?

____

b Who received the action?

____

Language Practice

Reflexive Pronouns

Personal Pronouns	Reflexive Pronouns
I	my**self**
you	your**self**
he	him**self**
she	her**self**
it	it**self**
we	our**selves**
you	your**selves**
they	them**selves**

Uso

Reflexivo – Indica que o sujeito pratica e recebe o efeito da ação do verbo. Nesse caso, o pronome vem logo após o verbo e concorda com o sujeito.

I hurt **myself** in the soccer game.

We gave **ourselves** a second chance to finish the project.

John sent **himself** a copy of the e-mail.

Enfático – Enfatiza o sujeito ou o objeto da oração. Não é parte essencial da oração e sua posição pode variar.

She talked to the king.

She **herself** talked to the king.

(ênfase no sujeito)

She talked to the king **herself**.

(ênfase no sujeito)

She talked to the king **himself**.

(ênfase no objeto)

Idiomático – O pronome vem precedido de **by**, formando uma expressão que significa "sozinho", "sem ajuda".

He lives **by himself**.

I did my homework **by myself**.

Mary baked a cake **by herself**.

A Underline the correct alternative.

1 Carlos made this T-shirt **by himself** / **by herself**.

2 Daniel, did you take these photos all by **yourselves** / **yourself**?

3 Leticia and Anna, if you want more juice, help **yourselves** / **yourself**.

4 The leopard can defend **himself** / **itself**.

5 My father always talks to **myself** / **himself**.

6 Alicia and Brian collected the coins **themselves** / **ourselves**.

B Complete the sentences with the appropriate reflexive pronoun.

1 The reader lost ________________ in the middle of the book. He found it very interesting.

2 The old lady ________________ helped the firemen rescue the little girl.

3 They usually go to school by ________________.

4 I made ________________ a cup of tea before going to sleep.

5 Ask ________________ what you can do to improve your grades.

6 We painted the school wall ________________.

C Rewrite the sentences. Insert reflexive pronouns according to the instructions in parentheses.

Example: She looked in the mirror. (reflexive)
She looked at herself in the mirror.

1 Karen and Tom walked in the park. (idiomatic)

____

2 Marion is singing in the shower. (reflexive)

____

3 I painted my room. (emphatic – subject)

____

4 You must take protection from the rain. (reflexive)

____

5 My little brother can tie his shoes. (idiomatic)

____

6 I talked to Sharon Stone. (emphatic – object)

____

Go to page 170 for Extra Practice.

The Genitive Case (Possuidor + ' / Possuidor + 's)

Uso

O caso genitivo expressa posse. Geralmente é usado para pessoas e animais em lugar da construção com **of**.

Mary's room (the room of Mary)

the dog's eyes (the eyes of the dog)

Nomes próprios terminados em **s** recebem **'s**: Denis's car. Mas os nomes clássicos recebem apenas **'**: Moses' laws, Jesus' disciples.

Particularidades:

Substantivos não terminados em **s** recebem **'s**.

Alan**'s** car

the man**'s** shirt

the women**'s** dresses

Substantivos no singular terminados em **s** recebem **'s**.

the boss**'s** car

the bus**'s** door

Substantivos no plural terminados em **s** recebem apenas **'**.

the boys**'** shoes

the ladies**'** room

Substantivos compostos são tratados como substantivos simples.

my mother-in-law**'s** house

O caso genitivo também é usado:

› para mencionar lugares

We're going to the barber**'s**.
(the barber's shop)

› com expressões de tempo, espaço ou peso

two week**'s** holiday

a month**'s** salary

the boat**'s** length

› para indicar posse comum

John and Mary**'s** house
(os dois possuem a mesma casa)

› para indicar posse individual

John**'s** and Mary**'s** houses
(cada um possui a sua casa)

D Write ' or 's.

1 My father ________ friends will arrive tomorrow.

2 My sisters ________ boyfriends are playing soccer.

3 The kids ________ toys are in the garage.

4 The ladies ________ hats are very expensive.

5 Those men ________ cars aren't very economical.

6 Your neighbor ________ cat is in my kitchen.

7 The girl ________ book is on the desk.

8 Where's Mr. Andersen ________ book?

E Rewrite these sentences inserting ' or 's where necessary.

Example: Mary and Tom father is Italian. Tom and Mary are brother and sister.
Mary and Tom's father is Italian.

1 I intend to have two week holiday next month.

____

2 My brothers friends are going to Rome with us.

____

3 Bob and Sally mothers are waiting for them in the hall.

____

4 The children shoes are in the garage.

____

F Choose the correct alternative.

1 My step sister ________ car is old. She needs to buy a new one.

a ☐ ' b ☐ 's c ☐ X

2 I'm going to take three week ________ holiday.

a ☐ 's b ☐ ' c ☐ X

3 Giulia ________ and Fred ________ apartments are on sale.

a ☐ ' / 's b ☐ 's / X c ☐ 's / 's

4 The teacher is going to correct the students ________ notebooks at home.

a ☐ ' b ☐ 's c ☐ X

Go to page 172 for Extra Practice.

READING

Before Reading

Approaching the text

A Discuss the questions below in Portuguese.

1. English philosopher Thomas Hobbes mentioned, "Man is man's wolf." What do you think this means?
2. Do you believe man respects other forms of life?

B Learning about the author.

George Orwell – Pen name of Eric Blair, 1903-1950. English novelist, essayist, and political satirist. Two of Orwell's most famous novels are *Animal Farm* and *1984*.

Vocabulary

Look up these words in the glossary.

1. slavery ____________________
2. strength ____________________
3. prevent ____________________
4. steal ____________________
5. truth ____________________

ANIMAL FARM

Comrades, consider this: we live in misery, work like hell and die young. After we are born, we receive just enough to keep us alive. Then we have to work until we have no more strength to keep standing. We live like slaves – that is the real truth.

Why are we in this miserable condition? Because human beings steal nearly all products of our labor. That, comrades, is the cause of our problems: man. Man is the only real enemy we have.

Man is the only creature that consumes without producing. He does not give milk, he does not lay eggs, he is too weak to plow by himself. He cannot run fast enough to catch rabbits. Yet, he is the lord of all animals. He puts other animals to work, and gives back to them the bare minimum to prevent starvation. The rest, he keeps for himself.

For myself, I do not grumble. I am a 12-year-old pig. I will soon die. But I warn you: whatever goes upon two legs is your enemy. Whatever goes upon four legs, or has wings, is a friend...

Based on ORWELL, George. *Animal Farm*. Harlow: Addison Wesley Longman Ltd., 1996.

Vocabulary

grumble: resmungar
lay eggs: botar ovos
plow: arar
starvation: inanição
warn: avisar, alertar
whatever: o que quer que

After Reading

A Look at the text and complete the information.

1 two kinds of animals: ______

2 the age of the speaker: ______

3 the author of the text: ______

B Find out what the words in bold refer to.

1 "For **myself**, I do not grumble."

a ☐ the pig

b ☐ the speaker and the audience

c ☐ the reader

2 "Man is the only creature that consumes without producing. **He** does not give milk, he does not lay eggs [...]"

a ☐ man

b ☐ creature

c ☐ the only creature

C Give the meaning of the words in bold in the sentences below.

1 (1st paragraph) "After we are born, we receive just enough to keep us **alive**. Then we have to work [...]" ______

2 (2nd paragraph) "Why are we in this miserable condition? Because human beings steal **nearly** all products of our labour." ______

3 (4th paragraph) "[...] whatever goes upon two legs is your enemy. Whatever goes upon four legs, or has **wings**, is a friend..." ______

D Check what man can't do, according to the pig.

1 ☐ lay eggs

2 ☐ work

3 ☐ steal

4 ☐ run fast

5 ☐ consume

6 ☐ grumble

7 ☐ walk

8 ☐ catch rabbits

9 ☐ plow by himself

10 ☐ give milk

E Some of the statements below are wrong. Find the mistakes and rewrite the statements.

In the pig's opinion...

1 animals' lives are wonderful. ______________________

2 human beings exploit animals. ______________________

3 man is a friend. ______________________

4 man lays eggs. ______________________

5 he will die soon. ______________________

6 animals live like slaves. ______________________

F Answer the questions according to the text.

1 What is the cause of the animals' problems?

____

2 Does man consume without producing?

____

3 What does man give back to the animals?

____

4 What is a friend?

____

5 According to the pig, is man the lord of all animals?

____

G Read, think and write.

1 What do you think of English philosopher Thomas Hobbes's idea?

"Man is man's wolf."

Do you agree with it? Why/Why not?

____

____

2 The animal that is speaking has a strong feeling against humans. Find in the text the sentence that best expresses this feeling.

____

____

VOCABULARY EXPANSION

A Complete the sentences. Use the words in the box.

whatever: o que quer que
whenever: sempre que
wherever: onde quer que
whoever: quem quer que

1 You can call me __________ you need a friend.

2 __________ she goes, her dog follows her.

3 __________ your teacher asks you to do, do it quickly.

4 __________ asks me for help, I help immediately.

5 __________ you do, do it carefully.

B Read the box and complete the sentences.

Special Difficulties

to lie	**lied**	**lied**	mentir
to lie	**lay**	**lain**	deitar-se, jazer, encontrar-se (situar-se)
to lay	**laid**	**laid**	pôr, colocar

1 Jonathan __________ to me about his age.

2 Dogs don't __________ eggs.

3 Brazil __________ in South America.

4 Yesterday, I __________ under a tree in the park.

5 Don't __________ to children. They will notice it.

C Rewrite the sentences. Follow the example.

Example: My brother is sixteen years old.
My brother is a sixteen-year-old boy.

1 Sally is twelve years old.

____

2 This house is twenty years old.

____

3 Ross is seven years old.

____

4 This chair is fifty years old.

____

A **Read the classified ad below. Then match the sentences in the box and talk to a classmate.**

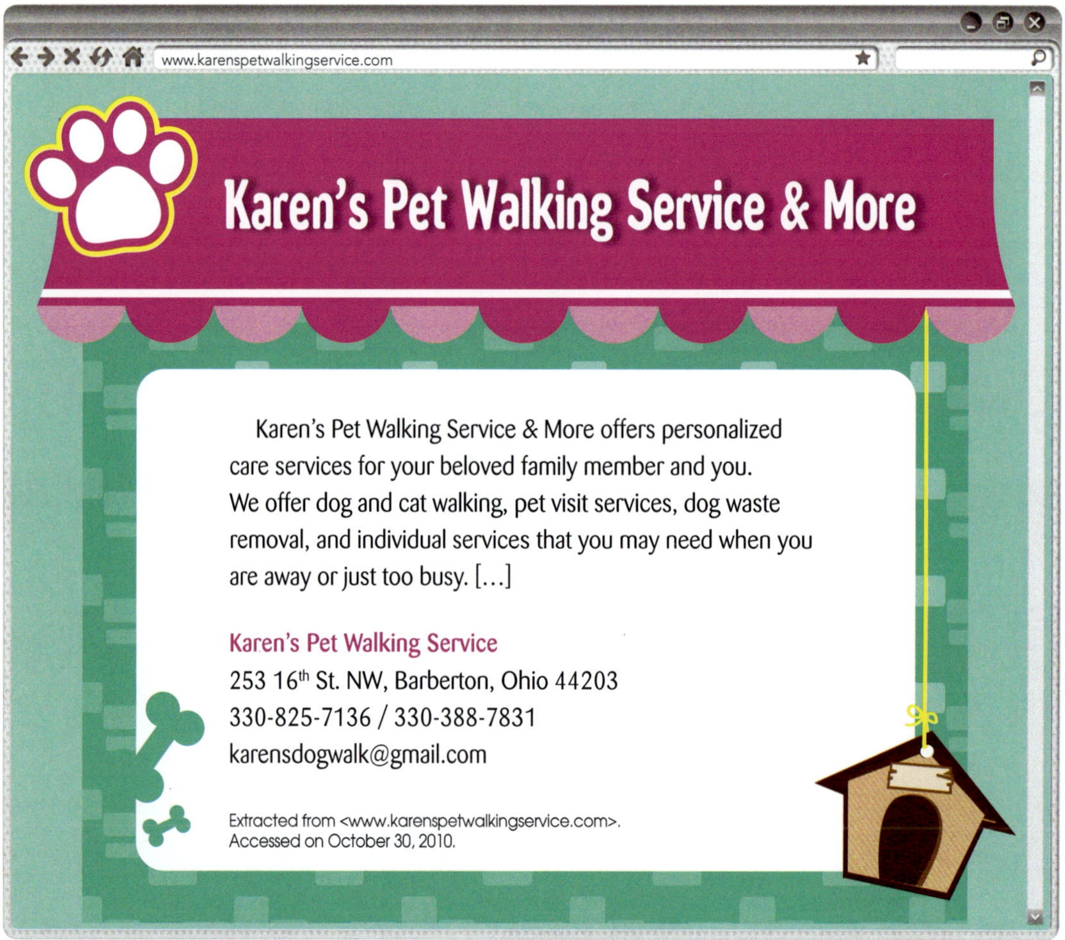

Karen's Pet Walking Service & More offers personalized care services for your beloved family member and you. We offer dog and cat walking, pet visit services, dog waste removal, and individual services that you may need when you are away or just too busy. [...]

Karen's Pet Walking Service
253 16th St. NW, Barberton, Ohio 44203
330-825-7136 / 330-388-7831
karensdogwalk@gmail.com

Extracted from <www.karenspetwalkingservice.com>. Accessed on October 30, 2010.

A	B
What's Karen good at? What does she do for a living? How can I contact her?	You can either call her or send her an e-mail. She's good at walking dogs. She's a pet sitter.

B **NOW IT'S YOUR TURN!**
Ask a classmate about his or her skills and abilities.

1 What are you good at?

2 What do you want to do for a living?

3 How can I contact you?

WRITING

Think about your abilities and what you would like to do to make some money. Then write a classified ad.

12 Anabolic Steroids

Language in Context

A **Complete the information. Read the dialogue and check your answers.** 24

1 Names: ______________________

2 The boy's occupation: ______________________

Derek: Celine! Lara! Where have you been? I haven't seen you lately.
Celine: Well, we've been very busy.
Derek: Working?
Celine: Yes, I've got a part-time job at the country club restaurant.
Derek: Cool. Do you like it?
Celine: I've just started but I think it's fine.
Derek: What about you, Lara?
Lara: I've been working in a community center. Working with children.
Derek: Really? What do you do?
Lara: I read stories to them. It's all volunteer work. Celine is there too.
Derek: That's nice.
Lara: Would you like to join us, Derek?
Derek: Sure! If you need a hip-hopper.
Lara: Why not? I'm sure the kids will love some music.

B **Give your opinion.**

1 Celine makes money working in a restaurant. How does Lara make her living?

2 What can a hip-hopper do in a community center?

Vocabulary

I've just started: acabei de começar
join in: participar

C **Think about it. Compare the sentences and answer the questions.**

A	I didn't see you yesterday. We were very busy this morning.
B	I haven't seen you lately. We've been very busy lately.

1 What is the difference between the verbs in groups A and B?

2 Is it possible to know when the actions happened?

LANGUAGE PRACTICE

Present Perfect (I)

Have/Has + verbo no **Past Participile**		
I **have** You **have** He **has** She **has** It **has** We **have** You **have** They **have**	work**ed**.	**Afirmativa:** He **has worked** hard. **Interrogativa: Has** he **worked** hard? **Negativa:** He **has not worked** hard. **Formas abreviadas: 's** (has) **hasn't** (has not) **'ve** (have) **haven't** (have not)
Past Participle (ver lista na página 396)		
Observe: (regular verbs) to work – worked – **worked**; to dance – danced – **danced** (irregular verbs) to see – saw – **seen**; to tell – told – **told**		

Uso

O *Present Perfect* expressa ações que ocorreram em um tempo indefinido no passado, que podem ter terminado ou ainda estar ocorrendo.

I **have** work**ed** hard.
(Trabalhei/Tenho trabalhado muito.)

Mas, se o tempo for mencionado ou sugerido, usa-se o *Simple Past*.

I work**ed** hard yesterday.
(Trabalhei muito ontem.)

I work**ed** hard when I was young.
(Trabalhei muito quando era jovem.)

157

UNIT 12

A Rewrite the verbs in bold in the Present Perfect. Use the box for help.

Infinitive	Simple Past	Past Participle
to arrive	arrived	arrived
to bring	brought	brought
to be	was/were	been
to help	helped	helped
to send	sent	sent
to sell	sold	sold
to write	wrote	written

1 Sally **wrote** letters in English. ____________________

2 They **brought** some old pictures of their family members. ____________________

3 Our family **is helping** poor people who live in the streets. ____________________

4 The company I work for **sends** lots of mail to the USA. ____________________

5 They **didn't arrive** because of the rain. ____________________

6 We **are** very busy. ____________________

7 Jack **sold** many of his old books. ____________________

8 Mike **is** a volunteer at his neighborhood. ____________________

B Complete the sentences. Use the Simple Past or the Present Perfect.

1 They ____________________ (to be) in the restaurant an hour ago.

2 I ____________________ (to write) books for children.

3 She ____________________ (to arrive) in São Paulo last month.

4 The doctor ____________________ (to send) me some medicine.

5 My friends ____________________ (to bring) all their paintings last summer.

6 I ____________________ (to see) Tom 10 minutes ago.

7 My parents ____________________ (to be) to Lençóis Maranhenses many times.

8 Dennis ____________________ (to write) me a letter last month.

9 Jennifer ____________________ (to send) me a postcard from Manaus in January.

10 The children ____________________ (to bring) many toys to the classroom.

11 All the family ____________________ (to help) to clean the new house last weekend.

12 My grandparents ____________________ (to sell) their apartment at the beach last year.

13 Many people ____________________ (to help) poor families in our city.

C **Complete Lara's report on the children she works with. Use the correct verb form of the Simple Past or the Present Perfect.**

Daily Report,

Today was a special day because we ________________ (to have) three birthdays in the group. Jennifer finally ________________ (to come) after three absences. Kamal ________________ (to be) absent for two days and Bob for three. I hope they come next class.

Sheila ________________ (to be) not feeling well when she ________________ (to arrive) this morning, but she ________________ (to take) some medicine and was soon feeling OK.

We ________________ (to read) three books so far this week and the kids seem to enjoy this activity.

Lara Elliott

Reading class volunteer

Richfield Community Center
1439 Broadview Rd

Present Perfect (II)

O *Present Perfect* pode ser usado com:

since (desde): I have worked here **since** June. (Trabalho aqui desde junho.)

for (por): She has worked here **for** five months. (Ela trabalha aqui há cinco meses.)

just (ação recente): They have **just** arrived. (Eles acabaram de chegar.)

ever (já): Have you **ever** seen that movie? (Você já viu aquele filme?)

never (nunca): I have **never** seen her. (Eu nunca a vi.)

already (já): They have **already** arrived. (Eles já chegaram.)

yet (já; ainda): Has he arrived **yet**? (Ele já chegou?)
He has not arrived **yet**. (Ele ainda não chegou.)

lately (ultimamente): We have not seen you **lately**. (Não o temos visto ultimamente.)

many times (muitas vezes): I have talked to her **many times**.
(Falei com ela muitas vezes.)

Present Perfect Continuous

Have/Has been + verbo + **ing**

Afirmativa: He **has been** travel**ing**.

Interrogativa: Has he **been** travel**ing**?

Negativa: He **has not been** travel**ing**.

Uso

O *Present Perfect Continuous* enfatiza a continuidade de uma ação que começou no passado e que se prolonga até o presente.

It **has been** raining hard. (Tem chovido muito.)

D Rewrite the sentences. Put the adverbs in the correct position.

1 I have had lunch. (already)

____

2 Sally has done her homework. (not/yet)

____

3 The kid has arrived. (just)

____

4 You have worked hard. (lately/?)

____

5 They have traveled abroad. (never)

____

E Answer the questions.

Examples: Have you ever arrived late? Yes, I have./No, I haven't.

Has your friend arrived yet? Yes, he/she has.
No, he/she hasn't.

1 Have you ever been to Rio de Janeiro?

____

2 Has your best friend studied hard lately?

____

3 Have you been working a lot recently?

____

4 Have you lived in the same house since you were born?

____

F Choose the appropriate words to complete the sentences below.

1 I haven't finished my exercise ☐.

a yet b just

2 He has ☐ sent his postcards.

a yet b already

3 She has ☐ made a cake.

a just b lately

4 We have been waiting for you ☐ an hour.

a for b ever

5 They have lived in Miami ☐ 2001.

a for b since

6 I haven't seen you ☐.

a never b lately

Go to page 173 for Extra Practice.

READING

Before Reading

Approaching the text

Discuss the questions below in Portuguese.

1 Do you believe it is important to have a healthy body? Why?/ Why not?

2 What is necessary in order to have a healthy body?

3 Have you ever heard of anabolic steroids? What are they? What do you know about them?

Vocabulary

Find the meaning of the words below. Use the glossary.

1 loss ____________________

2 stroke ____________________

3 toll ____________________

4 hope ____________________

Group task

Take a look at the text and check the best answer.

1 Where can you find this text?

a ☐ In a newspaper.

b ☐ In a magazine.

c ☐ On the internet.

2 The text is:

a ☐ a newspaper article.

b ☐ a letter.

c ☐ a magazine article.

www.nida.nih.gov

NIDA (National Institute on Drug Abuse) Community Drug Alert Bulletin
Anabolic Steroids

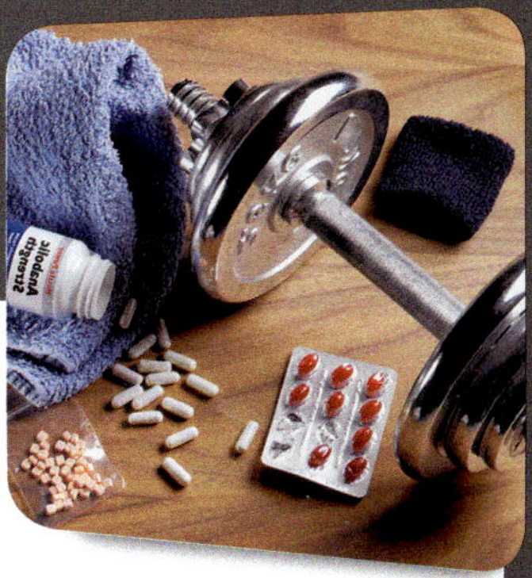

Home | About | Services | Contact Us

25

Dear Colleague,

Since the 1950s, some athletes have taken anabolic steroids to build muscles and boost their athletic performance. Increasingly, other segments of the population also have been taking these synthetic substances. The *Monitoring the Future* study, an annual survey of drug abuse among middle and high school students across the country, showed a significant increase from 1998 to 1999 in anabolic steroid abuse among middle schoolers. During the same year, the percentage of 12th-graders who believed that taking these drugs causes "great risk" to health declined from 68 percent to 62 percent.

Studies show that, over time, anabolic steroids can indeed take a heavy toll on a person's health. Abuse of oral or injectable anabolic steroids is associated with increased risk for heart attacks and strokes, and the abuse of most oral anabolic steroids is associated with increased risk for severe liver problems, including hepatic cancer. People who share needles or use nonsterile injection techniques put themselves at risk for contracting dangerous infections, such as HIV/AIDS, hepatitis B and C, and bacterial endocarditis.

Anabolic steroid abuse can also cause undesirable body changes. Men may develop enlarged breasts and women's bodies may become masculinized. Both sexes can develop acne and hair loss.

[...] Our objective is to keep the Nation's communities up-to-date concerning the risks of abusing anabolic steroids and science-based approaches to preventing and treating such abuse.

Sincerely,
Alan I. Leshner, Ph.D.
Director

Extracted from <www.nida.nih.gov>.
Accessed on December 5, 2010.

Vocabulary

approach: método
breast: seio
change: mudança
increasingly: cada vez mais
needle: agulha
over time: ao longo do tempo
undesirable: indesejável

After Reading

A Read the text and find the following information.

1 name of the institution the author is a member of:

____

2 period when there was an increase in anabolic steroid use among teenagers:

____

B Check the meaning of the words in bold.

1 (1st paragraph) "Since the 1950s, some athletes have taken anabolic steroids to build muscles and **boost** their athletic performance."

a ☐ preservar

b ☐ aumentar

c ☐ resgatar

2 (1st paragraph) "The *Monitoring the Future* study, an annual **survey** of drug **abuse** among middle and high school students across the country, showed a significant increase from 1998 to 1999 in anabolic steroid abuse among middle schoolers."

a ☐ sobrevivência – abuso

b ☐ sorver – abusar

c ☐ pesquisa – abuso

3 (4th paragraph) "Our objective is to keep the Nation's communities up-to-date concerning the risks of abusing anabolic steroids and **science-based approaches** to preventing and treating such abuse."

a ☐ métodos com base científica

b ☐ ciência baseada em métodos

c ☐ métodos da ciência básica

C Look at the text and find the names of:

1 some parts of the body:

____

2 some dangerous infections:

____

3 some problems associated with the abuse of oral anabolic steroids:

____

D Choose the best word for the definitions below.

1 having great weight; difficult to carry or lift

a ☐ heavy

b ☐ light

2 to be sure of the truth; have faith in

a ☐ unbelieve

b ☐ believe

3 good condition of the body or mind

a ☐ health

b ☐ sickness

4 extending far upwards; distant from the base to the top

a ☐ high

b ☐ low

5 the act, fact or process of losing

a ☐ gain

b ☐ loss

E Answer the questions.

1 Who wrote the letter?

____

____

2 Which body changes can anabolic steroid abuse cause?

____

____

3 Who is the probable addressee of this letter? How can you tell?

____

____

4 What is the objective of NIDA?

____

____

Vocabulary Expansion

A Find opposites or synonyms. Use words from the text.

Opposites

1 The HIV infection rate in our community has **decreased** in the last two years.

____

2 There is a **small** possibility of contagion if you wear a mask. ______________________

Synonyms

1 Every summer, high temperatures **increase** the consumption of electrical energy.

____

2 The Ministry of Health is conducting an **investigation** to identify why the consumption of illicit drugs is not decreasing. ______________________

3 The main **goal** of the campaign is to inform the public about the risks of self-medication. ______________________

4 Special measures have been taken to **impede** the spread of the disease among the population. ______________________

5 The number of young couples buying their own house has **dropped**.

____

6 Megan is worried about her son's alcohol **misuse**. ______________________

B Read the example and answer the questions.

Example: What's a science-based method?

It's a method based on science.

1 What's computer-based education?

____

2 What's an evidence-based investigation?

____

3 What's a content-based course?

____

C Choose the best alternative to complete each sentence.

1 The death of Albert Einstein was a great ________ for 20th century science.

a ☐ loss b ☐ share c ☐ people

2 The audience enjoyed his ________ very much last night.

a ☐ public b ☐ percentage c ☐ performance

3 He is interested in anything ________ the exploration of space.

a ☐ concerning b ☐ according c ☐ related

4 James has a ________ case of dandruff that no shampoo has been able to resolve so far.

a ☐ athletic b ☐ severe c ☐ principal

5 The new medicine produced some ________ side-effects that scientists had not foreseen.

a ☐ undesirable b ☐ corrective c ☐ up-to-date

D Read the information in the box and complete the sentences.

False Cognates

divert: mudar o curso ou destino	**own:** próprio	**pull:** puxar
have fun: divertir-se	**proper:** adequado	**push:** empurrar

1 You must have your ________________ pen and pencil to take the test.

2 The boy was ________________ the girl's hair.

3 The farmers want to ________________ water from the river to the field.

4 Don't ________________. There are many people entering the elevator.

5 Your clothes are not ________________ for a job interview.

6 They always ________________ when they travel by plane.

E Find the correct meaning of the words in bold.

a quantidade exagerada

b exagerado no modo de vestir

c superar

d movimentos e emoções exagerados

e exceder-se

over: acima; demais

1 ☐ You are working too hard. Please, don't **overdo** it and get sick again.

2 ☐ Celine started to lose weight when she **overcame** the temptation of eating pies.

3 ☐ They were **overdressed** for the wedding ceremony last night.

4 ☐ Sometimes she **overreacts** to difficult situations.

5 ☐ Some addicts die of drug **overdose**.

Language in Use

A **Read the medicine package. Then talk to a classmate. See the examples.**

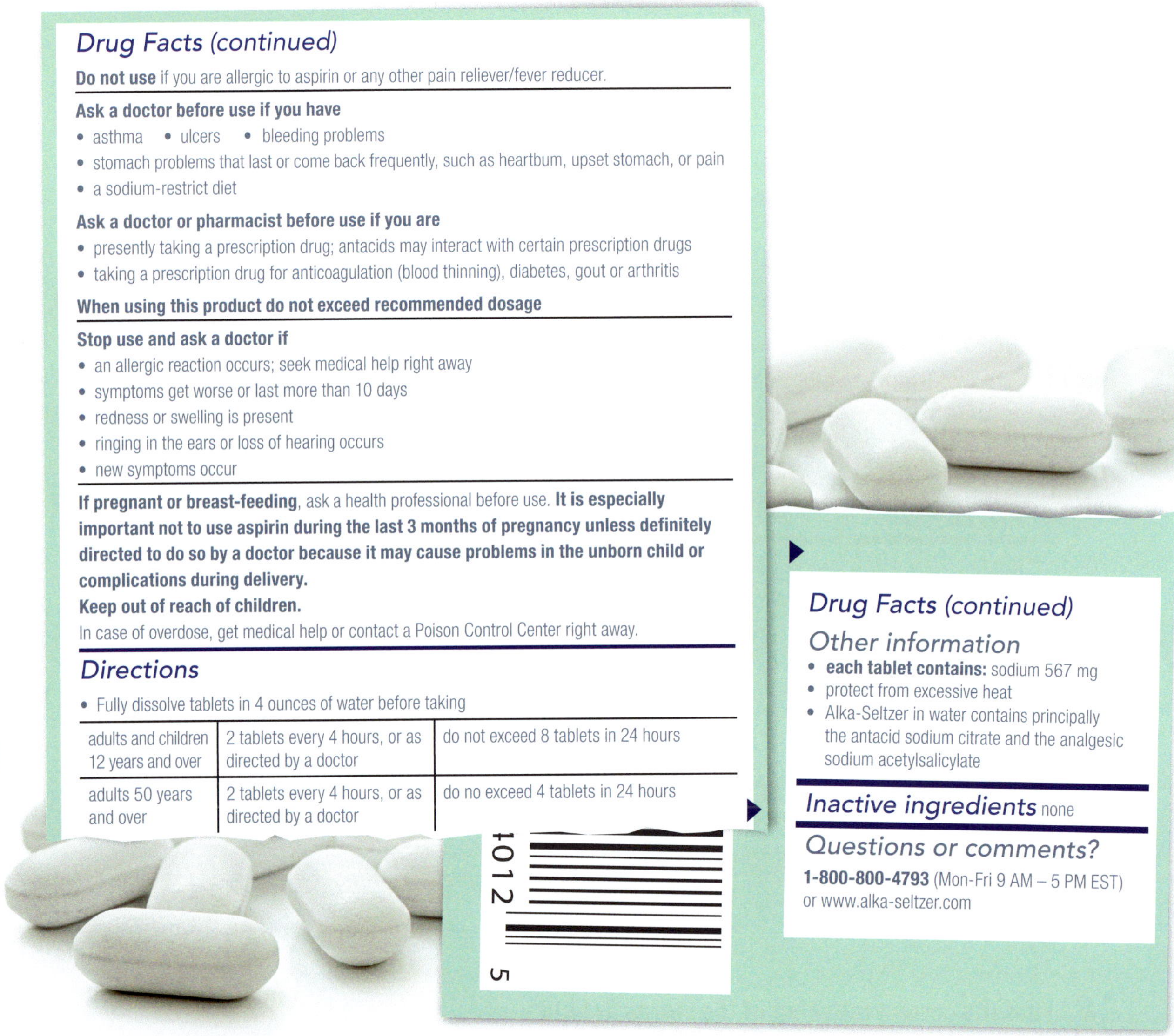

Drug Facts (continued)

Do not use if you are allergic to aspirin or any other pain reliever/fever reducer.

Ask a doctor before use if you have
- asthma • ulcers • bleeding problems
- stomach problems that last or come back frequently, such as heartbum, upset stomach, or pain
- a sodium-restrict diet

Ask a doctor or pharmacist before use if you are
- presently taking a prescription drug; antacids may interact with certain prescription drugs
- taking a prescription drug for anticoagulation (blood thinning), diabetes, gout or arthritis

When using this product do not exceed recommended dosage

Stop use and ask a doctor if
- an allergic reaction occurs; seek medical help right away
- symptoms get worse or last more than 10 days
- redness or swelling is present
- ringing in the ears or loss of hearing occurs
- new symptoms occur

If pregnant or breast-feeding, ask a health professional before use. **It is especially important not to use aspirin during the last 3 months of pregnancy unless definitely directed to do so by a doctor because it may cause problems in the unborn child or complications during delivery.**
Keep out of reach of children.
In case of overdose, get medical help or contact a Poison Control Center right away.

Directions

- Fully dissolve tablets in 4 ounces of water before taking

adults and children 12 years and over	2 tablets every 4 hours, or as directed by a doctor	do not exceed 8 tablets in 24 hours
adults 50 years and over	2 tablets every 4 hours, or as directed by a doctor	do no exceed 4 tablets in 24 hours

Drug Facts (continued)

Other information
- **each tablet contains:** sodium 567 mg
- protect from excessive heat
- Alka-Seltzer in water contains principally the antacid sodium citrate and the analgesic sodium acetylsalicylate

Inactive ingredients none

Questions or comments?
1-800-800-4793 (Mon-Fri 9 AM – 5 PM EST) or www.alka-seltzer.com

A: What should I do if...
I have asthma?
I have ulcers?
I am taking drugs for diabetes?
my symptoms last more than 10 days?
I take an overdose?

B: You should ask a doctor before using this medicine.

B **NOW IT'S YOUR TURN!**

Ask a classmate what you should do if redness or swelling is present, if loss of hearing or ringing in the ear occur, and if symptoms get worse.

WRITING

Write a paragraph to the company that makes the medicine. Inform the company that you have a symptom not mentioned on the package. Describe the symptom. Then ask for advice on what you should do.

EXTRA PRACTICE 6

A Write the appropriate reflexive pronoun.

1 When did you get hurt? I hurt ________________ when I was cleaning the kitchen.

2 Dennis and Karen! Go wash ________________ before dinner.

3 We have to congratulate the students. They created this NGO by ________________.

4 Grandpa said to ________________, "I'm really getting old."

5 Julia looked at ________________ in the mirror before leaving for work.

6 A: You look tired today.
B: I'm tired because I cleaned the house by ________________.

7 A: Did you go to the party last night?
B: Yes, and we really enjoyed ________________.

8 A: Are you talking to me?
B: No, I'm talking to ________________.

9 The girls bought a present for ________________ yesterday.

10 Tom was horrified when he saw ________________ in the mirror.

11 Mom usually sings to ________________ when she's working.

12 My brother is very selfish. He only thinks of ________________.

13 We were frightened last night because the door opened by ________________.

14 A: Why are you so happy?
B: Because we did the homework by ________________.

15 You look very upset. Give ________________ a holiday.

16 A: Did you take German lessons?
B: No, I taught ________________.

17 Look, the dog is washing ________________ in the lake.

18 We went to the cafeteria to buy ________________ some lunch.

B Underline the correct reflexive pronoun.

1 Do you consider **yourself** / **himself** too funny?

2 My mom never gives **yourself** / **herself** a day off.

3 What do you teens see when you look at **herself** / **yourselves**?

C Choose the correct alternative.

1 Frances doesn't know how to fix the computer. I'll do it ________.

a ☐ himself
b ☐ itself
c ☐ myself

2 A: Did the kids give any of the apples to Carla?
B: No, they ate all the apples ________.

a ☐ themselves
b ☐ herself
c ☐ itself

3 I want you to do the job ________.

a ☐ myself
b ☐ himself
c ☐ yourself

4 The players ________ are cleaning the field.

a ☐ itself
b ☐ themselves
c ☐ himself

5 Sandra doesn't believe Roy is telling the truth. I ________ believe he is.

a ☐ myself
b ☐ himself
c ☐ herself

6 I must speak to your father ________.

a ☐ themselves
b ☐ herself
c ☐ himself

7 The Queen ________ went to the kitchen to have lunch.

a ☐ itself
b ☐ herself
c ☐ yourselves

8 I am so happy! I spoke to the Prime Minister ________.

a ☐ yourself
b ☐ itself
c ☐ himself

D Complete the sentences. Use ' or 's and the words in parentheses.

1 Joe gave ______________________ (Sally) red book to Amanda.

2 My ______________________ (parents) car is very old.

3 The ______________________ (women) dresses are very expensive.

4 Let's go to ______________________ (grandma) next Saturday. It's her birthday.

5 A rover was sent to examine ______________________ (Mars) surface.

6 My ______________________ (friends) children always misbehave in class.

7 ______________________ (Dan, Carla, and Tom) shoes were behind the sofa.

8 ______________________ (Bob and Julia) daughter is very beautiful.

9 My ______________________ (aunt) husband is waiting for us.

10 Those ______________________ (sailors) ship is leaving the country tomorrow.

11 The ______________________ (presidents) wives are having tea in the garden.

12 Have you seen the ______________________ (kids) books?

13 That ______________________ (man) feet were hurt in the accident.

14 Those men hooked a fish that was a ______________________ (boat) length.

15 My ______________________ (father-in-law) shoe shop caught fire last night.

E Write the verbs in parentheses in the correct verb tenses.

1 We ______________________ (to study) English now.

2 They ______________________ (to watch) TV in their room 5 minutes ago.

3 I always ______________________ (to go) to school on foot.

4 She never ______________________ (to read) the newspaper in the morning.

5 Jennifer ______________________ (to write) letters to her friends at this moment.

6 I ______________________ (to write) many letters to my friends.

7 He ______________________ (to invite) many people to our party.

8 I ______________________ (to read) a good book last week.

9 The boys ______________________ (to be) to the zoo.

10 We ______________________ (to go) to the zoo next week.

11 My brother ______________________ (to send) me an e-mail yesterday morning.

12 While my father ______________________ (to work) someone stole his motorcycle.

13 The baby usually ______________________ (to sleep) at 8:30 p.m.

F **Rewrite the sentences below in the negative and interrogative forms.**

1 Carol has brought sandwiches for the kids.

2 You have arrived very late for our lessons.

3 They have found a treasure under their house.

4 She has been to the park lately.

5 Americans have sent many astronauts to the moon.

6 Frank has helped me a lot.

7 Josie has sung at Mark's bar for a decade.

8 The boys have been to the museum.

G Write C for the correct interrogative sentences and W for the wrong ones. Then, correct the mistakes.

1 The students have been to the library.
Do the students been to the library? ☐

____

2 You have tried really hard.
Have you tried really hard? ☐

____

3 She has done her best.
Does she do her best? ☐

____

4 We have been to a game.
Have we been to a game? ☐

____

H Rewrite the sentences below in the Present Perfect Continuous.

Examples: I have worked hard.
I have been working hard.
She has swum a lot.
She has been swimming a lot.

1 They have traveled abroad.

____

____

2 I have lived here.

____

3 He has spoken too much.

____

4 We have worked for him.

____

5 You have written many poems.

____

Teen Business
Do's and Don'ts

This article is all about providing great tips and suggestions to help younger teens earn some money and get work experience by starting their own neighborhood businesses.

Do get the advice of an adult family member before starting your business.

Don't try to compete directly with any big businesses; the key to finding success with your business is to find a niche – find something that is lacking and fill it.

Do make detailed plans about how you will run your business, including the types of services you will perform (babysitting, lawn care, errands, tutoring, etc.), prices, cancellation notices, payment options, and the like. And **do** consider writing a mission statement or philosophy to help guide your actions.

Don't get too discouraged if your business starts slowly; it takes time to get your business known.

Do consider coming up with a cool name for your business – it will make you seem more professional.

Don't let any of your customers cheat you out of your money. And **do** consider enlisting an adult family member to help you handle any customer disagreements.

Do consider developing agreements for each customer to sign. In fact, **do** get everything you do or plan to do in writing.

Don't let a competing teen stop you from opening a similar business. If you don't want to compete, **do** consider forming a partnership. With multiple partners, you'll have a bigger network of potential customers and perhaps more time flexibility because you'll be sharing the load. But **do** be aware that having partners can also add lots more hassles and aggravations.

Do use every available resource to spread the word about your new business, including posting flyers around the neighborhood, in community centers and religious organizations, and in local stores. But remember that the best source will be the network of your family, friends, and neighbors – and current customers, once you get your business established.

[...]

Don't fall in the trap of thinking that starting your own business will be extremely lucrative and fun; running your own business is a lot of hard work, but it will be great experience for future jobs and college applications.

Do be prepared to leave your friends behind when you go to work; and **don't** ever skip a customer appointment to hang out with your friends – your business has to come first.

Don't spend all the money you make from your business; **do** put some money aside to save for the future.

[...]

Extracted from <www.quintcareers.com>. Accessed on September 10, 2010.

13 The Gifts (Part I)

Language in Context

A **Complete the information. Read the cartoon and check your answers.** 26

1 Place

____

2 Relationship

____

3 Subject

____

B **Give your opinion.**

1 Have you ever forgotten about somebody's birthday?

2 How did you feel about this?

3 Has anybody important to you ever forgotten about your birthday?

4 Are birthdays important to you?

C **Think about it. Read the sentences and answer the questions.**

They had seen the earrings at the store.
Her birthday had been the day before.

1 What do these sentences have in common?

2 When did the actions happen?

Vocabulary

a pair of earrings: um par de brincos
the day before: no dia anterior

Language Practice

Past Perfect

Had + verbo no Past Participle		
I You He She It We You They	**had left**.	**Afirmativa:** He **had left.** **Interrogativa: Had** he **left**? **Negativa:** He **had not left.** **Formas abreviadas: 'd** (had); **hadn't** (had not)

Uso

O *Past Perfect* expressa uma ação que aconteceu no passado antes de outra que também aconteceu no passado. Geralmente é usado com **after, before, when,** etc.

The kids **had slept** before we arrived.

He **had left** when you called him.

Clara **had lived** in Spain before she moved to Paris.

Past Perfect Continuous

Had been + verbo terminado em ing
Afirmativa: They **had been** work**ing**. **Interrogativa: Had** they **been** work**ing**? **Negativa:** They **had not been** work**ing**.

Uso

O *Past Perfect Continuous* expressa uma ação que estava acontecendo no passado antes de outra ação no passado.

I **had been working** before you called.

John failed the final test because he **hadn't been attending** class.

We **had been waiting** there for more than one hour when he finally arrived.

A Write the verbs below in the Past Perfect. (See the irregular verbs list on page 396.)

1 to save ____________________
2 to be ____________________
3 to calculate ____________________
4 to plan ____________________
5 to give ____________________
6 to see ____________________
7 to have ____________________
8 to go ____________________
9 to make ____________________
10 to write ____________________

B Complete the sentences using the Past Perfect and the verbs in parentheses.

1 When she called me I ____________________ (to sleep) for two hours.
2 She told me she ____________________ (to fall) from a tree.
3 The kids ____________________ (to leave) before I arrived.
4 She lost the book Paul ____________________ (to give) her.
5 I washed the dishes after they ____________________ (to have) dinner.
6 He didn't have any money because he ____________________ (to lose) his wallet.
7 Justin and Taylor knew Orlando so well because they ____________________ (to visit) the city many times.

C Put the verbs in parentheses in the Past Perfect Continuous.

When I arrived home yesterday Dad (1) (to cook) dinner, Mom (2) (to make) a chocolate cake, Tim, my youngest brother, (3) (to clean) the garage, Theresa (4) (to water) the flowers and Ted (5) (to walk) the dog. I was in shock. What happened to them?

1 ____________________
2 ____________________
3 ____________________
4 ____________________
5 ____________________

D **Read this e-mail message from Alice Robin to her mother, Mrs. Barbara Bells. Put the verbs in parentheses in the Past Perfect to complete the message.**

From: alice.robin@jeetnet.com
To: Mother
Subject: Last night

Links | Send

Mom,

I had the weirdest experience last night. When I arrived home from work some things really caught my eye.

Harry ________________ (to cook) dinner,

Liz ________________ (to clean) the kitchen table,

Danny ________________ (to wash) the dog, and Cathy ________________ (to water) the flowers.

They never do that!

Harry was reading the newspaper in the library and the kids were watching TV. Everything was so strangely quiet and, you know, my house is never quiet.

When asked if there was anything left for me to do, Danny said I could take the garbage to the garage. So I did.

When I opened the garage door and turned on the light, I saw they ________________ (to prepare) a surprise birthday party for me. Our neighbor Helen ________________ (to make) a chocolate cake and the girls ________________ (to decorate) the garage with balloons.

That was really a big surprise and I was so happy. I thought they had forgotten about my birthday.

Well, that was it.

Wasn't that nice?!

Love,

Alice

E **Read the phrases below and match them to form complete sentences.**

He had left the party before

after they had drunk a lot.

but she gave him a magazine.

I arrived.

When I interrupted him,

She told me her name

after I had asked her twice.

he had been talking for more than an hour.

They started dinner

He had asked for a newspaper,

1 ____

____

2 ____

____

3 ____

____

4 ____

____

5 ____

____

Go to page 198 for Extra Practice.

F Make questions. Then answer them using the Past Perfect.

1 We arrived at work. Before that we ate breakfast.

Had we eaten breakfast before ______________________________?

____

2 They left the house. Before that they turned off the lights.

____

____

3 George and Mary came to this class. Before that they didn't study English.

____

____

4 She had a test. Before that she reviewed all her notes.

____

____

5 Carol arrived. Before that I left.

____

____

6 He got to his house. Before that the program didn't start.

____

____

7 She finished her work. Before that I began mine.

____

____

G Explain the differences between these two sentences. You may do it in Portuguese.

a The bomb exploded when the bomb team arrived.

b The bomb had exploded when the bomb team arrived.

____

____

____

____

____

READING

Before Reading

Approaching the text

A Discuss the questions below in Portuguese.

1 What can people do in the name of love?

2 Have you ever made sacrifices for someone you loved?

B Read the box and learn about the author.

O. Henry (1862–1910) is the pen name of William Sydney Porter, an American author of short stories.

C Take a look at the text on page 183. Check the type of text.

The text is...

1 ☐ a chronicle.

2 ☐ a narrative.

3 ☐ a tale.

Vocabulary

Find the meaning of the words below. Use the words in the boxes.

expenses | penny | flat | stairs | fall | ransack

1 moeda de 1 centavo ______

2 apartamento ______

3 cair ______

4 vasculhar ______

5 escada ______

6 despesas ______

27

The Gifts

part I

One dollar and eighty-seven cents. Three times Della counted it. That was all she had saved.

And the next day would be Christmas. Only $1.87 to buy a present for Jim!

There was clearly nothing to do but lie down and cry. So Della cried.

Her home was a poorly furnished flat at $8 per week and their income, a mere $20 per week.

Della finished her cry. She stood by the window and looked out. She had been saving every penny she could for months, with this result. Expenses had been greater than she had calculated. She had planned to buy something for him.

Something fine and rare.

Suddenly she stood before the mirror: her eyes were shining brilliantly. Rapidly she pulled down her hair and let it fall to its full length. Della's beautiful hair reached below her knee.

There were two possessions which they were both proud of. One was Jim's gold watch that had been his grandfather's. The other was Della's hair.

She took her old brown jacket and her old brown hat. She walked out the door and ran down the stairs to the street.

She entered a shop that had the sign:

"Hair Goods of All Kinds."

"Will you buy my hair?" asked Della.

"I buy hair," said the owner. "Let me take a look at it."

"Twenty dollars," said the owner, lifting the mass with a practiced hand.

"Give it to me quick," said Della.

The next two hours, she ransacked the stores for Jim's present.

She found it at last. It was a platinum chain. It would look beautiful on Jim's watch in the place of his old leather strap. It cost twenty-one dollars, and she hurried home with the 87 cents.

Based on HENRY, O. *The Gift of the Magi.* New York: HarperCollins, 2006.

Vocabulary

gift: presente
income: renda
lie down: deitar(-se)
lift: levantar
sign: placa
watch: relógio de pulso

After Reading

A Match the words with the pictures.

1 ☐ gloves
2 ☐ chain
3 ☐ leather strap
4 ☐ combs
5 ☐ couch
6 ☐ overcoat
7 ☐ mirror

a

b

c
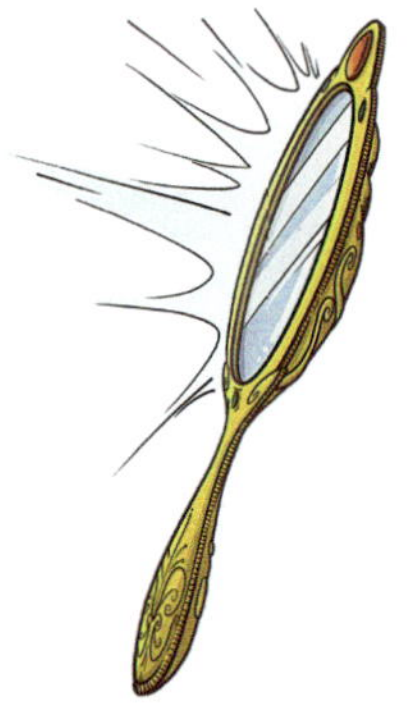

d

e
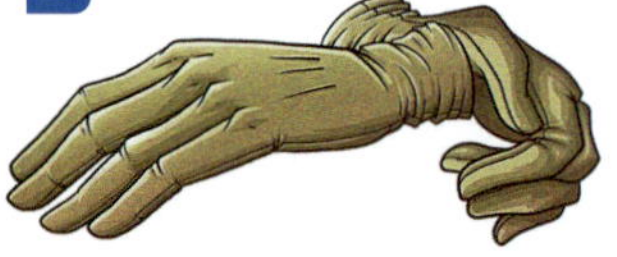

f

g

B Find the numbers that show...

1 the amount Della had saved. ______________________
2 the amount they paid for their flat. ______________________
3 their income. ______________________
4 the amount Della received for her hair. ______________________
5 the price of Jim's present. ______________________

C Complete the sentences.

1 And the next day would be ______________________________.

2 Her home was ______________________________.

3 The two possessions they were proud of were ______________________________.

D The story you have read was published in 1906. Read the story and make inferences. Answer in Portuguese.

1 Who was Jim? Explain.

____

2 What was the weather like? Explain.

____

3 On which floor did they live? Explain.

____

4 Why did Della cry?

____

Vocabulary Expansion

A Complete the sentences with the missing phrasal verbs. Use the box for help.

Phrasal Verbs

look: olhar; parecer
look after: cuidar, tomar conta
look at: olhar para
look for: procurar
look up: consultar (uma lista, um dicionário)

1 The mother stood by the door and ______________ her children.

2 You ______________ great! Let me ______________ you again.

3 She can't go with us because she has to ______________ the kids.

4 Can you ______________ these words in the dictionary, please?

5 Phoebe ______________ old and tired after the accident.

6 The teacher is ______________ a book to read.

B Read the box. Choose the best alternative.

1 I don't like tomatoes **but** the doctor told me I have to eat them.

a ☐ mas b ☐ exceto

2 We can help many people but we can't **save** the world.

a ☐ economizar b ☐ salvar

3 Everybody **but** me is going to the concert.

a ☐ mas b ☐ exceto

4 Della had **saved** only $1.87 to buy Jim a present.

a ☐ economizado b ☐ salvo

Words with Two Meanings

but: mas; exceto
save: salvar; economizar

C Complete the sentences. Use the boxes for help.

What (que)
Usado antes de substantivos no plural.

What a (que)
Usado antes de substantivos no singular ou substantivos incontáveis.

1 ______________________ nice people they are.

2 ______________________ difficult problem this is!

3 ______________________ wonderful stories she writes.

4 ______________________ beautiful chain she has bought!

5 ______________________ delicious cup of coffee!

D Complete the sentences. Use the words in the box.

above: acima
below: abaixo
over: por cima
under: embaixo

1 Look at the sky ______________________ us.

2 The cat was hidden ______________________ the sofa.

3 In Finland the temperature in winter is usually ______________________ zero.

4 The horse jumped ______________________ the fence.

5 From the top of the building we can see the streets ______________________.

6 In the desert the temperature can reach ______________________ 40 degrees during the day.

7 The magician kept a rabbit ______________________ her hat.

8 It's hard to see things ______________________ water.

Go to page 199 for Extra Practice.

LANGUAGE IN USE

A Take a look at the ad below. Then read the dialogue.

A: How much is a vest top for girls?
B: It's nine dollars and ninety-nine cents.
A: What's the regular price?
B: Twenty-two dollars.
A: How much do I save?
B: You save twelve dollars and one cent.

B NOW IT'S YOUR TURN!

Ask a classmate about other items in the ad. Look at the example above.

WRITING

Write an e-mail to a friend informing him or her of the special sale. Tell him or her:

- that you tried to call him or her but you got no answer;
- what you bought;
- how much you paid;
- what the regular price was;
- how much you saved;
- not to miss the special sale because this is the last day.

14 The Gifts (Part II)

LANGUAGE IN CONTEXT

A **Complete the information. Read the cartoon and check your answers.** 28

1 Place: ______________________

2 Relationship: ______________________

B **Give your opinion.**

1 Is Jeff the boss or the employee?

2 How do you know?

3 What kind of employee is Jeff?

4 Is Jeff trying to fool Mrs. Jones? Is he successful at that?

C **Think about it. Read the sentences and answer the questions.**

A	B
I have a good reason.	I may have a good reason.
My mother is sick.	My mother may be sick.
This is true.	This may be true.

1 *May* is the name of the fifth month of the year. But what does it mean in the sentences in group B?

2 What's the difference in meaning between the two groups of sentences?

Vocabulary

nope: não

sick: doente

Language Practice

Modal Verbs

May/might, should/ought to		
Os verbos modais dão um significado específico ao verbo principal.		
Formas	May/Might	Should/Ought to
Afirmativa	He **may** stay here. He **might** stay here.	We **should** go now. We **ought to** go now.
Interrogativa	**May** he stay here? **Might** he stay here?	**Should** we go now? **Ought** we **to** go now?
Negativa	He **may not** stay here. He **might not** stay here.	We **should not** go now. We **ought not** go now.
Formas abreviadas	**mightn't**	**shouldn't/oughtn't**

Uso

May/Might (pode, podia, poderia)

Expressam: pedido, possibilidade, permissão, dedução.

May, no sentido de permissão, pode ser substituído por **be allowed to** e é conjugado em todos os tempos.

May I go?

It **may** rain.

He **might** be sick.

He **was allowed to** leave.

Your wallet **might** be in the kitchen.

We **are allowed to** play cards on the bus.

I **may not** have time to do it.

Nota
- **may** – informal
- **might** – formal

Should/Ought to (deveria)

Expressam: dedução, conselho, lembrança de um dever.

You **should** be happy.

He **ought to** sleep now.

They **should** study hard.

I **ought to** help her with her shopping.

They **shouldn't** get angry.

A Read the sentences below. Choose their correct meaning.

a possibility/permission

b advice

1 [ ] Your boss is mad at you. You should arrive earlier tomorrow.

2 [ ] We may help you if we have some time left.

3 [ ] You ought to talk to her.

4 [ ] They might help her. I'm sure Mom won't mind.

5 [ ] She should travel in the morning; it's safer.

6 [ ] Tell Ted that he may leave now.

B Rewrite the sentences. Follow the example.

Example: You may leave now.
You are allowed to leave now.

1 She may walk around the park.

____

2 We may enter this room.

____

3 They may arrive late tonight.

____

4 The kid may play in the living room.

____

5 You may help us if you arrive early.

____

C Underline the correct alternative.

1 They **may** / **are allowed to** get there on time if they hurry.

2 She doesn't exercise much, but she really **ought to** / **might**.

3 **Ought to** / **May** I use your telephone?

4 Parents **should** / **might** spend much more time with their children.

5 Nobody knows what **might** / **ought to** happen in the future.

6 The students **ought to** / **aren't allowed to** enter class after 7:35 a.m. because classes start at 7:30 a.m.

D Check the best alternative.

1 She is crying because her mother said she ________ go out with her friends today.

a ☐ is allowed to
b ☐ should
c ☐ ought to
d ☐ may not

2 You look pale today. You ________ see your doctor.

a ☐ should
b ☐ oughtn't to
c ☐ mightn't
d ☐ are allowed to

3 My team ________ win this championship, but I don't think it will.

a ☐ may not
b ☐ shouldn't
c ☐ might
d ☐ might not

4 The teacher ________ to give us an easier test next time.

a ☐ may
b ☐ might
c ☐ should
d ☐ ought

5 We ________ arrive late to the show because we won't find any empty seats.

a ☐ should
b ☐ shouldn't
c ☐ are allowed to
d ☐ might

Used to vs. Be Used to

Uso

Used to é frequentemente confundido com **be used to**. Observe as diferenças:

Used to + **infinitivo**: expressa uma situação passada, que não ocorre mais.

I **used to play** soccer, but I don't anymore. (Eu jogava futebol, mas não jogo mais.)

He **used to study** hard. (Ele estudava muito, mas não estuda mais.)

Be used to + (verbo + **ing** ou **objeto direto**): expressa costume (presente, passado ou futuro).

I **was used to playing** soccer. (Eu estava acostumado a jogar futebol.)

I **am used to working** here. (Estou acostumado a trabalhar aqui.)

I **will be used to the noise.** (Vou me acostumar ao barulho.)

E **Complete the sentences with the correct form of the verbs in parentheses.**

1 He used to ______________________ (go out) a lot, but now he rarely goes to the movies.

2 Did you use to ______________________ (live) on this street?

3 I am used to ______________________ (drive) in São Paulo.

4 He was used to ______________________ (swim) every day.

5 I am not used to ______________________ (get up) early.

6 My father used to ______________________ (smoke) when he was young.

7 She is used to ______________________ (ride) her bike to school.

8 They aren't used to ______________________ (drink) a lot of coffee.

F **Underline the correct alternative.**

1 Where did you use **living** / **to live** before you moved here?

2 Don't worry about the kids: they are used to **get up** / **getting up** early every day.

3 Customers didn't use **to shop** / **shopping** from home.

4 My cousin lives in Orlando and she is used **to going** / **to go** to Universal Studios.

5 She didn't use **to like** / **liking** him, but now they are friends.

6 There used to **being** / **be** a grocery store in the neighborhood in those days.

7 My family used to **travel** / **traveling** to the beach when I was a kid.

8 My uncle is not used to **living** / **live** in a big city.

READING

Before Reading

Approaching the text

Discuss the questions below in Portuguese.

1 Della sold her hair. Was it a good idea?

2 Would you do something like that for someone you loved?

3 Do you think Jim is going to like the surprise?

4 Would you like the surprise if you were Jim?

Vocabulary

Find the meaning of the words below. Use the words in the boxes.

gloves | overcoat | pretty | mirror | pocket

1 bonita ____________________

2 bolso ____________________

3 luvas ____________________

4 sobretudo ____________________

5 espelho ____________________

The Gifts

part II

When Della got home she looked at her reflection in the mirror. "I have a feeling Jim will not like this at all," she said to herself. "But what could I do with a dollar and eighty-seven cents?"

Jim was never late, so at 7 o'clock Della sat on the corner of the table near the door.

Then she heard his step on the stairs and she turned white for just a moment. "Please, God, make him think I am still pretty."

The door opened and Jim stepped in and closed it. He looked thin and very serious. Poor fellow, he was only twenty-two. He needed a new overcoat and he had no gloves.

Jim stopped inside the door, immovable. His eyes were fixed upon Della.

"Jim, darling," she cried, "don't look at me that way. I sold my hair. I wanted to buy you a present. I just had to do it. You don't know what a nice gift I've got for you."

"You've cut off your hair?" asked Jim.

"Cut it off and sold it," said Della. "Don't you like me just as well, anyhow?"

"You say your hair is gone?" he said, with an air almost of idiocy.

"It's sold, I tell you – sold and gone, too," said Della.

Jim drew a package from his overcoat pocket and gave it to Della. She opened the package. Then she saw the combs – the set of combs that she had worshipped in a window. They were expensive combs, she knew. And now, they were hers, but her hair was gone.

"My hair grows awfully fast, Jim!"

Jim had not yet seen his beautiful present. She held it out to him.

"Isn't it beautiful, Jim? I hunted all over town to find it. Give me your watch. I want to see how it looks on the chain."

But Jim didn't give his watch to her. He tumbled down on the couch and put his hands under the back of his head and smiled.

"Della," said he, "I sold the watch to get the money to buy your combs."

Based on HENRY, O. *The Gift of the Magi.* New York: HarperCollins, 2006.

Vocabulary

awfully: terrivelmente
idiocy: bobeira
package: embrulho
set of combs: conjunto de pentes
tumble down: despencar
window: vitrine

After Reading

A Find words in the text that are the synonyms of the words below.

1 (l. 1) arrived ______________________

2 (l. 4) close to ______________________

3 (l. 8) walked in ______________________

4 (l. 19) adored ______________________

5 (l. 23) gave ______________________

6 (l. 24) looked for ______________________

7 (l. 26) fell quickly ______________________

B Find the sentences in the text that were used to say:

1 "Seus olhos estavam fixos em Della."

____

2 "Você cortou o cabelo?"

____

3 "Cortei-o e vendi-o."

____

4 Jim desabou no sofá.

____

C Check Yes or No according to the information in the text.

		Yes	No
1	Quando Della chegou em casa, Jim já estava lá.		
2	Della achou que Jim não gostaria de vê-la daquele modo.		
3	Jim sempre chegava tarde em casa.		
4	Della ficou de pé esperando por Jim.		
5	Jim precisava de um casaco novo.		
6	Jim tinha somente vinte e dois anos.		
7	O conjunto de pentes que Jim deu a Della era caro.		
8	Della tinha dado seu cabelo de presente a alguém.		
9	Della tinha comprado um relógio para Jim.		
10	Jim chorou quando viu o presente de Della.		

D Answer the questions according to the text.

1 Where did Della wait for Jim?

____

2 What did she worry about while she waited for him?

____

3 Why did she sell her hair?

____

4 What present did she buy him?

____

Vocabulary Expansion

A The verb *to get* may have different meanings. Match the columns.

1 When Della got home. a ☐ bring

2 You don't know what a nice gift I've got for you. b ☐ arrive

3 I sold the watch to get the money to buy your combs. c ☐ acquire

4 Get me a glass of water, please. I'm thirsty. d ☐ obtain

B Find the synonyms of the words in bold. Use the words in the boxes.

took terribly sweetheart

1 Jim, **darling**, don't look at me that way. _______________

2 My hair grows **awfully** fast. _______________

3 Jim **drew** a package from his pocket. _______________

C Rewrite the sentences. Follow the example.

Example: He was a teacher. He was twenty-two years old.
He was a twenty-two-year-old teacher.

1 She was a scientist. She was fifty-five years old.

____

2 They were dancers. They were nineteen years old.

____

Language in Use

A **Read about the author of *The Gift of the Magi*. Then match the columns and talk to a classmate. See the examples.**

O. Henry

O. Henry is one of the most famous American short story writers.

O. Henry's real name was William Sydney Porter and he was born in Greensboro, North Carolina, on September 11, 1862.

At the age of 20 (1882), he moved to Texas, where he had various jobs. He married Athol Estes in 1887; they had a son and a daughter. His wife died from tuberculosis in 1897.

In 1894, while working for First National Bank in Austin, Porter was accused of stealing $4,000. He went to prison in Columbus, Ohio, for 3 years eventually.

While in prison Porter first started to write short stories and it's believed that he has found his writer's pseudonym there.

After Porter was released from prison in 1901, he changed his name to O. Henry and moved to New York in 1902.

From December 1903 to January 1906 O. Henry wrote one story a week for the *New York World* magazine, and published several short stories in other magazines.

O. Henry's short stories are famous for their surprise endings and humor.

O. Henry wrote such classic short stories as "The Ransom of Red Chief", "The Gift of the Magi", and "The Furnished Room".

In his later years, O. Henry had financial and health problems. An alcoholic, O. Henry died on June 5, 1910 in New York City, virtually broke.

Extracted from <www.literaturecollection.com>. Accessed on November 25, 2010.

A	B
What	his wife die of
When	do from December 1903 to January 1906
Where	be born in 1862
	live from 1882 to 1902
	die
	go in 1902
	write some of his stories
	go to Texas

Examples:

A: When was he born?

B: He was born in 1862.

A: Where did he live from 1882 to 1902?

B: He lived in Texas.

B **NOW IT'S YOUR TURN!**

Ask a classmate about his or her family. Look at the examples.

Examples: **A:** Where were your... born?

B: Where did your... live?

Writing

Write a small article for an encyclopedia describing an important person in the history of your community. You may take a look at some articles in different encyclopedias if you want.

EXTRA PRACTICE 7

A Complete the sentences. Use the Past Perfect and the verbs in parentheses.

1 When you arrived yesterday, I ____________ already ____________ (to leave).

2 She ____________ already ____________ (to sleep) when they phoned her.

3 When she went to the kitchen, we ____________ already ____________ (to wash) the dishes.

4 By the time he asked for a piece of cake, the kids ____________ already ____________ (to eat) all of it.

5 I wrote him a letter, but when it arrived there, he ____________ already ____________ (to move) to San Francisco.

6 We went to her place for dinner but, to our great surprise, she ____________ already ____________ her dinner.

B There are mistakes in some of the sentences below. Circle the mistakes and rewrite these sentences in the correct form.

1 We had finish the exercises when the teacher called us.

____

2 You told me you had saved some money.

____

3 When the guests arrived I had been writing a letter.

____

4 Roy told me he had fallen from a tree.

____

5 I had asked her five times to close the window when she saw her notebook was wet because of the rain.

____

6 She tells me that the children has eat all her chocolate bar.

____

7 We had not been working when she arrives at the office.

____

8 Mom said that I had not told her the truth.

____

C Complete the sentences. Use the words in the boxes.

above below over under above

1 The Minister of Finance is working hard to keep the inflation rate ______________ 4.1% this year. He doesn't want it to go higher than that.

2 High inflation rates impact society as a whole, but ______________ all they deeply affect the working class.

3 I remember that my secretary put my report on foreign investments ______________ this book, but it is not here any more.

4 Mr. Jaegger is planning to fly ______________ the English Channel with his experimental airplane. Some people say he won't succeed.

5 The reason why they say he won't succeed is that his airplane flies very low. It cannot fly ______________ 200 feet.

D Rewrite the sentences. Use the form indicated in parentheses.

1 He might work in the morning.

(interrogative) ____

2 You should call your friend today.

(negative) ____

3 I might help them.

(interrogative) ____

4 You ought not to pay her this week.

(affirmative) ____

5 The children may play outside after class.

(interrogative) ____

E Write A (advice) or D (deduction).

1 ☐ Look at Mary! She may be happy.

2 ☐ She doesn't exercise much, but she really ought to.

3 ☐ Parents should spend more time with their children.

4 ☐ Nobody knows what might happen in the future.

5 ☐ The children ought not to go out now. They have to finish their homework first.

6 ☐ He hasn't arrived yet. He must be late.

F Complete the sentences with the modal verbs given.

may | might | should | ought to

1 Your eyes are reddish. You ______________________________ have a fever.

2 I need a pencil. ______________________________ I use yours for a minute?

3 Mom is not sure, but she said she ______________________________ arrive a little late today.

4 I ______________________________ pass the examination, but I don't think I will.

5 She ______________________________ travel with her friends because she is feeling sick.

G Check the correct alternative.

1 The students _________ to study our history a bit more.

a ☐ ought

b ☐ should

2 You _________ give her a present. It's her birthday.

a ☐ ought not

b ☐ should

3 There's a special class tomorrow. You _________ arrive late.

a ☐ should not

b ☐ ought to

4 She _________ to be fat. Now she is thin.

a ☐ is used

b ☐ used

5 She _________ pay the bill, but she knows she _________.

a ☐ may not – ought to

b ☐ might – should

6 _________ I repeat the story?

a ☐ Might not

b ☐ Should

7 It _________ rain, but I don't think it will.

a ☐ might

b ☐ ought

www.careerdirections.ie

Home | Description | Aspects of Work | Work Activities | Personal Qualities and Skills | Pay and Opportunities
Entry Routes and Training | Qualifications | Adult Opportunities | Further Information

Hotel Accommodation Assistant

Introduction

Hotel accommodation assistants are responsible for preparing rooms and making sure they reach the required standard for arriving guests. Duties include making beds, cleaning the room and replacing linen, towels and toiletries.

Aspects of Work

Central Aspects	Secondary Aspects	Other Aspects
Being physically active and on your feet	Doing practical work not needing new skills	Providing a service to members of the public
Cleaning and clearing up	Being interested in household organisation and activities	Lifting or carrying heavy things
	Being well-organised and careful with practical tasks	Repeating the same short tasks
	Working evenings or weekends	

Work Activities

The hotel accommodation assistant works behind the scenes and provides a "home away from home" for guests, making their stay relaxed and enjoyable.

Professional maintenance of bedrooms and public areas in the hotel are the responsibility of the Accommodation Services Department. This involves the day-to-day upkeep of rooms and equipment, service of meals in guest bedrooms and other room services such as doing the laundry.

Personal Qualities and Skills

Personal qualities required for this career include the ability to anticipate guests needs, being of a trustworthy and discreet nature, having a good eye for detail and being active and in good health.

As a hotel accommodation assistant, you could have anywhere between 12 and 20 rooms to clean, so you'll be on your feet, bending, lifting and moving about all the time. [...] A polite and pleasant personality is important because you'll meet hotel guests as you do your work.

[...]

You should be able to work with people at all levels, follow procedures and demonstrate attention to detail.

[...]

Extracted from <www.careerdirections.ie>. Accessed on November 26, 2010.

15 Multiple Intelligences

Language in Context

A Complete the information. Read the cartoon and check your answers. 30

1 Place

____

2 Relationship

____

3 Boy's name

____

B Give your opinion.

1 Why does the little boy's mother think he is a genius?

2 Are kids more intelligent now than the kids in the past?

C Think about it. Read the sentences carefully and answer the questions.

I need no cards now.
I still have some cards.
You can give me some more cards.

1 Which sentence has a negative meaning?

2 The word "some" expresses quantity. Is it possible to know what the quantity is?

Vocabulary

stay: ficar
still: ainda

Language Practice

Indefinite Adjectives and Pronouns (I)

Some, any e **no** podem desempenhar a função de adjetivos ou de pronomes. Indicam quantidade ou número indefinido.

I need **some** money.

I need **no** money.

Do you need **any** money? (adjective)

No, I don't need **any**. (pronoun)

Uso

Some [algum(ns), alguma(s), um pouco] é usado em frases afirmativas.

I want **some** coffee. She wrote **some** letters.

Any [algum(ns), alguma(s), nenhum(a)] é usado em frases interrogativas e negativas.

Did she write **any** letters? She didn't write **any** letters.

No/None [nenhum(a)] são usados com o verbo na forma afirmativa. Dão sentido negativo à frase.

I have **no** money. (adjetivo) I have **none** either. (pronome)

Notas

> **Some** é usado em frases interrogativas para expressar um pedido, oferecimento ou quando se espera uma resposta positiva.

Would you like **some** coffee?

Do you need **some** money?

> **Any** é usado em frases afirmativas quando:

- significa **qualquer, quaisquer**;

  Call me at **any** time.

- é usado em frases afirmativas após **if**;

  If you have **any** questions, ask me.

- é usado em frases afirmativas com palavras de sentido negativo, como **seldom, rarely, never, without**, etc.

  He **seldom** has **any** money.

  He **never** has **any** good ideas.

A Underline the correct alternatives.

1 Jerry hasn't eaten **any**/**no** biscuits yet.

2 There is **some**/**no** car in front of the bank.

3 They built **any**/**some** houses last year.

4 She bought many books, but I bought **no**/**none**.

5 I can't buy this CD for you. I have **no**/**none** money.

6 Mother cooked **any**/**some** fish for lunch today.

7 Are you going to write **any**/**no** e-mails tomorrow?

8 She rarely drinks **no**/**any** coffee.

B Rewrite the sentences. Use the forms indicated in parentheses.

Example: I have no doubts.
(int.) Do you have any doubts?

1 We can call no friends for dinner tonight.

(aff.) ____

2 Did you see any notebooks in the classroom?

(neg.) ____

3 I had seen some gold coins in the empty room.

(neg.) ____

4 There is some sugar in the sugar bowl.

(int.) ____

5 She has planned to buy no expensive clothes.

(aff.) ____

Go to page 224 for Extra Practice.

Indefinite Adjectives and Pronouns (II)

Compostos de **some, any** e **no**		
Os compostos de **some**, **any** e **no** seguem as mesmas regras de uso apresentadas na página 203.		
Some	Any	No
someone/somebody something somewhere	anyone/anybody anything anywhere	no one/nobody nothing nowhere

C Check all correct answers.

1 Have you seen my glasses? I can't find them ________.

a ☐ nowhere b ☐ anywhere c ☐ somewhere

2 Is there ________ to eat in the kitchen?

a ☐ anything b ☐ anytime c ☐ nowhere

3 I know I've left my keys ________ around here.

a ☐ something b ☐ somebody c ☐ somewhere

4 There is ________ that I like in this store.

a ☐ anyone b ☐ nothing c ☐ anywhere

D Write *some*, *any*, *no* or the correct compound.

1 Don't put ________________ on the table.

2 I asked him for ________________ money, but he didn't have any.

3 ________________ has taken my umbrella. I can't find it.

4 Did you go ________________ last night?

5 There are ________________ students here. They must be ________________ else.

6 There is ________________ written on the wall, but I can't read it.

7 ________________ has arrived. Did you tell people the correct time?

8 The refrigerator is empty. We have ________________ to eat.

9 Have you read ________________ good books lately?

Go to page 225 for Extra Practice.

READING

Before Reading

Approaching the text

Discuss the questions below in Portuguese.

1 In your opinion, what is intelligence?

2 Are we all born intelligent?

3 Is it possible to improve one's intelligence?

4 How many different kinds of intelligence are there?

Vocabulary

Write the meaning of the words below. Use the glossary.

1 awake ______________________________

2 herd ______________________________

3 puny ______________________________

4 nearsighted ______________________________

5 jam ______________________________

6 summon ______________________________

31 Many Kinds of Minds: The Theory of Multiple Intelligences

Imagine for a moment that you're living in prehistoric times. You've been awakened in the middle of the night by the thundering noise of a herd of mastodons moving toward your encampment. Now, let's say for the sake of argument that you're able to bring any individual from the twentieth century into your primitive setting to help you out of this jam. Who's it going to be? Will it be Albert Einstein? Nope, too puny. How about James Joyce? Sorry, too nearsighted. What about Franklin Delano Roosevelt? Not in a wheelchair. The most "brilliant" men of the twentieth century would be of little use to you in your hour of need. On the other hand, if I suggested you summon someone like Michael Jordan or Arnold Schwarzenegger, I'd be closer to bailing you out of your predicament. The truth is that intelligence in that environment had more to do with quick reflexes, acute spatial orientations, speed, strength, and agility than $E = mc^2$, *Finnegans Wake*, or the *New Deal*.

Extracted from ARMSTRONG, Thomas. *7 Kinds of Smart*. New York: Plume/Penguin, 1993, p. 7.

In a traditional view, intelligence is defined operationally as the ability to answer items on tests of intelligence. [...] Multiple intelligences theory, on the other hand, pluralizes the traditional concept. An intelligence entails the ability to solve problems or fashion products that are of consequence in a particular cultural setting or community.

[...] We believe that human cognitive competence is better described in terms of a set of abilities, talents, or mental skills, which we call "intelligences". All normal individuals possess each of these skills to some extent.

Extracted from GARDNER, Howard. *Multiple Intelligences: The Theory in Practice*. New York: Basic Books, 1993, p. 15.

Franklin Delano Roosevelt

Presidente norte-americano de 1933 a 1945. Tirou seu país da Grande Depressão dos anos 1930 por meio de um complexo plano econômico conhecido como *New Deal*. Governou durante toda a Segunda Guerra Mundial. Contraiu poliomielite em 1931 e governou o país em cadeira de rodas.

James Joyce

Escritor irlandês, considerado um dos maiores do século XX. Autor do livro *Finnegans Wake*.

$E = mc^2$

Energia é igual à massa multiplicada pelo quadrado da velocidade da luz no vácuo. Essa equação, que resume a Lei da Relatividade, foi formulada por Albert Einstein.

Vocabulary

- **bail out:** resgatar
- **encampment:** acampamento
- **fashion:** criar; desenvolver
- **for the sake of argument:** a título de argumento
- **predicament:** apuro
- **set:** conjunto
- **setting:** cenário; ambiente
- **thundering noise:** barulho como o de um trovão

After Reading

A **Read and identify the kind of intelligence that best describes you.**

BODILY/KINESTHETIC
Ability to control body movements and make things (with one's hands).
People who like to move around, act, mime, dance, sports, crafts; use hands to create things, people who have physical coordination.
Professions: inventor, musician, surgeon, athlete, dancer, physical education teacher, actor, artisan.
Examples: Magic Johnson, Daiane dos Santos.

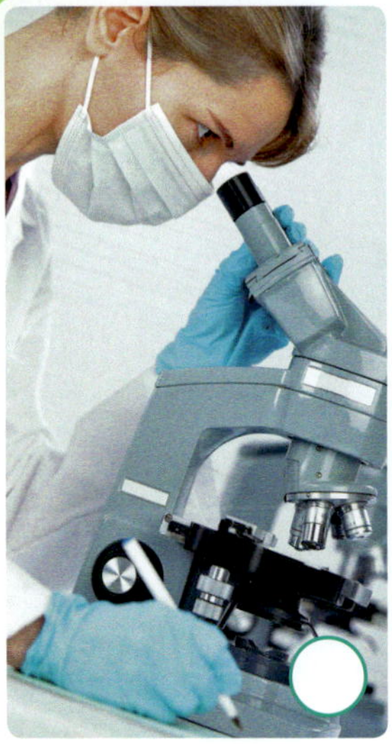

LOGICAL/MATHEMATICAL
Ability to use reason, logic, and numbers.
People who like to ask questions, solve problems, experiment, work with numbers, abstract and geometric shapes.
Professions: banker, lawyer, computer programmer, researcher, scientist, accountant, mathematician, engineer.
Example: Albert Einstein.

VERBAL/LINGUISTIC
Ability to use words and language.
People who like to listen, speak, write, explain, use humor, tell stories, convince someone of their point of view.
Professions: actor, comedian, poet, journalist, writer, teacher, public speaker, secretary, politician, lawyer.
Examples: Abraham Lincoln, Monteiro Lobato.

INTRAPERSONAL
Ability to self-reflect.
People who like to analyze themselves, work alone, set goals, recognize their own strengths, and understand their inner feelings and intentions.
Professions: psychiatrist, philosopher, theorist, researcher, religious leader.
Example: Sigmund Freud.

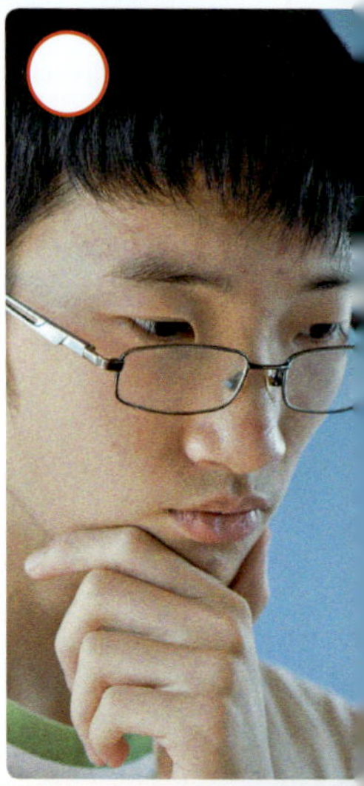

MUSICAL/RHYTHMIC
Ability to produce or create music.
People who like to sing, play musical instruments, listen to music, compose; can remember melodies; have rhythm.
Professions: dancer, music teacher, songwriter, composer, singer, musician, disc jockey.
Examples: Mozart, Caetano Veloso.

B **Answer the questions about yourself.**

1 Which types of intelligence have you developed? List them.

____

2 Which types do you want to be stronger at? List them.

____

3 Relate people you know to each type of intelligence.

____

C **Check Y (yes) or N (no).**
According to Howard Gardner's theory, we can say that:

1	We all have several types of intelligence.	☐ Y	☐ N
2	Our intelligence is fixed at birth.	☐ Y	☐ N
3	Different types of intelligence help us to solve problems.	☐ Y	☐ N
4	We can become "more intelligent".	☐ Y	☐ N
5	It is important to understand how we learn.	☐ Y	☐ N

INTERPERSONAL
Ability to understand other people.
People who like to communicate, lead, resolve conflicts, sell, cooperate, listen; people who can understand other people's points of view.
Professions: therapist, teacher, counselor, salesperson, politician, business person, religious leader.
Examples: Mother Theresa, Nelson Mandela.

VISUAL/SPATIAL INTELLIGENCE
Ability to perceive the visual.
People who like to read, write, paint, draw, and have good sense of direction.
Professions: sculptor, painter, inventor, visual artist, architect, designer, mechanic, engineer, navigator.
Examples: Di Cavalcanti, Amyr Klink.

NATURALIST
Ability to understand/observe nature.
People who like activities that involve nature, natural events, and biological science.
Professions: botanist, naturalist, physicist, geologist.
Example: Charles Darwin.

Vocabulary Expansion

A Read the box. Write the words that match the definitions.

multicolored | multiracial | multiform

1 Region with many races of people

____

2 Something that has many different forms or shapes

____

3 Something that has many different colors _______________

Prefix multi

O prefixo **multi** indica que algo consiste em muitas coisas de um determinado tipo:

multinational

multimillionaire

B Choose the best alternative to complete each pair of sentences.

1 Mr. Smith is a very competent ________.

Monica ________ many different subjects very well.

a teaches b teacher

2 They have gone to the party, but they didn't ________.

Cynthia was a very good ________ when she was young.

a dance b dancer

3 Richard is an honest ________.

People should never discuss ________ or religion.

a politics b politician

4 He is a good ________ student. He will be a good professional.

Dr. Johnson is the ________ in charge of this research.

a psychiatrist b psychiatry

C Complete the sentences. Use *both* or *together*.

both: ambos(as), os(as) dois (duas)

together: juntos(as)

1 Sally and Kelly are going to travel to Europe ______________.

2 ______________ of us have already done the exercises.

3 Don't worry. Let's do it ______________.

4 Sarah and Ernie always come to the meeting ______________.

5 Eddie bought ______________ books he needed.

Language in Use

A **Read the dictionary entry below. Then talk to a classmate.**

in·tel·li·gen·ce
(ĭn-tĕl′ə-jəns) n. *Abbr.* int.,
1.a. The capacity to acquire and apply knowledge.
b. The faculty of thought and reason. **c.** Superior powers of mind.
2. Information; news.
3.a. Secret information, especially about an enemy.
b. An agency or an office that gathers secret information.
c. Espionage agents or organizations.

Extracted from: *The American Heritage Dictionary of the English Language.* Boston: Houghton Mifflin Company, 1992, p. 938.

A: What's the meaning of intelligence?

B: It's the capacity to acquire and apply knowledge.

B **NOW IT'S YOUR TURN!**

Ask a classmate about the various meanings of the word *intelligence*.

Writing

Write a paragraph about your best friend, proving that he or she is intelligent. Don't forget to mention what kind of intelligence best describes him or her.

16 Child Labor

Language in Context

A **Complete the information. Read the dialogue and check your answers.** 32

1 Names of people

____

2 Activities

____

B **Give your opinion.**

1 What do Derek and Celine do in this place?

2 What does Lara want to do?

3 Do you think volunteer work can help a community? How?

C **Think about it. Read the sentences and answer the questions.**

We have many students who are volunteers.
The boy who is wearing a yellow T-shirt is our *capoeira* instructor.
They chose theater, which is their favorite activity.

1 All the sentences above have two clauses: a main clause and a subordinate clause. Identify them.

2 Which word begins each subordinate clauses?

3 Why is the subordinate clause in the last sentence introduced by a different word?

Derek: Wow, Lara! There are lots of kids here.

Lara: Yeah, Derek. And more and more come each day.

Derek: Are there instructors for everybody?

Celine: Yup. We have many students who are volunteers. Look. The boy who is wearing a yellow T-shirt is our *capoeira* instructor.

Lara: And the girl near the entrance is our theater director.

Derek: What kind of youngsters come here?

Celine: All kinds. The kids who have nothing to do in the afternoon or on weekends. Everything is planned by them and we haven't had any kind of problem.

Derek: Which activities do they choose?

Lara: *Capoeira*, hip-hop, guitar lessons and theater are their favorite.

Celine: We intend to have volleyball and choir singing, which many students have asked us about.

Derek: I'm a good hip hop dancer and I'm free on weekends. Is there a place for me?

Vocabulary

entrance: entrada
youngster: jovem

Language Practice

Relative Pronouns (I)

Os pronomes relativos introduzem orações subordinadas adjetivas. Essas orações definem, limitam ou acrescentam alguma informação ao substantivo da oração principal.

Uso

Who/That (que, quem) – Usados quando o antecedente do pronome relativo é uma pessoa.

The man [**who/that** arrived] is a pilot.

Which/That (que, o/a qual, os/as quais) – Usados quando o antecedente não é uma pessoa.

The book [**which/that** is on the bed] is mine.

The dog **which/that** I saw was hurt.

Sujeito/Objeto – O pronome relativo pode ser sujeito ou objeto da oração subordinada.

The man [**who** arrived] is a pilot.

The man [**who** I saw] is a pilot.

Objeto – Quando o pronome relativo é objeto, ele pode ser omitido.

The man [**X** I saw] is a pilot.

The dog [**X** I saw] was hurt.

Whom (que, quem) – Pode substituir **who**.

The man [**who** I saw]
The man [**that** I saw]
The man [**whom** I saw]
The man [**X** I saw]
} is a pilot.

Whom – Pode ser precedido por preposição.

The man to **whom** you were talking is Mr. Taylor.

A Complete the sentences. Use *who* or *which*.

1 That is the person ________________ sold me those ancient books.

2 This is the house ________________ I want to buy.

3 He is the mechanic ________________ has fixed my car.

4 The dogs ________________ you have at home are very dangerous.

5 The people ________________ have just arrived live in my neighborhood.

B Join the sentences with relative pronouns.

Example: Sheila is my friend. Sheila is a teacher.
Sheila, who is my friend, is a teacher.

1 I bought the shirt. The shirt was very expensive.

____

____

2 He has an apartment. His apartment was built in 2005.

____

____

3 Her younger son is ten years old. He plays the guitar very well.

____

____

C Read the sentences below. Follow the instructions.

1 Coloque as orações subordinadas entre colchetes.

2 Indique se o pronome relativo é sujeito (S) ou objeto (O) da oração.

a [ ] This is the evidence that his lawyer needed.

b [ ] The housewife that we asked the question to is over there.

c [ ] Einstein formulated a law that changed the course of science.

d [ ] The car that Paul bought was made in Italy.

e [ ] She is the dentist that talked about tooth decay.

f [ ] My brother is sleeping in the room that is near the kitchen.

g [ ] A girl that we know will help you.

h [ ] The boy who wrote me a letter lives in Japan.

D Underline the correct alternatives. More than one alternative may be correct for each sentence.

1 The woman (who / that / which) saved the baby was very courageous.

2 The keys (that / who / which) were on the table are mine.

3 That is the boy about (who / whom / that) I was talking.

4 This is the diary about (which / that / whom) she was talking.

5 The house (which / that / who) we bought was very expensive.

6 The girls (who / that / whom) you invited ate all the sandwiches.

E Complete the sentences with a relative pronoun. Write all the possibilities.

1 Is she the woman ______________________ you met yesterday?

2 You are the professional ______________________ we are looking for.

3 Martin is the German boy ______________________ speaks Portuguese.

4 The car ______________________ you had sold me was stolen last weekend.

5 She is the girl to ______________________ I gave the book.

Go to page 226 for Extra Practice.

Relative Pronouns (II)

Uso

Where (onde) – Usado para se referir a lugares.
The house **where** she lives is near the park.

Whose [cujo(s), cuja(s)] – Usado para indicar relação de posse.
The girl **whose** mother is an astronaut wants to talk to you.

F **Complete the sentences with *where* or *whose*.**

1 I went to a restaurant __________________ the food was cheap and delicious.
2 I met a woman __________________ son had studied at my school.
3 This is the park __________________ I used to come when I was a child.
4 This is the room __________________ the kids watch TV.
5 The man __________________ son is a lawyer was arrested yesterday.
6 The hotel __________________ I stayed was very expensive.

G **Circle the relative pronouns in the sentences below. Some sentences have no relative pronouns.**

1 Is that the house that you like?
2 Which do you prefer, cinema or theater?
3 That is the school where I study.
4 Who is your English teacher?
5 When is your birthday?
6 She is the girl whose shoes are black.
7 My friend whom I like very much is in hospital.

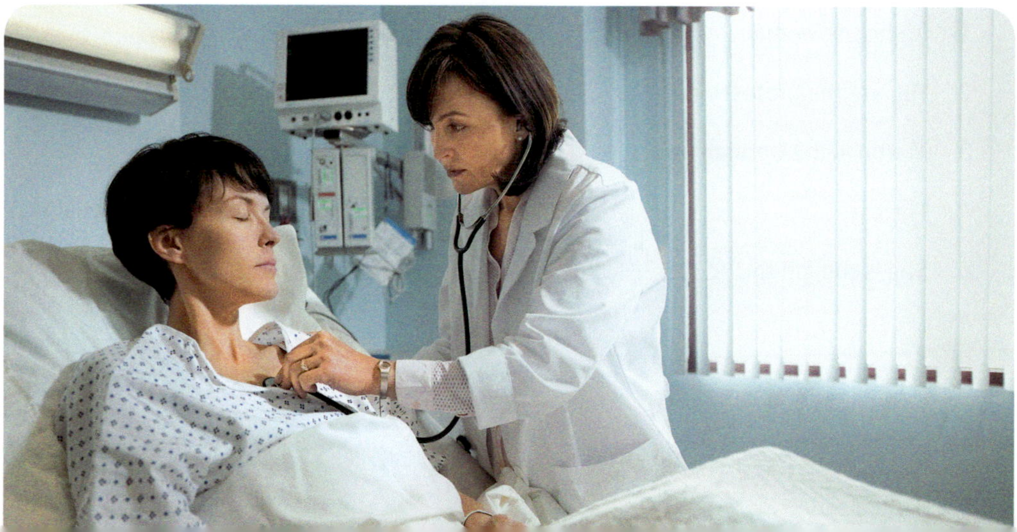

H **Choose the correct alternative to complete each sentence.**

1 The book ________ she wrote was a best-seller.

a ☐ which
b ☐ whose
c ☐ that
d ☐ *a* and *c* are correct

2 The player ________ won the competition is my brother.

a ☐ whom
b ☐ who
c ☐ which
d ☐ *a* and *b* are correct

3 The dress ________ you bought is very expensive.

a ☐ whose
b ☐ X
c ☐ that
d ☐ *b* and *c* are correct

4 The person ________ I most admire will be here tonight.

a ☐ which
b ☐ whom
c ☐ whose
d ☐ *b* and *c* are correct

5 That's the policeman ________ spoke to me last night.

a ☐ where
b ☐ that
c ☐ X
d ☐ *b* and *c* are correct

6 That's the dog ________ owner is Italian.

a ☐ which
b ☐ whose
c ☐ that
d ☐ *a* and *c* are correct

7 The house in ________ she lives is very small.

a ☐ where
b ☐ which
c ☐ that
d ☐ *a* and *b* are correct

8 The boy ________ mother works in the post office is very shy.

a ☐ who
b ☐ whom
c ☐ whose
d ☐ *a* and *b* are correct

9 The dogs ________ are in your garden belong to me.

a ☐ that
b ☐ which
c ☐ *a* and *b* are correct
d ☐ whose

10 Sandy and John are the students ________ have passed the exam.

a ☐ that
b ☐ X
c ☐ who
d ☐ *a* and *c* are correct

READING

Before Reading

Approaching the text

Discuss the questions below in Portuguese.

1 How many people in your class work?

2 What kind of jobs do they have?

3 How many hours do they work every day?

Vocabulary

Find the meaning of the words below. Use the glossary.

1 engaged ____________________

2 hazardous ____________________

3 labor ____________________

4 machinery ____________________

5 mine ____________________

CHILD LABOR

33

An estimated 158 million children aged 5 to 14 are engaged in child labor – one in six children in the world. Millions of children are engaged in hazardous situations or conditions, such as working in mines, working with chemicals and pesticides in agriculture, or working with dangerous machinery. They are everywhere but invisible, toiling as domestic servants in homes, laboring behind the walls of workshops, hidden from view in plantations.

In Sub-Saharan Africa around one in three children are engaged in child labor, representing 69 million children. In South Asia, another 44 million are engaged in child labor. Children living in the poorest households and in rural areas are most likely to be engaged in child labor. Those burdened with household chores are overwhelmingly girls.

Millions of girls who work as domestic servants are especially vulnerable to exploitation and abuse.

Extracted from <http://volunteers.unicefusa.org>. Accessed on August 16, 2009.

Child Labor in Brazil

Economic Activity (as % of total aged 7 to 14)	
Total	7.1
Male	9.5
Female	4.6
School Attendance (as % of total aged 7 to 14)	
Total	97.2
Male	96.9
Female	97.5
Sector of Work (as % of economically-active children aged 7 to 14)	
Agriculture	59.7
Services	31.3
Manufacturing	7.4
Other	1.7

Work Intensity (average weekly working hours in economic activity, children aged 7 to 14 years)	
Children Working Only	
Male	34.2
Female	34.6
Total	34.3
Children Working and Attending School	
Male	19.6
Female	18.8
Total	19.3

Source: VCW calculation based on "Pesquisa por amostragem de domicílios (PNAD)", 2003.
Extracted from <www.ucw-project.org>. Accessed on August 16, 2009.

[...] Labor often interferes with children's education. Ensuring that all children go to school and that their education is of good quality are keys to preventing child labor. [...]

Extracted from <www.unicef.org>. Accessed on December 16, 2010.

Vocabulary

chore: tarefa
ensuring: assegurando
household chores: serviços domésticos
overwhelmingly: predominantemente
toil: trabalhar arduamente

After Reading

A Find in the text:

1 the number of children engaged in work worldwide: ______________

2 the number of children engaged in work in Sub-Saharan Africa: ______________

3 the number of children engaged in work in South-Asian: ______________

B Choose the words that mean about the same as the words in bold.

1 (1st paragraph) "Millions of children are engaged in **hazardous** situations or conditions, such as working in mines, working with chemicals and pesticides in agriculture, or working with dangerous machinery."

a ☐ adequate b ☐ dangerous c ☐ slavery

2 (1st paragraph) "They are everywhere but invisible, toiling as domestic servants in homes, **laboring** behind the walls of workshops, hidden from view in plantations."

a ☐ working b ☐ forcing c ☐ reading

C Choose the meaning of the sentences below.

1 "They are everywhere but invisible [...] hidden from view in plantations."

a ☐ People rarely see them.

b ☐ They don't exist.

2 "Millions of girls who work as domestic servants are especially vulnerable to exploitation and abuse."

a ☐ They receive adequate payment to work as maids.

b ☐ They work as maids and can suffer from abuse.

D Read the sentences about child labor in Brazil. Write T (true) or F (false).

1 ☐ More girls than boys go to school.

2 ☐ More boys than girls work after school.

3 ☐ The average number of hours that boys work a week is 34.3.

4 ☐ 9.5 percent of boys between 7 and 14 years of age work in Brazil.

5 ☐ More children work in industries than in agriculture in Brazil.

6 ☐ Labor doesn't interfere with children's education.

Vocabulary Expansion

A **Rewrite the expressions. Follow the example.**

Example: a woman that screams a screaming woman

1 children who labor ____________
2 a hand that helps ____________
3 a child that sleeps ____________
4 mothers who work ____________
5 a dog that jumps ____________
6 girls who smile ____________

B **Complete the sentences. Use the expressions in the boxes.**

age: relativo a idade; era, época, século

at an early age | for ages | of full age | aged | aging | ageless

1 This wine was ____________ in oak barrels. (envelhecido)
2 She looked beautiful and ____________. (que não envelhece)
3 Rich and John can enter the ballroom because they are ____________. (maior de idade)
4 Because he was born in a poor family, he started working ____________. (cedo na vida)
5 My family has lived in this town ____________. (há séculos)
6 Lack of exercise contributes to the process of ____________. (envelhecimento)

C **Search the boxes below and find synonyms for the words.**

frequently | behind | captivity | vulnerable | nearly | nowhere | terrible
illegal | invisible | housemaid | above | everywhere
ahead | worst | work | unpaid | involved

1 horrific ____________
2 engaged ____________
3 illicit ____________
4 bondage ____________
5 almost ____________
6 toil ____________
7 often ____________
8 servant ____________

— He is a good runner.
— He started at an early age.

Language in Use

A **Read the poem below. Then match the columns and talk to a classmate. See the examples.**

www.stopchildlabor.org

Message

The Song of Iqbal

By Casse L. Forczek / © 1997

Message of the Month

My father sold me to a carpet man
I go to his factory at 4 a.m.
I'm working all day as hard as I can
I'm just a child workin' like a man

My father sold me to a carpet man
Who runs a factory in Pakistan
For a twelve-dollar debt he could not pay
I work like a slave for six cents a day

[...]

My name is Iqbal and I'm only five
I don't even know that I am alive
When I'm six I hope this torture will cease
Or is this the way it must always be?

[...]

Postscript

Iqbal had the dream to read and help other boys and girls. After being freed at ten years old, Iqbal Masih became an outspoken advocate for working children and was awarded the Reebok Human Rights Award in America at the age of 11. Back in Pakistan, he rallied and set free over 3,000 children. Then, at the age of 12, he was murdered on Easter Sunday in 1995.

Extracted from <www.stopchildlabor.org>. Accessed on November 30, 2010.

A	B
Who	sold
How much	bought
When	pay
	make

A: Who is the author of the poem?
B: The author is Casse L. Forczek.
A: How old is Iqbal?
B: He's only five.

B NOW IT'S YOUR TURN!

Ask a classmate about his/her daily schedule. Look at the examples.

What do you do after school?
Do you get an allowance?
What do you do with your money?

WRITING

Write a short poem (4 lines at minimum) about someone's hard life. Describe what he or she does, how much he or she makes, and what he or she wants to be in the future.

EXTRA PRACTICE 8

A Write *some*, *any*, *no* or *none*. More than one alternative may be possible.

1 There were __________ children in the park this morning.

2 We wanted to eat __________ bananas before dinner, but mother gave us __________.

3 I haven't had __________ coffee for three days.

4 They were looking for __________ old books in the garage.

5 I need __________ more eggs to make the cake.

B Rewrite the sentences. Follow the example.

Example: He didn't have any money.
He had no money.

1 We didn't buy any sugar. __________

2 He doesn't eat any apples. __________

3 You didn't make any mistakes. __________

4 She didn't hear any noise. __________

5 They don't eat any vegetables. __________

C Rewrite the sentences in which the indefinite adjective or pronoun is not used correctly.

1 Do you have some problems with the Chemistry exercises?

____

2 I offered him any money.

____

3 My sister was sad, but she had no problems.

____

4 May I offer you some coffee?

____

5 I went to your house last night, but there was anybody in.

____

D Check the correct alternative.

1 You can't sit down because there are ________ empty seats.

a ☐ no
b ☐ none
c ☐ some

2 Does he have ________ French books? No, he has ________.

a ☐ any, none
b ☐ any, no
c ☐ some, any

3 ________ students were playing the guitar yesterday.

a ☐ None
b ☐ Some
c ☐ Any

4 ________ of my brothers speak English. They speak French only.

a ☐ None
b ☐ Any
c ☐ No

5 I couldn't go out yesterday. My car had ________ fuel.

a ☐ any
b ☐ none
c ☐ no

6 Are there ________ doctors in the audience?

a ☐ some
b ☐ any
c ☐ none

7 Is there ________ I can do for you? No, ________.

a ☐ nothing, nothing
b ☐ anything, nothing
c ☐ anything, something

8 This taxi can take you ________ near the museum.

a ☐ some
b ☐ someone
c ☐ somewhere

9 Have you solved ________ mysterious cases?

a ☐ something
b ☐ any
c ☐ nothing

10 Are you waiting for ________? No, I'm waiting for ________.

a ☐ anyone, no one
b ☐ anybody, somebody
c ☐ nobody, anyone

E Combine the sentences. Use *who.*

Example: The man abandoned the child. He was punished.
The man who abandoned the child was punished.

1 The boy is sick. He is my brother's friend.

____

2 The old lady hit my car. She was my teacher.

____

3 Mary and Helen were talking to a man. He was the director of the company.

____

4 You met a boy at the bakery. He stole the jewels.

____

5 The girl studied with my brother. She is my friend.

____

F Complete the sentences. Use *which* and the information in the boxes.

It was later run over by a car. **It belonged to my grandfather.** **It was in the garage.** **It looks like a castle.** **Nobody knows them.**

1 I have been playing the piano _______________.

2 The kids have brought home a dog _______________.

3 He likes talking about subjects _______________.

4 I am looking for the red car _______________.

5 He is going to live in a house _______________.

G There are mistakes in some of the sentences. Underline the mistakes and write the correct form.

1 The girl which we saw was very beautiful. _______

2 That's the man whom was looking for you. _______

3 The car who Paul bought was made in Italy. _______

4 She is the dentist that talked about tooth decay. _______

5 The man who is the best soccer player in the world came here yesterday. _______

6 Millions of girls which work as unpaid domestic servants are under 18. _______

7 I read a survey about violence which was very critical of teenager attitudes. _______

8 The information who was shown in the survey was not completely true. _______

H When possible, substitute the underlined words.

Example: She is the lady that you helped some days ago.
Other possibilities: who – whom – X

1 The research that you've proposed is very important.
Other possibilities: ______________________

2 São Paulo, which is a big city, is very beautiful.
Other possibilities: ______________________

3 The doctor that was in the hospital is my father.
Other possibilities: ______________________

4 Helen, who is British, was the first to arrive.
Other possibilities: ______________________

5 The exercise which you've proposed is very difficult.
Other possibilities: ______________________

6 The girl who I met yesterday is Canadian.
Other possibilities: ______________________

7 The boy whose father is a judge was arrested yesterday.
Other possibilities: ______________________

8 He was the first person that I met when I arrived here.
Other possibilities: ______________________

I Answer the questions. Use *whose* and the information in parentheses.

Example: Who is Maria? (the girl/brother/rock singer)
Maria is the girl whose brother is a rock singer.

1 Who is Dr. Jungen? (the man/son/pilot)

____

2 Who is Giovanna? (the girl/mother/my neighbor)

____

3 Who is Kylie? (the woman/husband/a Brazilian engineer)

____

4 Who is Pietro? (the boy/father/my Italian teacher)

____

J Check the correct alternative.

1 I don't like people ________ are against the idea of saving water.

a ☐ which b ☐ that c ☐ X d ☐ whom

2 The woman ________ son is sick is very sad.

a ☐ whom b ☐ whose c ☐ where d ☐ X

3 I don't want to talk about the people and the things ________ I like.

a ☐ which b ☐ who c ☐ that d ☐ where

4 Mr. Swanson, ________ is near the door, is a physicist.

a ☐ that b ☐ who c ☐ X d ☐ whom

5 The man to ________ many students are talking was my teacher.

a ☐ who b ☐ that c ☐ whom d ☐ which

6 The book ________ she gave you is mine.

a ☐ which b ☐ X c ☐ whose d ☐ who

7 Gary's letters, ________ I have kept, contain lovely poems.

a ☐ who b ☐ whose c ☐ which d ☐ that

8 The player ________ won the competition is my brother Peter.

a ☐ who b ☐ X c ☐ which d ☐ when

9 Peter, ________ is my brother, won the competition.

a ☐ who b ☐ that c ☐ X d ☐ whose

10 The dress ________ you bought is very expensive.

a ☐ where b ☐ which c ☐ whose d ☐ who

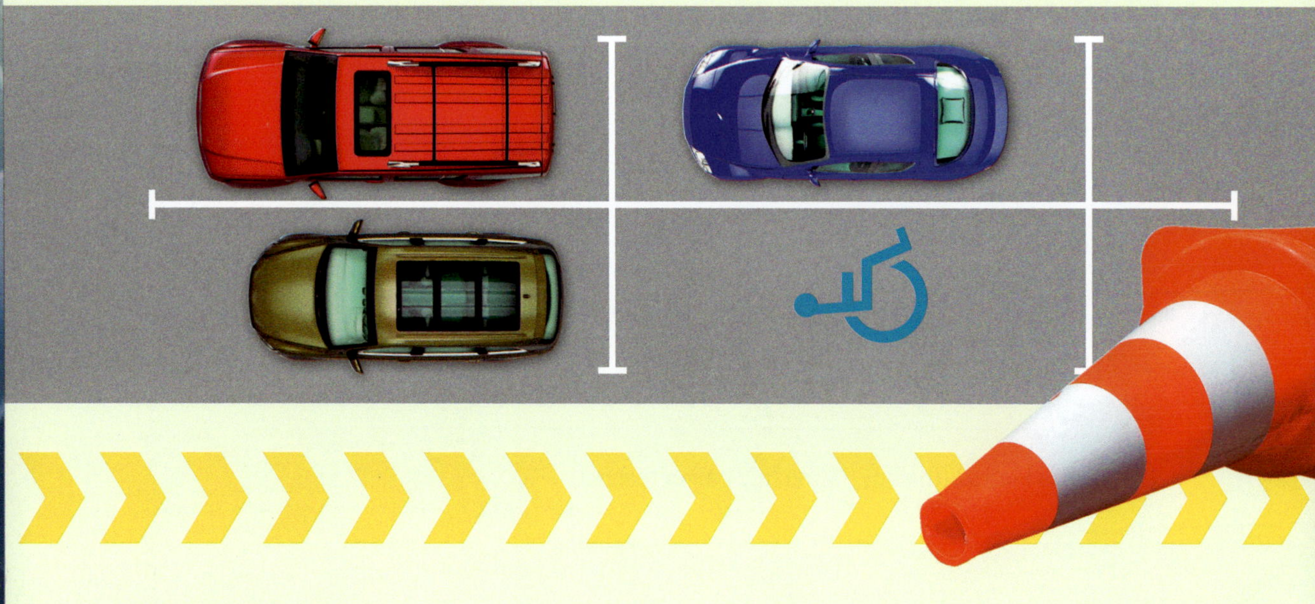

Car Park Attendant

Also known as: Parking Attendant

Introduction

Car park attendants organize the parking of cars in car parks. They may also collect parking fees, direct drivers to free spaces, and be responsible for the security of the cars.

Work Activities

Car park attendants' work largely depends on the type of car park they work in. Some work in only one car park and others drive to different ones during the day.

Some attendants supervise outdoor car parks, working from a small hut at the entrance. When customers arrive, they pay the attendant who then gives them a ticket. An attendant also often directs drivers to free spaces in the car park.

[...]

In some car parks, including multi-storey and some supermarket car parks, attendants work from a small booth at the exit and take payments from drivers as they leave. They find out how much to charge by taking the driver's entrance ticket and putting it into a machine; this reads the ticket and shows the price to charge.

In some car parks there are reserved places for regular users. Attendants may deal with bookings for these and set out cones. There may also be a security role for attendants in some car parks – patrolling the car park and using closed-circuit televisions (CCTV). Attendants may also have to check that the car parks are kept clean and tidy.

A lot of the work is outside in all weather conditions.

Personal Qualities and Skills

[...]

You may need number skills to work out the length of time that customers have spent in the car park, how much they owe and how much change to give them when they pay.

As a car park attendant you should be reliable and trustworthy. You should have a responsible attitude towards security and safety. You should be self-reliant and able to work on your own. You also need to be polite and friendly when dealing with the public.

Pay and Opportunities

Pay rates for car park attendants vary among employers.

The pay rates given below are approximate.

Parking attendants earn in the range of £14,500 to £16,000 per year [...].

Some car park attendants work a 39-hour week, others work more, and some work part-time. [...]

Extracted from <www.careers-scotland.org.uk>. Accessed on November 30, 2010.

17 The Father and His Daughter

Language in Context

James Thurber, who was an American, was born in Columbus, Ohio. He was blinded in the left eye during a game at the age of 8. After that, he could no longer participate in games with other children. As an adult he became a writer, cartoonist, humorist, and satirist.

He was born in 1894 and died in 1961.

Learn one of his famous sentences:

"I hate women because they always know where things are."

Vocabulary

be blinded: ficar cego
no longer: nunca mais

A Complete the information. Read the text and check your answers.

34

1 Place of birth: ____________ 2 Age at which he was blinded: ________

B Give your opinion.

1 When you listen to Thurber's sentence, do you think that he really hated women or that he was being humorous?

C Think about it. Compare the sentences and answer the questions.

The boy who is wearing a yellow T-shirt is our *capoeira* instructor.
James Thurber, who was American, was born in Columbus, Ohio.

1 What is a visible difference between the two sentences?

2 Separate the subordinate clauses.

3 Which of the subordinate clauses is not essential to the meaning of the sentence?

Language Practice

Relative Pronouns (III)

Uso

Orações entre vírgulas (oração subordinada adjetiva explicativa) – Quando a oração subordinada adjetiva não é essencial para o significado da oração principal, ela vem entre vírgulas; o pronome relativo não pode ser omitido e não se usa **that** para introduzi-la.

James Thurber, **[who was an American writer]**, was blinded in the left eye.

Mount Tambora, **[which is in Indonesia]**, erupted in 1815.

A Complete the sentences with the appropriate relative pronoun.

1 George Orwell, ____________ wrote *Animal Farm*, was an English writer.
2 I love studying Math, ____________ is the most difficult subject.
3 Martin, ____________ is German, is my friend.
4 Laura's dog, ____________ was very docile, died last week.
5 I keep my French books, ____________ are very old, in the attic.
6 My father, ____________ is very tall, is a firefighter.
7 The *Titanic*, ____________ was a very big ship, collided with an iceberg.
8 *Romeo and Juliet*, ____________ is my favorite play, was written by Shakespeare.

Go to page 250 for Extra Practice.

B Choose the correct alternative.

1 The old woman, ______ was sick, looked very pale.

a ☐ which b ☐ X c ☐ who

2 They were sitting in the room, ______ was overcrowded.

a ☐ which b ☐ who c ☐ X

3 He called to a nurse, ______ lived nearby.

a ☐ who b ☐ which c ☐ X

Relative Pronouns (IV)

Uso

Casos especiais

That – É o único pronome relativo usado:

› após **the first, the last** e superlativos;

You are the first person **[that has said this to me].**

She is the smartest girl **[(that) I know].**

› após **all, every, some, any, no** e seus compostos;

All **[that glitters]** is not gold.

Nothing **[(that) you say]** will convince her.

› quando há antecedentes diferentes.

Tell me about the people and the places **[(that) you know].**

Nota

› **That** pode ser omitido quando exerce a função de objeto.

Preposições – Quando uma preposição antecede o pronome relativo:

› usa-se apenas **whom** ou **which** (pessoa ou não pessoa, respectivamente);

› não se pode omitir o pronome.

The man **[about whom we were talking]** is near the door.

The dog **[to which you gave the food]** is better now.

C Match the columns to make complete sentences.

1 This is the first time
2 I told him everything
3 John Lennon, who was a rock singer,
4 *Les Misérables*, which is a famous play,
5 She will talk about the places and food

a ☐ was shown in São Paulo.
b ☐ died in New York City.
c ☐ (that) I have seen you crying.
d ☐ (that) she likes.
e ☐ (that) I dislike about him.

D Underline all the correct alternatives.

1 You can't believe anything (which – that – X) she says.
2 Alice, (that – who – X) is Canadian, is my neighbor.
3 That is the man to (whom – that – X) I gave the money.
4 The mine from (X – which – whom) they extract gold belongs to the government.
5 She was the last person (that – which – X) I saw before going to sleep.
6 Nobody (who – that – X) he loved came to his wedding.
7 This is the most expensive car (that – which – X) I've ever bought.
8 Don't touch anything (which – that – X) is in that room.

E Check the correct alternative.

1 Joseph, to ________ I gave the flowers, is my gardener.

a ☐ whom
b ☐ who
c ☐ whose
d ☐ which

2 Joseph, ________ gave me the flowers, is my gardener.

a ☐ that
b ☐ X
c ☐ who
d ☐ whom

3 *Island Escape*, ________ is a nice ship, travels along the Brazilian coast in February.

a ☐ X
b ☐ that
c ☐ which
d ☐ whose

4 My mother, ________ likes swimming, is afraid of the sea.

a ☐ whom
b ☐ that
c ☐ X
d ☐ who

5 The boy ________ was talking to you is my brother.

a ☐ X
b ☐ which
c ☐ that
d ☐ whose

READING

Before Reading

Approaching the text

Discuss the questions below in Portuguese.

1 Do you know any children between 5 and 8 years of age?

2 Do they give their things to other children freely?

3 If you got several books on your 7th birthday, would you give some of the books to a friend?

Vocabulary

Look up the words below in the glossary.

1 neighbor ____________________

2 so ____________________

3 after all ____________________

4 learn ____________________

5 library ____________________

6 look up ____________________

35

The Father and his Daughter

A little girl received so many books on her seventh birthday that her father told her to give one or two of her new books to a little neighbor named Robert.

Now, taking books, or anything else, from a little girl is like taking candy from a baby. But the father, who was very persuasive, convinced the little girl, and Robert got two of her books. "After all, that leaves you with nine," said the father, who thought he was a philosopher and a child psychologist.

A few weeks later, the father went to his library to look up a word in the *Oxford English Dictionary*. However, he couldn't find volume V-Z, and then he discovered that three other volumes were missing, too. "They should all be here," he thought. "Where are they?" He questioned all family members, and soon learned what had become of the four missing volumes.

"A man came to the door this morning," said his little daughter, "and he didn't know how to get from here to Torrington, or from Torrington to Winsted, and he was a nice man, much nicer than Robert, and so I gave him four of your books. After all, there are thirteen volumes in the *Oxford English Dictionary*, and that leaves you with nine."

Based on THURBER, James. "The Father and his Daughter." In: *Fables for Our Times*. London: Mandarin Books, 1991.

Vocabulary

anything else: qualquer outra coisa
leave: deixar
miss: faltar
question: perguntar
should: deveria(m)
soon: logo

After Reading

A Mark the meaning of the words in bold.

1 (1st paragraph) "A little girl received **so many** books [...] that her father told her to give one or two of her new books to a little neighbor [...]"

a ☐ tal
b ☐ muitos
c ☐ tantos

2 (2nd paragraph) "Now, taking books [...] from a little girl is **like** taking candy from a baby."

a ☐ gosta
b ☐ como
c ☐ partir

3 (3rd paragraph) "[...] the father went to his library to look up a word in the *Oxford English Dictionary*. **However**, he couldn't find volume V-Z [...]"

a ☐ Também
b ☐ Quase
c ☐ Porém

B What are the words in bold related to?

1 (2nd paragraph) "[...] said the father, **who** thought he was a philosopher and a child psychologist." ______

2 (3rd paragraph) "[...] he discovered that three other volumes were missing, too. '**They** should all be here,' he thought." ______

C Answer the questions according to the text.

1 Who was nicer: the little boy or the man?

______

2 How many books had the girl received?

______

3 Was the father's library inside his house?

______

4 How many volumes did the girl give the man?

______

VOCABULARY EXPANSION

A **Use the suffix *ment* to write new words.**

	Verb	Noun	Translation
1	move	________	________
2	develop	________	________
3	improve	________	________
4	arrange	________	________
5	govern	________	________
6	invest	________	________

Suffix ment

Acrescentado a alguns verbos, forma substantivos que se referem a ações, processos ou estados.

*agree – agree**ment***

B **Choose the appropriate words to complete the sentences.**

False Cognates

actually: de fato, realmente
nowadays: atualmente
library: biblioteca
bookstore: livraria
data: dados, informações
date: data; encontro
sort: classificar; separar
luck: sorte

1 Our teacher has to ________ all his students' papers next week.

2 Mark not only went to her party, but he ________ organized it.

3 Phil and June have a ________ on Sunday.

4 The policemen need some more ________ to complete the investigation.

5 ________ kids spend too much time playing electronic games.

6 Noah is studying at the ________ now.

C **Com o auxílio do quadro, escreva definições para as palavras abaixo.**

1 arrangement 2, 11 ____________________

2 nowadays 8, 13 ____________________

3 blind 3, 9, 15 ____________________

4 sort 1, 12 ____________________

5 psychologist 4, 6, 14 ____________________

6 actually 5, 7, 10 ____________________

1 arrange	2 put	3 without
4 the person	5 in reality	6 who studies
7 in fact	8 at the present	9 the ability
10 really	11 in order	12 in groups
13 time	14 the mind	15 to see

LANGUAGE IN USE

A Read the ads below and match the columns to make questions. Then answer the questions you have made.

Work with a classmate to make a review of the first ad. Although it is an authentic ad found in the internet, the language is not very good. What mistakes can you find?

A	B	C
Which	sells	flowers
Where	can you buy	cakes
What		instruments
		on the internet

B NOW IT'S YOUR TURN!

Ask other questions about the ads to a classmate. Use the glossary for help.

WRITING

Work with a classmate. Make an ad for the internet.

18 Paralympic Games

Language in Context

A **Complete the information. Read the dialogue and chek your answers.** 36

1 What they are talking about

____

2 Number of athletes in 1960

____

Jarred: Are the Paralympic Games something new? I've heard about them just recently.

Ricky: Not really. Olympic Games for athletes with disabilities were officially organized for the first time in Rome, in 1960.

Jarred: You mean, there were no games before 1960?

Ricky: Well, unofficially, the games started in 1948. But they were only for some types of athletes.

Jarred: Were there many competitors in 1960?

Ricky: Yes. 400 athletes.

Jarred: Have the games grown since then?

Ricky: A lot! By 2016 more than 40,000 athletes will have competed in the games.

B **Give your opinion.**

1 Did you know that the Paralympic Games existed?

2 What is the level of Brazilian participation in the Paralympic Games?

Vocabulary

disability: deficiência
known: conhecido

C **Think about it. Compare the sentences and answer the questions.**

a Before 1960, disabled athletes **had competed** unofficially.

b In 1960, four hundred athletes **competed** in the Paralympic Games.

c In 2016, many athletes **will compete** in the Paralympic Games.

d By 2016, forty thousand athletes **will have competed** in the Paralympic Games.

1 What period of time does each sentence express: past, present, or future?

2 What are the differences in form and meaning between sentences **c** and **d**?

3 Which happened first: the action in sentence **a** or **b**?

Language Practice

Future Perfect

Will have + verbo no **Past Participle**

Afirmativa: He **will have left** when you arrive there.
Interrogativa: Will he **have left** when you arrive there?
Negativa: He **will not have left** when you arrive there.
Forma abreviada: won't (will not)

Uso

O *Future Perfect* indica que uma ação terá ocorrido (ou não) antes de determinado momento no futuro.

By 5 o'clock, I **will have arrived** home.
Até as 5 horas, (já) terei chegado em casa.

By January, she **will have bought** her house.
Até janeiro, ela (já) terá comprado a casa dela.

They **won't have fixed** the TV by 7 o'clock.
Eles (ainda) não terão consertado a TV até as 7 horas.

A Write the Future Perfect of the verbs in parentheses.

1 By the time you come back, they ______________ (see) the movie.

2 I ______________ (tell) her the good news by the time you meet her.

3 ______________ you ______________ (finish) the job by April?

4 He ______________ (arrive – neg.) by 4:00.

5 By tomorrow, at this time, she ______________ (meet) Charles.

6 Sheila ______________ (read) the book by the time you get home.

7 ______________ the children ______________ (have) lunch by the time Grandma arrives?

8 By December, I ______________ (buy) a new apartment.

B Combine the sentences. Follow the example.

Example: We will talk to him at 2 o'clock. You will arrive at 3 o'clock.
By the time you arrive, we will have talked to him.

1 She will make a cake at 3 o'clock. You will arrive at 4 o'clock.

____

2 He will talk to her in the morning. We will arrive in the afternoon.

____

3 The show will start at 8 o'clock. You will arrive at 8:15.

____

Go to page 252 for Extra Practice.

Verb Tense Review

Verb Tense	Example
Present Continuous	He **is swimming** now.
Past Continuous	He **was swimming** 5 minutes ago.
Future with Going to	He **is going to swim** next week.
Future Continuous	He **will be swimming** at 5 o'clock.
Simple Present	He **swims** every morning.
Simple Past	He **swam** yesterday.
Simple Future	He **will swim** tomorrow.
Imperative	Don't **swim** now!
Present Perfect	He **has swum** for 2 hours.
Present Perfect Continuous	He **has been swimming** since 2 o'clock.
Past Perfect	He **had already swum** when I talked to him.
Past Perfect Continuous	He **had been swimming** before we arrived.
Future Perfect	He **will have swum** by 6 o'clock.

C Underline the appropriate alternative.

Right now, I (was read – am reading) the newspaper and my wife (is making – makes) dinner. We do the same thing every day. I (read – is reading) while she (makes – made) dinner. Tomorrow, we will (doing – do) the same thing: she (will cook – cook) and I (am reading – will read) the newspaper.

D Write the verbs in parentheses in the correct verb tense.

1 They ______________________ (to get) married three months ago.

2 I ______________________ (to hurt) myself in the accident last week.

3 She ______________________ (to teach) English for ten years.

4 Karl ______________________ (to live) in Italy since last year.

5 Ted always ______________________ (to run) around the block in the morning.

6 He usually ______________________ (to take) the children to school.

7 The kids ______________________ (to play) in the garden now.

8 I ______________________ (to meet) my friends at 5 o'clock tomorrow.

9 Mom ______________________ (to make) lunch when I arrived yesterday.

10 She ______________________ (to finish) the exercise by the time I get home.

E Match the columns to make complete sentences.

1	They are going to the movies	a	[ ]	It is raining.
2	She told me the story	b	[ ]	since 5 o'clock.
3	They have gone to the museum	c	[ ]	They are good for your health.
4	She will be riding a horse	d	[ ]	when I arrived.
5	They will have finished the project	e	[ ]	You are going to fall.
6	He is studying	f	[ ]	many times.
7	He had been working	g	[ ]	every morning.
8	We have watched TV	h	[ ]	before I woke up.
9	Be careful!	i	[ ]	last night.
10	He was cooking dinner	j	[ ]	by 6 o'clock.
11	They usually	k	[ ]	for two hours.
12	Alice had left	l	[ ]	after school.
13	Eat your vegetables!	m	[ ]	in the evening.
14	Don't go out now!	n	[ ]	work in the afternoon.
15	I go to school	o	[ ]	today.

Go to page 253 for Extra Practice.

READING

Before Reading

Approaching the text

Discuss the questions below in Portuguese.

1 What are the Olympic Games?

2 What are the Paralympic Games?

3 What is the importance of the Paralympic Games?

Vocabulary

A Match the synonyms.

1	goal	a	☐	objective
2	to take place	b	☐	place
3	venue	c	☐	to happen

B Look up these words in the glossary.

1 competitor ______________________

2 injury ______________________

3 emphasize ______________________

4 join ______________________

PARALYMPIC GAMES

A Paralympic competitors

Paralympic competitors are athletes with disabilities. Much like Olympians, Paralympians compete for gold, silver, and bronze medals against the best disabled athletes in the world.

The Paralympics have always taken place in the same country, and in the same year as the Olympic Games – every four years. Since the Seoul Games (1988), they have taken place shortly after the Olympics, using the same sporting venues and facilities.

The games have emphasized the importance of physical activity for people with disabilities and have promoted equality, inclusion, and accessibility.

The first sports competition for disabled people happened in 1948, in England. A neurosurgeon organized games involving World War II veterans with spinal cord injuries. Throughout the years more and more competitors from other countries joined the games, which only became official in 1960.

In 1960, in Rome, 400 athletes from 23 countries participated in the games. In Atlanta, in 1996, they numbered 3,195 from 103 countries. By 2016, about 40,000 competitors will have participated in the games. These athletes will have shown the world the power of their determination.

B Paralympic philosophy

Athletes with disabilities should have opportunities to pursue their goals in sport equivalent to those of non-disabled athletes.

C Curiosities

The Paralympics are the second largest sporting event in the world. The Paralympic summer sports include archery, athletics, basketball, boccia, cycling, equestrian events, football, judo, sailing, shooting and swimming, among others. The Paralympic winter sports are alpine skiing, ice sledge hockey, Nordic skiing, and wheelchair curling.

Based on <www.atlanta.olympic.org>; <www.paralympic.org>. Accessed on November 20, 2010.

Vocabulary

become: tornar-se
disabled: pessoa com deficiência
facilities: instalações
pursue: perseguir

After Reading

A **Text organization.**
Look at the text on page 245 and mark the correct information below.

1 Number of paragraphs:

☐ 3 ☐ 4
☐ 5 ☐ 7

2 Inclusion of pictures or boxes:

☐ Yes ☐ No

3 Inclusion of legends:

☐ Yes ☐ No

B **What do the words in bold refer to?**

1 (4th paragraph) "[...] more and more competitors from other countries joined the games, **which** only became official in 1960." ______________________

2 (5th paragraph) "In Atlanta, in 1996, **they** numbered 3,195 from 103 countries."

____

C **Choose the best alternative to complete each sentence.**

1 The Paralympic Games have taken place ________ the Olympics.

a ☐ shortly after b ☐ shortly before c ☐ likewise

2 Paralympian athletes compete for medals ________ Olympians.

a ☐ inclusion b ☐ much like c ☐ months later

3 The best ________ athletes in the world compete in the Paralympic Games.

a ☐ disabilities b ☐ disabled c ☐ disabling

4 The expression used for *lesão na coluna espinhal* is:

a ☐ injury cord spinal b ☐ cord injury c ☐ spinal cord injury

5 The Olympic and Paralympic Games have used the same sporting ________ since the Seoul Games.

a ☐ venues b ☐ modalities c ☐ medals

6 The Paralympic Games became official in ________.

a ☐ 1988 b ☐ 1960 c ☐ 1948

D Answer the questions.

1 When and where did the first sports competition for people with disabilities happen?

____

2 What have the Games promoted?

____

3 What have the games emphasized?

____

E Read item *b* "Paralympic Philosophy" and discuss the implications of this sentence with your friends. Do it in Portuguese.

VOCABULARY EXPANSION

A Complete the sentences. Add the prefix *dis* to the words in parentheses.

Prefix dis

Descreve um processo, uma qualidade ou um estado negativo.
*to **dis**connect (verb), **dis**honest (adj.), **dis**ability (noun)*

1 Leona looked at the stranger with _______________ (trust) and fear.

2 Grandpa's speech was full of words in _______________ nowadays (use).

3 I _______________ (like) meat but, unfortunately, it is all we have to eat.

4 Money _______________ (appear) from my pockets easily!

5 You must not _______________ (obey) your parents.

B Choose the correct meaning of the words in bold.

1 OFFICIAL a oficial b funcionário público

1.1 [ ] An **official** will come and explain the rules to us.

1.2 [ ] Members of the Parliament are on an **official** visit to India.

2 SUBJECT a assunto b matéria, disciplina escolar

2.1 [ ] Math is her favorite school **subject**.

2.2 [ ] What is the **subject** of our meeting today?

C **Read the boxes and complete the sentences with the words given. Use a dictionary for help.**

therefore **because** **unless** **while** **afterwards** **although**

1 She asked me to take care of the children ______________ she was out.

2 ______________ the singer was expected to be here, he never showed up.

3 Emma has put on some weight. ______________ she can't eat cakes or pies anymore.

4 Those students will fail ______________ they study hard.

5 ______________ I knew them, I did what I could for them.

6 Ernie made himself a hot chocolate and ______________ went to bed.

Connectives

São palavras usadas para ligar as ideias expressas em duas frases.

*I like her, **but** she doesn't like me.*

Language in Use

A **Read the letter published in the newspaper *The Gazette Newspaper of Montreal*. Match the columns to make questions. Then answer the questions you have made.**

The Gazette

Montreal, October 28, 1996.

Farewell Letter to a Friend

Judy Sklar Rasminsky

Dear Joanne,

I just heard that you sold your house. It's a beautiful house, and I knew you'd sell it eventually, but this is much too fast for me.

It's barely been three months since you told us Stan had a new job and you were leaving Montreal, and in that short time you've organized the house to sell, found a school for Jeremy, taken Jessica to university, packed, and rented a house in Connecticut.

Of course, it's been much too hectic for you to spend any time with me. I feel lucky that we had that one lunch together when you explained why you were going.

The news didn't come as a great surprise. Of all of our friends, you and Stan were the ones with the most opportunities to leave.

[...]

I wish you luck in your new life. May you have friends who love you as I do. I will miss you terribly. And I will miss the Montreal we knew together. ■

Judy

Extracted from <www.challengingbehavior.com>. Accessed on November 30, 2010.

A	B	C
Who	did	Joanne sell
Why	is	Joanne
What	are	Joanne and Stan leaving Montreal

B **NOW IT'S YOUR TURN!**

Ask more questions about the letter to a classmate. Use the glossary for help.

WRITING

Write Joanne's reply to Judy's letter. Include more information about Joanne and Stan's departure from Montreal.

Extra Practice 9

A Underline the correct alternatives. Sometimes more than one alternative is correct in each item.

1 David fixed the table (who, that) was broken.

2 The horses (which, who, that, X) were in the stable belonged to the farmer.

3 She bought a violin (whom, X, which, who) cost 1,500 dollars.

4 That's the lady to (whom, which, that, who, X) we gave the keys.

5 Children (that, who, X, whom) don't brush their teeth may have many cavities.

6 The book (that, X, who, which, whom) he's reading belongs to me.

B Choose the correct alternative.

1 He has a house, ________ was built in 1940.

a ☐ that b ☐ whose c ☐ who d ☐ whom

2 Dr. Braun, ________ works in the laboratory, has received a Nobel Prize.

a ☐ whose b ☐ X c ☐ whom d ☐ who

3 Technology, ________ brings us comfort, is the result of scientific investigation.

a ☐ that b ☐ who c ☐ which d ☐ X

4 The woman ________ baby is sleeping is an excellent mother.

a ☐ that b ☐ whose c ☐ who d ☐ whom

5 The salesman, ________ showed us the products, is sick.

a ☐ whose b ☐ X c ☐ who d ☐ which

6 Helen, ________ husband is in England, is taking an English course now.

a ☐ who b ☐ which c ☐ that d ☐ whose

C Match the words with the adequate definitions.

1 handicapped	a	☐	object of efforts or ambition
2 ignore	b	☐	for that reason
3 goal	c	☐	place fixed for a contest or match
4 shortly after	d	☐	someone who has a physical or mental disability
5 sporting venue	e	☐	disregard, take no notice of
6 therefore	f	☐	soon after, in a short time after

D Complete the sentences with the correct relative pronoun.

1 William Shakespeare, ________________ was an English playwright, wrote *Romeo and Juliet*.

2 The Theory of Relativity, ________________ changed the course of modern science, was thought up by Albert Einstein.

3 Venice, ________________ is called the city of lovers, is in Italy.

4 Julia, about ________________ we're talking, has written two books.

5 My father, ________________ was born in Spain, doesn't speak a word of Spanish.

6 We often visit our uncle in Dublin, ________________ is in Ireland.

7 Jeff is studying a gas ________________ damages the ozone layer.

8 Their leader is the one ________________ marches in front of the group.

9 Gypsies are a nomadic people ________________ came from the Indian subcontinent.

10 The singer ________________ we listened to is Australian.

E Choose the alternative that best completes each sentence below.

a who / whom / that / X

b who / that

c which / that

d which / that / X

e whom

1 I called the director, [ ] was very understanding.

2 The girl [ ] we know will help us.

3 There is the housewife [ ] we asked a question to.

4 Where is the car [ ] you liked?

5 This is the medical exam [ ] her doctor needed.

6 She is the dentist with [ ] we talked about tooth decay.

7 The girl to [ ] we are writing lives in Germany.

8 The motorcycle [ ] Joan received was made in Japan.

9 It's a poem [ ] my grandmother taught me.

10 My sister is studying in the room [ ] is near the bathroom.

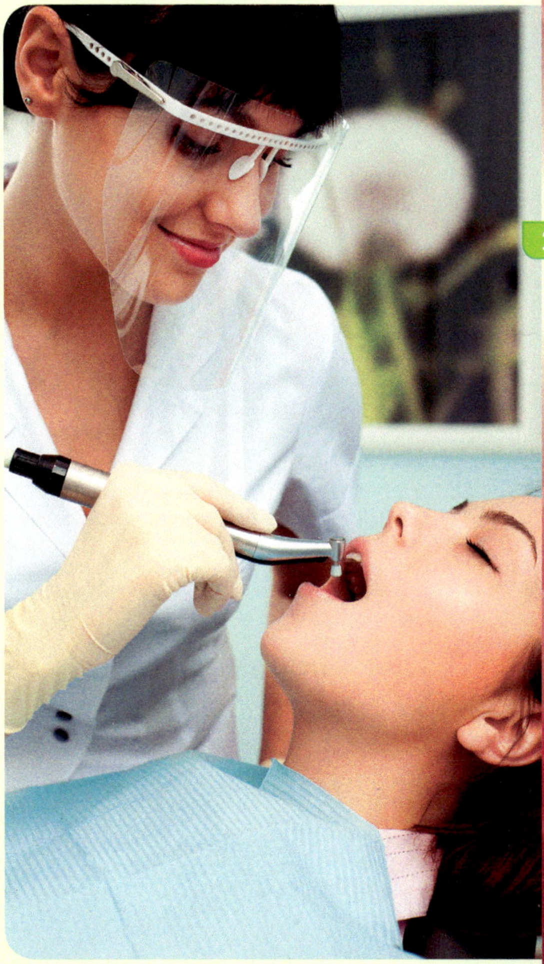

F Connect the sentences using *which*. Follow the example.

Example: I like the violin. It is broken.

The violin, which I like, is broken.

1 The dentist bought a new chair. It is very expensive.

____

2 He gave me red roses. They were beautiful.

____

3 The car is in front of the house. It is mine.

____

G Put the sentences into the form indicated in parentheses.

1 I will have finished the test by 4 o'clock. (neg.)

____

2 He will have sold his car by the end of this week. (int.)

____

3 She will have taken the kids to the park by 10. (neg.)

____

4 They will have gone to Miami by March. (int.)

____

5 She will have finished dinner by the time you arrive. (neg.)

____

6 It will have stopped snowing by February. (int.)

____

7 My father will have cooked lunch by 1 o'clock. (neg.)

____

H Write the Future Perfect of the verbs in parentheses.

1 We ______________ (to meet) the new teacher by the end of this week.

2 By 2 o'clock tomorrow she ______________ (to read) my letter.

3 By the time he comes back, I ______________ (to finish) my homework.

4 I ______________ (to have) lunch by the time he arrives.

5 They ______________ (to talk) by the time I get there.

I Sublinhe os erros de alguns dos tempos verbais e corrija-os.

1 Will you have finished everything by the time I come back from school?

___

2 By this time next year, I have graduated.

___

3 By the time I am 60, I'll have visited most countries in the world.

___

4 We are late. By the time we get to the party, everyone will leave.

___

5 By the time we come back to Brazil, Sally will have have her baby.

___

6 Janet must be angry. By the time we meet her, she waits for us for one hour.

___

J Choose the best alternative to complete each sentence.

a will go
b don't like
c rains
d waiting for
e just left
f were studying
g makes
h is taking
i want
j am writing

1 Sue [ ] the most delicious cakes in the world.
2 Tomorrow after work, I [ ] to the beach.
3 While you [ ] at home, your friends were in class.
4 Do you [ ] to come over for dinner tonight?
5 I [ ] a book about my adventures in Africa.
6 I [ ] to live in London because it [ ] a lot there.
7 A: Are you [ ] Mr. Britt?
B: Yes, I am.
A: Sorry to tell you, but he has [ ].
8 Look, that man [ ] your magazine away!

K Choose the best alternative to complete the sentences.

1 What ________ you ________ when the accident happened?

a ☐ will – do
b ☐ will – have done
c ☐ is – doing
d ☐ were – doing

2 It ________ hard yesterday. We can ________ skiing tomorrow.

a ☐ snowed – to go
b ☐ snows – goes
c ☐ snowed – go
d ☐ was snowing – went

3 They ________ in China three weeks ago.

a ☐ arrive
b ☐ arrived
c ☐ will arrive
d ☐ will have arrived

4 My brother ________ in India for more than a year.

a ☐ has lived
b ☐ was live
c ☐ had lived
d ☐ can to live

5 She ________ her job because she ________ always ________.

a ☐ loses – did – complain
b ☐ losed – is – complain
c ☐ lost – was – complaining
d ☐ is lose – can – complain

6 Silence, please! Mom ________.

a ☐ had slept
b ☐ is sleeping
c ☐ sleeps
d ☐ will slept

7 I have ________ to the Modern Art Museum many times.

a ☐ be
b ☐ went
c ☐ was
d ☐ been

8 I had ________ pictures of the Iguaçu Falls before I went to Foz do Iguaçu. They are much more beautiful than in the pictures.

a ☐ seen
b ☐ saw
c ☐ sawed
d ☐ seeing

9 When you called yesterday I ________ my favorite TV program.

a ☐ was watching
b ☐ watched
c ☐ am going to watch
d ☐ watch

10 When I arrive in São Paulo next week I ________ in a hotel.

a ☐ stay
b ☐ to stay
c ☐ have stayed
d ☐ will stay

PHYSICAL EDUCATION

The students that went to physical education school in the past had little choice: they could work as physical education teachers — and few of them found employment in sports clubs.

Things are quite different today. Physical education is recognized as an ally of healthcare and of esthetics. Thus, the area of physical fitness offers employment positions for many professionals. The best opportunities are in fitness centers and spas, but the physical educator can also work independently as a personal trainer.

Another area with plenty of jobs is that of groups with special needs. Employers in this area are entities and NGOs that care for children with special needs and take care for the elderly. São Paulo and Rio de Janeiro are the two best markets for these specializations.

In Southern Brazil, tourism promotes the specialization in recreation and leisure activities. Professionals that also have knowledge and experience in hiking, horseback riding, canoeing, and other sports can find excellent jobs.

Based on
GUIA DO ESTUDANTE. São Paulo: Abril, 2008.
<www.guiadasprofissoes.com.br>;
<www.vestibular.brasilescola.com>;
<http://guiadoestudante.abril.com.br>;
<www.portaldeensino.com.br>.
Accessed on November 26, 2010.

Vocabulary

ally: aliado(a)
elderly: idosos
employment: emprego
fitness center: academia de ginástica
healthcare: cuidados com a saúde
hiking: caminhada
leisure: lazer
NGO: Non-Governmental Organization (Organização Não Governamental)
physical fitness: condicionamento físico
plenty of: muitos(as)
(take) care: cuidar

19 Medical Advertising in the Future

Language in Context

A Listen to the text. Complete the information and number the pictures.

38

The text is about ______________________________.

a 

b 

c 

d 

e 

f 

g 

h 

i 

B Give your opinion.

1 Do commercials really have an influence on our lives?

2 Do you know anyone who is influenced by commercials? What types of commercials are they?

3 Have you ever bought anything because of a commercial? What?

C Think about it.
Compare the sentences and answer the questions.

a If I study more, I'll pass the test.

b If I studied more, I would pass the test.

1 Which of the actions will most probably happen? The action in sentence **a** or in sentence **b**?

2 What verbal tenses were used in sentence **a**?

3 What verbal tenses were used in sentence **b**?

Language Practice

Sentences with *Would*

Would + verbo / Would have + Past Participle

Would é um verbo modal e, sozinho, não tem tradução. Assim como os outros *modal verbs*, ele aparece sempre ligado a outro verbo.
Afirmativa: I **would go** to the party. (Eu iria à festa.)
I **would have gone** to the party. (Eu teria ido à festa.)
Interrogativa: Would you **go** to the party? **Would** you **have gone** to the party?
Negativa: I **would not go** to the party. I **would not have gone** to the party.
Forma abreviada: wouldn't (would not)

A Rewrite the sentences. Use the following structures:

to meet – met – met
to run – ran – run
to sell – sold – sold
to teach – taught – taught

a ***would*** **+ verb**

b ***would have*** **+ Past Participle**

1 I will visit her.

a ______________________________

b ______________________________

2 They will not sell the house.

a ______________________________

b ______________________________

3 Will she run to the park?

a ______________________________

b ______________________________

4 He will not meet us.

a ______________________________

b ______________________________

5 Will they invite us?

a ______________________________

b ______________________________

Conditional Sentences (I)

A oração condicional (*if clause*) expressa uma condição e vem sempre ligada a uma oração principal (*main clause*).

If she comes, I will talk to her.
[*If clause*]

I will talk to her **if she comes.**
[*If clause*]

As estruturas condicionais podem expressar:

Condição provável: If he has money, he will buy a car.

Condição improvável: If he had money, he would buy a car.

Condição impossível: If he had had money, he would have bought a car.

B Write the correct verb form to indicate a probable condition.

1 If we protest, they ______________________ (to cut down – neg.) the trees.

2 If you pay attention, you ______________________ (to learn) the lesson.

3 If she has money, she ______________________ (to go) to the movies.

4 We ______________________ (to save) time if we take a taxi.

5 He ______________________ (to find) his book if he looks for it in his bedroom.

C Write the correct verb form to indicate an improbable condition.

1 If you asked her, she ______________________ (to tell) the story.

2 If he studied, he ______________________ (to pass) the test.

3 I ______________________ (to teach) you if I had time.

4 They ______________________ (to play) in the park if it didn't rain.

5 We ______________________ (to help) her if she asked us.

D Write the correct verb form to indicate an impossible condition.

1 If he had accepted the idea, he ______________________ (to approve) the project.

2 I ______________________ (to go) to the market if it hadn't rained.

3 She ______________________ (to come) to the party if you had invited her.

4 If I had known about your birthday, I ______________________ (to buy) you a present.

5 If you had arrived earlier, you ______________________ (to get) a good seat.

E Choose the correct verb form.

1 They ________ a new car if they win the lottery.

a ☐ will buy

b ☐ would buy

2 I ________ the house if you bought some paint.

a ☐ would have painted

b ☐ would paint

3 If they had asked, I ________ their refrigerator.

a ☐ will fix

b ☐ would have fixed

4 If we ________ late, she will look after the children.

a ☐ arrive

b ☐ arrived

5 I would make a chocolate cake if I ________ the recipe.

a ☐ have

b ☐ had

6 She would have been tired if she ________ hard.

a ☐ had worked

b ☐ worked

7 If she had studied harder, she ________ her college test.

a ☐ would have passed

b ☐ will pass

8 The gate ________ if you press the button.

a ☐ would unlock

b ☐ will unlock

F Escreva os números das frases do exercício E que correspondem a cada uma das condições estudadas.

Provável	Improvável	Impossível

Go to page 276 for Extra Practice.

READING

Before Reading

Approaching the text

Discuss the questions below in Portuguese.

1 Do you remember any medical drug advertisement?

2 Have you ever taken any medicine because you saw it on TV or on the internet?

3 Should people take medical drugs without a doctor's prescription?

Vocabulary

Read the synonyms below.

Vocabulary

tool: instrument, piece of equipment
trend: tendency

Medical Advertising in the Future

39

For many years, prescription drug makers promoted their products exclusively to healthcare professionals. But, about 15 years ago, some manufacturers began to produce ads targeted to consumers.

In 1996, a study by industry drug consultant Scott-Levin showed that some medicines are announced as products that the person can buy and take without any professional guidance. Three-quarters of the doctors surveyed said that their patients talked about drugs they had seen on TV or on the internet.

If this trend continues, maybe in the future you will see the ad below in a magazine.

Based on <www.wesoomi.com>. Accessed on December 8, 2010.

Vocabulary

advertising: anúncio, propaganda
guidance: orientação
manufacturer: fabricante
set: engessar
survey: estudo, pesquisa

After Reading

A Observe as páginas 260 e 261 e responda.

1 Qual é o assunto do texto?

____

2 Sobre o que é o anúncio?

____

B Localize as expressões abaixo no texto e no anúncio.

1 [...] consultores médicos estão a apenas um telefonema de distância.

____

2 Compre nosso *kit* Engesse uma Fratura.

____

3 [...] deduziremos $10.00 do preço total.

____

4 [...] fabricantes de remédios vendidos com receita médica [...]

____

C Read the sentences and choose the best alternative.

1 "[...] some medicines are announced as products that the person can buy and take without any professional guidance."

Some ads suggest that:

a ☐ the person should have professional guidance to take medicines.

b ☐ everyone can buy products without professional guidance.

c ☐ professional guidance will be necessary if the medicines are announced.

2 "Our 24/7 medical consultants are only a phone call away."

The numbers 24/7 refer to:

a ☐ the number of medical consultants.

b ☐ the number of hours in a day and of days in a week.

c ☐ the number of phone calls received every day.

D **Answer the questions according to the texts.**

1 Who should prescribe medicines?

____

2 What is the fracture kit used for?

____

3 What would be a good Christmas present?

____

Vocabulary Expansion

A **O verbo *to stop* pode assumir diferentes significados.**
Leia o quadro e depois sublinhe as alternativas apropriadas.

To stop
Sheila ***stopped drinking*** *coffee.* (parou de tomar)
Sheila ***stopped to drink*** *coffee.* (parou para tomar)

1 Kids, stop (to talk – talking) and do your homework!

2 Johnny was thirsty, so he stopped (drinking – to drink) some water.

3 Fiona stopped (to read – reading) when her mother entered the room.

4 Kirk fell from that tree and I stopped (to help – helping) him.

5 It was cold and he stopped (making – to make) some hot tea.

6 Many people are now trying to stop (smoking – to smoke).

7 Those employees stop (working – to work) at 5:30 p.m.

8 She stopped everything she was doing (to buy – buying) him a present.

B **Find the meaning of *for* in the sentences below. Use the box for help.**

1 [ ] My friend is saving money for a new project.

2 [ ] I'm doing this for her safety.

3 [ ] The swimmers turned and headed for the shore.

4 [ ] The teacher said that we should read for pleasure.

5 [ ] Kids must be prepared for life.

For
a) objetivo: para
b) destino: para
c) intenção: por, pelo

C Match the words in English to their meanings in Portuguese.

1	guidance	a ☐	ferramenta
2	surveyed	b ☐	direcionado(a)
3	fooled	c ☐	sem
4	targeted	d ☐	equipamento; estojo
5	kit	e ☐	estudado(a), pesquisado(a)
6	tool	f ☐	receita médica
7	without	g ☐	orientação; direção
8	prescription	h ☐	enganado(a)

D Read the examples, write similar sentences and translate them.

Examples: (to cry) There is no need to cry.
(Não há necessidade de chorar.)

(to worry) There is no reason to worry.
(Não há razão para se preocupar.)

1 (to shout) ______________________________

____

2 (to be surprised) ______________________________

____

3 (to hurry) ______________________________

____

4 (to be nervous) ______________________________

____

LANGUAGE IN USE

A Study the map. Then match.

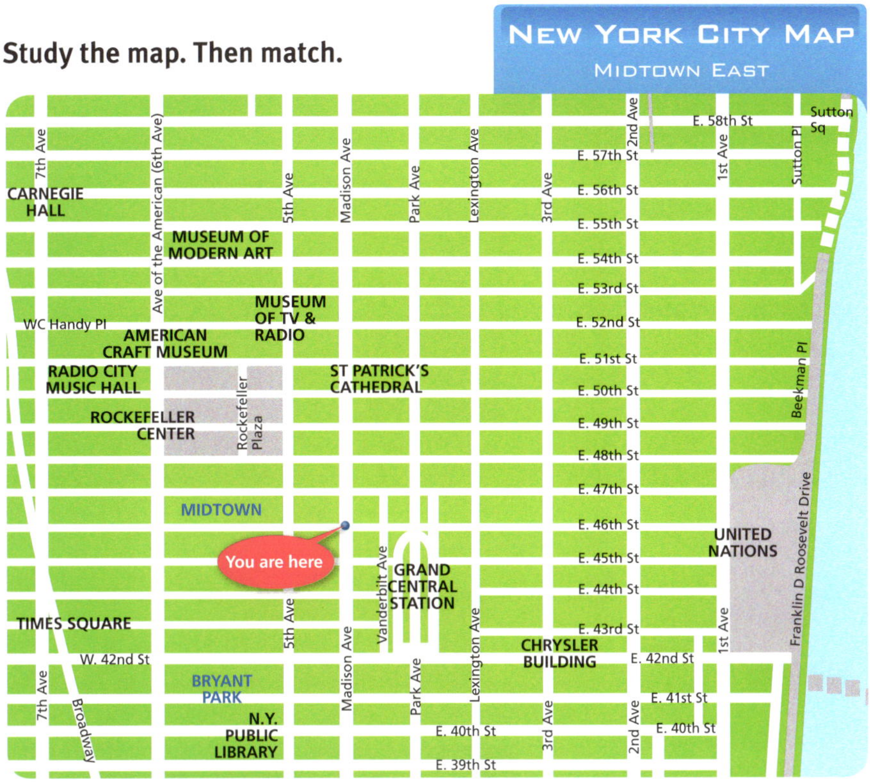

1 Where is your hotel?

2 How do you get to Times Square?

3 Is Carnegie Hall far from Times Square?

a ☐ Yes. It's thirteen blocks north.

b ☐ It's on the corner of 46th Street and Madison Avenue.

c ☐ You walk three blocks west, turn south on 7th Avenue, and walk three more blocks.

B NOW IT'S YOUR TURN!

Talk to a classmate about going places in New York. Use the sentences in exercise A as examples.

WRITING

Your hotel is on the corner of 54th Street and Park Avenue. You are going to the public library. Write a note to a friend, telling him or her to meet you there. Give directions to get to the library.

20 Global Warming

Language in Context

A **Complete the information. Read the text and check your answers.** 40

1 Type of text

____

2 Weather forecast for the following year

____

Dear Phil,

In response to your letter of last May 16, I would not plant rice if I were you. Rice will not grow well unless there is abundant rainfall. Rice planters lose money when there is little water.
Weather specialists forecast a very dry year next year. So choose something that doesn't need much water. Or else, you can plant rice provided that you irrigate your land.

Yours cordially,
Jeff Owens — Agriculture Consultant

B **Give your opinion.**

1 What's Phil's profession?

2 Does Phil plant rice now?

3 What did Phil ask of Jeff Owens?

C **Think about it. Compare the sentences and answer the questions.**

a I would not plant rice if I were you.

b Rice will not grow unless there is abundant rainfall.

c You can plant rice provided that you irrigate your land.

1 Underline the conditional clauses.

2 *If* is not used in sentences **b** and **c**. What words introduce the conditional clauses?

____

____

Vocabulary

forecast: prever
unless: a menos que
provided that: desde que

Language Practice

Conditional Sentences (II)

Uso

Podemos verificar vários tipos de ocorrência com as estruturas condicionais:

Modals – Verbos modais como **may, might, can** e **could** podem ser usados.

If you go out in the rain, you **may catch** a cold.

If we had asked her, she **could have** come.

Imperative – Usado para dar uma ordem ou instrução.

If you have problems, **call me.**

Simple Present – Usado para expressar leis naturais e verdades universais.

If you heat iron, **it melts.**

Were – Pode ser usado em lugar de **was** para a 1ª pessoa do singular.

If **I were** your mother, I would punish you.

Unless (se não, a menos que), **provided that** (desde que) – Podem ser usados em lugar de **if not** e **if**.

Unless we study, we won't pass the examination.

Provided that we study, we will pass the examination.

If – Em condições impossíveis, **if** pode ser omitido invertendo-se o sujeito com o verbo auxiliar.

If he had a car, he would ride to work.

Had he a car, he would ride to work.

A Transform the sentence. Use the tips in parentheses.

If you make an effort, you will win the game.

1 (made) ______________________________

2 (had made) ______________________________

3 (had you) ______________________________

4 (may) ______________________________

B Choose the best alternative.

1 Don't ________ me to help you if you get in trouble.

a ☐ will ask
b ☐ ask
c ☐ would ask
d ☐ asked

2 Birds ________ south if the weather is cold.

a ☐ would fly
b ☐ flew
c ☐ would have flown
d ☐ fly

3 I ________ if I were 16.

a ☐ would vote
b ☐ will vote
c ☐ voted
d ☐ vote

4 If she knew about your past, she ________ very upset.

a ☐ would be
b ☐ would have been
c ☐ was
d ☐ will be

C Complete the sentences. Use the phrases in the boxes.

ask for another one | it melts | unless you pay them | if he had been kind to me | if I were you

1 I would have talked to him ____.
2 If you heat ice, ____.
3 If your hamburger tastes bad, ____.
4 I would sell this car ____.
5 They won't work on Sunday ____.

Go to page 278 for Extra Practice.

D Underline the correct alternative.

1 If he (had loved – loves) me, he might buy me some flowers.

2 I won't buy a new house unless I (win – won) the lottery.

3 Rice planters (may lose – would lose) money if there is little water.

4 Had he known the truth, he (would have told – will tell) us.

5 If I (had been – were) you, I wouldn't talk to Dad now.

6 (Raise – Will raise) your hands if you have a question.

7 If you visited them, they (might be – will be) very happy.

8 They (won't go – will go) to the movies unless I help them first.

E Write the correct forms of the verbs in parentheses.

1 If the kids disturb you, ______________________ (call) me.

2 Rice ______________________ (grow) if there is abundant rainfall.

3 If they had arrived earlier, they ______________________ (see) the show.

4 Plants ______________________ (grow – neg.) if you leave them in the dark.

5 She ______________________ (come – neg.) unless we invite her.

6 I would not meet him if I ______________________ (be) you.

7 If he ______________________ (like – neg.) pasta, I wouldn't cook spaghetti.

8 If I ______________________ (have) enough money, I might go to Europe.

Reading

Before Reading

Approaching the text

Discuss the questions below in Portuguese.

1 What is global warming?

2 What can cause global warming?

3 What is the impact of global warming on our lives (climate, rainfall, health, etc.)?

Vocabulary

A Match the words with their definitions.

drought carrier southwards inner

1 ____________________: animal que passa doenças de uma pessoa para outra; transmissor

2 ____________________: a parte interna; próximo ao centro

3 ____________________: período durante o qual não há chuvas; seca; estiagem

4 ____________________: em direção ao sul

B Look up these words in the glossary.

1 average ____________________

2 disease ____________________

3 increase ____________________

4 spread ____________________

5 threaten ____________________

6 widespread ____________________

41

Global Warming Impacts

1 Global warming refers to an average increase in the Earth's temperature, which, in turn, causes changes in the climate.

2 When scientists talk about climate change, there is, for the most part, a scientific consensus that human action is causing a warming of the Earth. For centuries we've been clearing forests and burning coal, oil, and gas – pouring carbon dioxide and other gases into the atmosphere faster than plants and oceans can suck them up.

3 Scientists don't know for sure what global warming will bring, but they are able to forecast.

4 If climatic trends continue unabated, global warming will threaten our cities and farms, as well as forests, beaches, wetlands, and other natural habitats.

5 The impact on health will be immediate, with its most direct effect in the tropics. In Africa, for example, where a form of sleeping sickness is currently confined to the inner part of the continent, its carrier (the tsetse fly) would go southwards. Unless we are able to prevent it, there may be severe consequences for humans and cattle.

6 Many infectious and parasitic diseases spread by insects, snails, and ticks would become more widespread, taking with them yellow fever, malaria, and many other diseases.

7 The changing climate is expected to increase both evaporation and precipitation.

8 In those areas where evaporation increases more than precipitation, drought will take place: soil will become drier, rivers will carry less water, and lake levels will drop. Drought will also increase the risk of malnutrition. The consequence is higher chances of getting tuberculosis, leprosy, and polio. Water shortage will cause a deterioration in hygiene and public health. Poorer sanitation and contaminated water can spread cholera, typhus, and other diseases.

9 Unless we start looking for global solutions right now, living on the planet will be a difficult task in the future.

"We're now geological agents, capable of affecting the processes that determine the climate."

(George Philander, climate expert at Princeton University)

Extracted from PHILANDER, S. George. *Is the Temperature Rising?* Princeton: Princeton University Press, 1992; <http://yosemite.epa.gov>. Accessed on December 3, 2010.

Vocabulary

burn: queimar
coal: carvão
drop: cair
pour: despejar
shortage: escassez
sleeping sickness: doença do sono
suck up: aspirar, sorver
unabated: sem diminuição
wetland: pântano

After Reading

A Observe the pictures and captions. Write the words in Portuguese.

snail

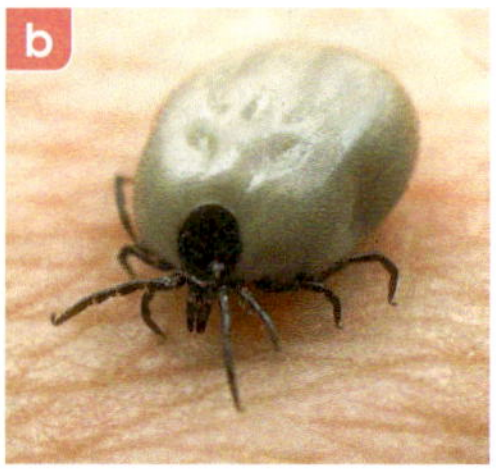

tick

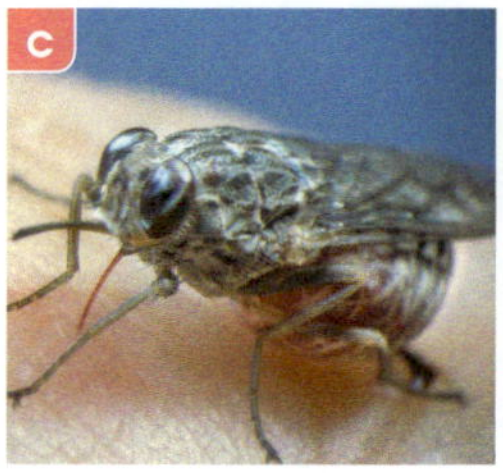

tsetse fly

cattle

B Look at the text and find the names of 8 diseases (paragraphs 5, 6, and 8).

C Observe the words in bold in the sentences below. Check the correct alternative.

1 (5th paragraph). "[...] a form of sleeping sickness is **currently** confined to the inner part of the continent [...]"

a ☐ correntemente b ☐ atualmente

2 (5th paragraph). "Unless we are able to **prevent** it, there may be severe consequences for humans and cattle."

a ☐ evitar b ☐ prever

3 (2nd paragraph). "For centuries we've been **clearing** forests [...]"

a ☐ desmatando b ☐ clareando

D Check Yes or No according to the text.

		Yes	No
1	Mudanças no clima aumentam a temperatura da Terra.		
2	Se a temperatura do planeta continuar a aumentar, haverá um impacto imediato sobre nossa saúde.		
3	Caracóis e carrapatos são transmissores de doenças.		
4	Uma mudança climática vai, certamente, aumentar a evaporação.		
5	Atualmente a doença do sono espalha-se pela África.		
6	In Africa, if the global temperature increased, humans and cattle would go southwards.		
7	For centuries people have been clearing forests and burning coal, oil, and gas.		
8	Drought will also increase the risk of malnutrition.		

E Group Discussion.

O texto menciona as consequências da seca. Quais poderiam ser as consequências do aumento das chuvas?

Vocabulary Expansion

A Complete the chart and the diagram.

formation	malformation	má-formação
nourishment		desnutrição
	maltreatment	maus-tratos
nutrition		
administration		

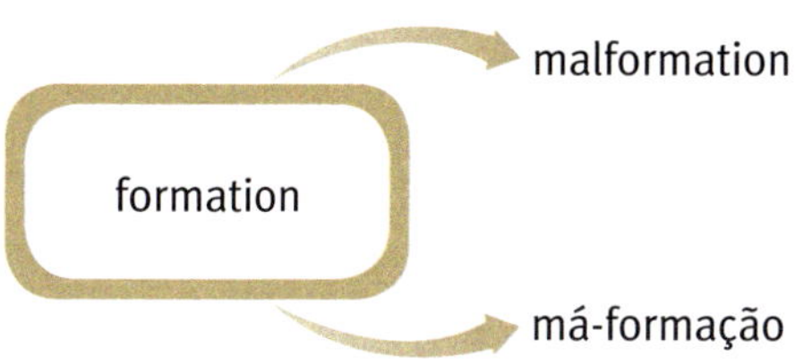

B Complete the sentences. Use the words in the second column of the chart in exercise A.

Prefix mal

Indica coisas desagradáveis, ruins ou imperfeitas; ações malsucedidas.

adjusted – ***mal****adjusted*

1 Forty percent of the population suffers from ______________________ (nutrition).

2 The animals at this zoo died because of ______________________ (treatment).

3 Who is responsible for the ______________________ (nourishment) of these children?

4 Last month he accused the local authorities of ______________________ (administration).

5 Military aircraft can't fly in ______________________ (formation).

C Choose the correct meaning of the words in bold.

1	enfrentar	a ☐	He went on **stage** and started to sing.
2	fase	b ☐	They are not accepting any job applications at this **stage**.
3	palco	c ☐	I am too tired to **face** another problem like this.
4	remédio	d ☐	She had a beautiful and delicate **face**.
5	medicina	e ☐	He wasn't sure if he wanted a career in **medicine**.
6	rosto	f ☐	The young child died because there was no **medicine**.

D Complete the sentences. Use the box for help.

Phrasal Verbs

to come: vir	**to give:** dar
to come across: encontrar por acaso	**to give in:** ceder
to come out: ser publicado(a)	**to give out:** distribuir
to come up: surgir	**to give up:** desistir

1 The thieves ______________________ the very moment the police arrived.

2 Because of the accident, they had to ______________________ their dreams.

3 I ______________________ your brother at the party last weekend.

4 Ann is going to ______________________ lots of candy to kids on Halloween.

5 Kirk's new book will ______________________ next year.

6 That subject has ______________________ at a meeting in the office.

LANGUAGE IN USE

A **Read the text. Then answer the questions.**

www.nytimes.com

SÃO PAULO JOURNAL

An elite pastime that became a passion of the masses

By ALEXEI BARRIONUEVO Published: October 7, 2008

SÃO PAULO, Brazil — Walking into Brazil's new soccer museum is like entering a hall filled with busts of Greek gods. Suspended on glass screens some eight feet tall in the darkened chamber are the outlines of a dozen or so of Brazil's soccer legends in action.

Underneath, the players' names are printed in capital letters. For most, one name is enough.

Ronaldo... Didi... Falcão... Tostão... Garrincha... and the most famous of all, Pelé.

[...]

The new museum is Brazil's first truly national soccer museum, a reminder in this soccer-mad nation of how Brazilians — winners of five World Cups — became the most successful footballers the world has known.

[...]

The museum tells the story of both sport and country, where the national pastime has come to represent and inspire the multiracial, samba-loving soul of the people. In Brazil, stuffy European soccer was transformed into "the beautiful game" of magical passing and dribbling that has won the country world renown.

[...]

Another room pays homage to Brazil's fans. They dance shirtless, beating drums to samba rhythms on huge video screens, with cacophonous surround sound that makes you feel as if you are among the crowd.

[...]

History aside, the museum offers a bit of fun as well. Visitors can kick a soccer ball while a radar gun measures its speed, and later retrieve a photo capturing the moment from the museum's website. And they can don 3-D glasses to watch the star player Ronaldinho dribble a ball all over his body to a thumping rock soundtrack.

Extracted from <www.nytimes.com>.
Accessed on December 10, 2010.

1 Where is the new Brazilian soccer museum?

____

2 What is written underneath the big outlines in the entrance of the museum?

____

B **NOW IT'S YOUR TURN!**

Ask other questions about the article to a classmate. Use the glossary for help.

WRITING

Write a paragraph in your notebook explaining why the soccer museum is or isn't important to Brazilians.

Extra Practice 10

A Complete the chart about conditional sentences.

Condição	Oração condicional (if)	Oração principal
	presente simples	will + verbo
improvável		
	passado perfeito	+ verbo no particípio passado

B Identify the condition expressed in each sentence. Use A (*probable*), B (*improbable*) or C (*impossible*).

1 [ ] If you had locked the car, nobody would have stolen it.

2 [ ] I will drive you home if I find my driver's license.

3 [ ] If he doesn't get here soon, we will start the meeting without him.

4 [ ] If I knew her address, I would send her a postcard.

5 [ ] We wouldn't go out if it snowed hard.

C Rewrite the sentences according to the information in parentheses.

1 If he finds the money, he will give it to me. (improbable condition)

____

2 They will win the game if they play well. (impossible condition)

____

3 If it rained, we wouldn't go to the beach. (possible condition)

____

4 You would have arrived earlier if you had taken a taxi. (possible condition)

____

5 If you teach me, I will learn how to drive. (improbable condition)

____

6 I will eat the cake if you make it. (impossible condition)

____

D Choose the best alternative to complete each sentence.

1 We ________ in the afternoon if I have time.

a ☐ will talk b ☐ would talk c ☐ would have talked

2 They ________ the room if she had come back.

a ☐ will leave b ☐ would leave c ☐ would have left

3 I would visit my friends if I ________ time.

a ☐ have b ☐ had c ☐ had had

4 He would answer your question if he ________ the answer.

a ☐ knows b ☐ knew c ☐ had known

5 They ________ you the whole story if you had had time to listen to them.

a ☐ will tell b ☐ would tell c ☐ would have told

6 She will hurt herself if she ________ over the gate.

a ☐ jumps b ☐ jumped c ☐ had jumped

7 You ________ the flight if you didn't arrive earlier.

a ☐ will miss b ☐ would miss c ☐ would have missed

8 If he doesn't talk to me, I ________ at him any more.

a ☐ won't look b ☐ wouldn't look c ☐ wouldn't have looked

9 I will spend some time in Europe if I ________ a vacation.

a ☐ have b ☐ had c ☐ would have

10 She ________ get sick if she stays in the sun.

a ☐ had b ☐ would c ☐ may

11 We will go to the beach if it ________ hot.

a ☐ is b ☐ was c ☐ had been

E Complete the sentences with the correct verb forms.

1 I ______________ (trust) you if you didn't tell so many lies.

2 You ______________ (get) lost if you don't pay attention to where you are going.

3 If he hadn't read so many books, he wouldn't ______________ (be) a good writer.

4 If I had gone to the bank, I ______________ (talk) to the manager.

5 You would like this book if you ______________ (read) it.

6 If he ______________ (come) here, I would give him a kiss.

7 She will start crying if I ______________ (criticize) her.

8 If he ______________ (get – neg.) out of here, I would have called the police.

9 If he ______________ (drop) the vase, it will break.

10 The cats would have escaped if you ______________ (open) the door.

F Rewrite the sentences using *unless*.

Example: You won't be a healthy person **if** you **don't** eat vegetables.
You won't be a healthy person unless you eat vegetables.

1 Don't write to Mark if you don't like him.

____

2 He wouldn't be rich if he didn't work hard.

____

3 The kids won't come back for lunch if you don't call them.

____

G Check the correct inversion.

1 If I were tired, I would take a rest.

a ☐ Were I tired, I would take a rest.

b ☐ Would I take a rest if I were tired.

2 If he had studied, he would have passed the final exams.

a ☐ Had he studied, he would have passed the final exams.

b ☐ Were he studied, he would have passed the final exams.

H Match the parts of the sentences.

1 If you are late,
2 Rice grows
3 Wood floats if
4 Don't wait for him
5 If you want to have dinner,

a [ ] ... if it rains.
b [ ] ... wash your hands.
c [ ] ... take a taxi.
d [ ] ... if he is late.
e [ ] ... you put it in water.

I Match the definitions to the correct words.

1 a mixture of gases surrounding the Earth

a [ ] centuries b [ ] atmosphere

2 heating a higher degree

a [ ] warming b [ ] soil

3 conditions or practices to maintaining health and preventing diseases

a [ ] contaminated b [ ] hygiene

4 condition caused by lack of food

a [ ] evaporation b [ ] malnutrition

J Choose the adequate alternative.

1 You won't enjoy yourself unless you ________ during spring.

a ☐ will travel
c ☐ travel
b ☐ had traveled
d ☐ would travel

2 If you like skiing, you ________ to Colorado.

a ☐ go
c ☐ would go
b ☐ can go
d ☐ would have gone

3 If it rains, he ________ fishing.

a ☐ goes
c ☐ would go
b ☐ would have gone
d ☐ won't go

4 If it rains, he ________ fishing.

a ☐ can't go
c ☐ go
b ☐ couldn't
d ☐ didn't

5 I would go if I ________ you.

a ☐ am
c ☐ was
b ☐ were
d ☐ will be

6 ________ known, she would have stayed for the film.

a ☐ If she
c ☐ Had she
b ☐ May she
d ☐ If she was

7 I'll visit London ________ I have enough money.

a ☐ unless
c ☐ provided that
b ☐ if not
d ☐ could

Tourism

As is the case in many areas, you can take a two-year or a four-year course in Tourism. There are many post-graduation courses for tourism careers both in Brazil and abroad. It all depends on what you want to do.

Tourism graduates can work in travel agencies. They organize tours with detailed information on means of transportation, lodging options, places to visit, and local attractions. Some tour agents offer specialized packages, such as educational tourism or ecotourism.

Tourism professionals can also work with the marketing side of tourism. They can make market analyses in order to meet the needs of the clients. They create projects to advertise a city, a state, or a region. They announce a product to attract visitors and investments.

On the planning side, tourism specialists identify the tourism possibilities of a place (they call it a destination). They analyze the environmental and the cultural impacts of tourism activities on the place.

Tourism specialists also organize events, such as fairs, exhibits, seminars, and conferences. This is known as business tourism.

Based on GUIA DO ESTUDANTE. São Paulo: Abril, 2008. <www.guiadasprofissoes.com.br>; <www.vestibular.brasilescola.com>; <http://guiadoestudante.abril.com.br>; <www.portaldeensino.com.br>. Accessed on December 18, 2010.

Vocabulary

abroad: no exterior
advertise: fazer propaganda
both... and: tanto... quanto
conference: congresso
environmental: ambiental
exhibit: exposição
lodging: acomodações
meet the needs: atender às necessidades

21 Culture Shock

Language in Context

A Complete the information. Read the dialogue and check your answers. 42

1 Mood: ______________________
____

2 Situation: ______________________

John: Did anybody lock the doors, Mila?
Mila: Yes, John. I locked them myself. Let's go.
Jessy: Dad, look!
John: Just a minute, Jessy. Where's the dog, Mila?
Mila: He was taken to Grandma's. Jessy took him in the morning.
Jessy: Dad, look, look!
John: Wait a moment, Jessy.
Jessy: But, Dad. That man...
John: Wait, Jessy! Did you stop the newspaper, Mila?
Mila: Yes, John. The newspaper was stopped, all the lights were turned off and the neighbors were informed. Can we go now?
John: Yes, we can.
Mila: Afraid not.

B Give your opinion.

1 What was Jessy trying to do?

2 Did the family go on a trip?

C Think about it. Compare the sentences below and answer the questions.

A (Active Voice)	B (Passive Voice)
Jessy took the dog.	The dog was taken.
Mila stopped the newspaper.	The newspaper was stopped.
The thief stole the car.	The car was stolen.

1 Observe the sentences in group **A**. Underline the subjects and circle the objects.

2 Observe the sentences in group **B**. Underline the subjects.

3 What happened to the verbs and objects when changing from the active to the passive voice?

Vocabulary

lock: trancar
turn off: desligar, apagar

LANGUAGE PRACTICE

Passive Voice (I)

To be + Past Participle (no mesmo tempo do verbo principal da forma ativa)
John broke the vase. → The vase was broken. broke ↓ Simple Past; was ↓ Simple Past; broken ↓ Past Participle

Uso

A voz de um verbo mostra se o sujeito faz ou recebe a ação.

Voz ativa – o sujeito faz a ação: **He wrote** a message in French.

Voz passiva – o sujeito recebe a ação: **A message was written** in French.

A voz passiva é usada quando o agente/autor da ação é desconhecido, não é importante ou quando não se deseja mencioná-lo ou enfatizá-lo. É usada principalmente em textos técnicos, científicos, formais e em reportagens.

A Com base nas informações acima, complete o quadro abaixo.

Tempo verbal	Voz ativa	Voz passiva
Simple Present	writes/write	is written/are ______
Simple Past	wrote	was written/ ______
Present Continuous	is/are writing	is/are being ______
Past Continuous	was/were writing	______
Present Perfect	has/have written	has/have been ______
Past Perfect	had written	______
Simple Future	will write	______
Modal	can write	can be ______

B **Rewrite the sentences in the passive voice.**

1 The students were writing a beautiful song.

____

2 The teacher taught the major points of the lesson.

____

3 A tornado has smashed several houses in southern Oklahoma.

____

4 He slammed the skateboard into the wall.

____

5 Don't worry. Someone will open the door.

____

6 They grow coffee in Kenya.

____

7 People are destroying the forests in Indonesia.

____

Go to page 302 for Extra Practice.

Passive Voice (II)

Observações

Quando uma frase passa da voz ativa para a voz passiva:

- o objeto da voz ativa passa a ser sujeito da voz passiva.

  (sujeito) (objeto) (sujeito)

  Someone stole **my bag**. **My bag** was stolen.

- pode-se mencionar quem realizou a ação usando-se a preposição **by**.

  My bag was stolen **by someone**.

- se houver dois objetos (direto e indireto), qualquer um deles pode ser o sujeito da passiva.

  John told **me a story**.

  I was told a story (by John).

  A story was told to me (by John).

C Rewrite the sentences into the Passive Voice without *by*.

1 They sent the letters yesterday.

2 Someone has revised the agenda for the next meeting.

3 The monkey is eating the bananas.

4 They make good shoes in Franca, São Paulo.

5 The committee has approved the new medical program.

6 He is selling that big house on the corner.

D Rewrite each sentence in the two possible passive forms.

Example: She sent us a letter.
We were sent a letter.
A letter was sent to us.

1 They will give the kids new shoes.

2 I have asked John a question.

3 The salesperson showed me an expensive book.

4 Grandma told me a secret.

Go to page 303 for Extra Practice.

READING

Before Reading

Approaching the text

Discuss the questions below in Portuguese.

1 Have you ever traveled or wanted to travel abroad?

2 Where would you like to go?

3 How would you feel if you had to live abroad for one year?

Vocabulary

A Read the synonyms below.

keep: maintain
likewise: in the same way
once: one time
skill: ability
soon: in a short period of time
wear off: weaken

B Look up these words in the glossary.

1 hard ______________________

2 laugh ______________________

3 survival ______________________

4 stay ______________________

Culture Shock

43 Adjusting to a new culture and way of life is both exciting and challenging – you will experience some highs and lows during your time abroad. During these times of difficulty, just remind yourself that these cultural differences are the reason we all love to travel – to experience the unknown!

Remember, it's just a phase.

Stages of Cultural Adjustment

There are typically three stages that most people go through.

1. Honeymoon – You will probably experience an initial period of excitement and happiness, due to new things around you. You will constantly be reminded that you are in a new culture and are many miles from home.
2. Shock – As you adjust to the routine of daily life, that initial sense of adventure will wear off. During this phase you may start to miss your friends and family. During this time, you may find it hard to keep a positive attitude. You may be tempted to withdraw from people around you or even become hostile. At this point it is helpful to know that for most people this phase doesn't last too long.
3. Adjustment – The second phase will soon give way to the third phase – your true adjustment to the foreign culture. Once the values and characteristics of people become more familiar to you, life will become easier and you will really begin to experience the other culture.

Survival Skills

- Stay positive.
- Give yourself a chance.
- Try not to withdraw from your new friends. Make a special effort to have fun and most importantly: remember all of the reasons that brought you to the other country in the first place!
- Be open and friendly and people will respond likewise.
- Maintain a sense of humor and an open mind. Keep in mind that even the worst experience will make your friends and family laugh when you are back home.

Based on <www.workinaustralia.net>; <www.ciee.org>; <www.cord.edu>. Accessed on December 20, 2010.

Vocabulary

due to: devido a
keep in mind: ter em mente
last long: durar muito tempo
withdraw: afastar-se

After Reading

A **Look at the main title, the section titles, and the blocks of text. Then answer the questions below in Portuguese.**

1 Que tipo de texto é esse?

2 Qual é o público-alvo do texto?

3 Qual é o objetivo do texto?

B **Transparent words.**
Read the text and underline the transparent words.

1 How many did you find: about 15 ☐ or more than 20 ☐?

2 Look at the words in the boxes and circle the ones you found.

culture | shock | adjust | difference | reason | phase | initial | period
constantly | routine | adventure | positive | attitude | hostile | familiar
characteristics | chance | special | effort | respond | sense | humor

C **Understanding words and phrases.**

1 Choose the meaning of the underlined words in the sentence.

"[...] you will experience some ☐ highs and lows during your time ☐ abroad."

a happy times and sad times
b just happy times
c far from one's family
d in a foreign country

2 What kind of word is "experience" in the sentence above?

a ☐ A verb.
b ☐ A noun.

3 Write the meaning in Portuguese of the underlined words in the sentence below.

"[...] you may start to miss your friends and family." ____________________

D **Understanding the text.**

1 Uma das sentenças no início do texto tem como objetivo tranquilizar o possível viajante. Identifique-a e transcreva-a.

____

2 O texto menciona um motivo pelo qual todos gostamos de viajar para outros países e conhecer outras culturas. Identifique o motivo e transcreva-o.

____

Vocabulary Expansion

A **Read the information in the chart.**

Alguns adjetivos podem terminar em **ed** ou **ing**, mudando ligeiramente de significado.

bored: entediado(a)	**boring:** entediante
challenged: desafiado(a)	**challenging:** desafiador
excited: empolgado(a)	**exciting:** empolgante
interested: interessado(a)	**interesting:** interessante

The kids were **excited** about the trip to the beach. Our trip to the beach was **exciting**.

B **Transform the words in parentheses into adjectives.**

1 A: Do you want to know more about Australia?

B: Sure, my friends and I are very ____________ (interest) in it.

2 A: I don't want to talk about this film. It's so ____________ (bore).

B: I don't agree with you. In my opinion, it is very ____________ (interest).

3 A: The more difficult the task, the better.

B: You're right. I like ____________ (challenge) tasks, too.

4 A: The children look ____________ (bore) today. What happened?

B: They have nothing ____________ (excite) to do.

C **Give the correct meaning of the words in bold.**

1 When you live abroad you **miss** your family and friends.

2 Could you please come here, **Miss** Brown?

a ☐ senhorita

b ☐ sente falta

3 If you run that way, your shoes won't **last** very long.

4 They were the **last** two passengers to leave the plane.

a ☐ durar

b ☐ últimos(as)

5 Sometimes it's very **hard** to understand you.

6 Those nuts are as **hard** as rocks. I can't crack them.

a ☐ difícil

b ☐ duras

D Read the verbs and phrasal verbs in the box. Then join the phrases to make complete sentences.

Phrasal Verbs

to turn: girar; virar(-se)	**to turn down:** recusar
to turn against: voltar-se contra	**to turn off:** desligar
to turn around: virar-se	**to turn on:** ligar
to turn away: expulsar; rejeitar	**to turn out:** resultar; acontecer
to turn back: voltar para	

1	The house is too quiet today.	a	☐	Please, turn off the radio!
2	It was a good offer but...	b	☐	look at me?
3	I have to study.	c	☐	Turn on the TV, please.
4	Can you turn around and...	d	☐	Things didn't turn out the way she had expected.
5	She is unhappy.	e	☐	I had to turn it down.
6	The snow forced them...	f	☐	were turned away.
7	He's managed...	g	☐	to turn back.
8	The machine will start...	h	☐	to turn his wife against you.
9	Fans who tried to photograph the pop star...	i	☐	turning this wheel.

— She turned pale when she saw me. She thought I was a ghost.

LANGUAGE IN USE

A **Read the tale and then answer the questions.**

The Old Woman and the Doctor

An old woman became almost totally blind from a disease of the eyes and after consulting a doctor she made an agreement with him in the presence of witnesses that she should pay him a high fee if he cured her, while if he failed he was to receive nothing. The doctor accordingly prescribed a course of treatment, and every time he paid her a visit he took away with him some article from the house, until, at last, when he visited her for the last time, and the cure was complete, there was nothing left.

When the old woman saw that the house was empty, she refused to pay him his fee; and, after repeated refusals on her part, he sued her before the magistrates for payment of her debt. On being brought into court she was ready with her defense.

"The claimant," said she, "has stated the facts about our agreement correctly. I undertook to pay him a fee if he cured me, and he, on his part, promised to charge nothing if he failed. Now, he says I am cured; but I say that I am blinder than ever, and I can prove what I say. When my eyes were bad I could at any rate see well enough to be aware that my house contained a certain amount of furniture and other things; but now, when according to him I am cured, I am entirely unable to see anything there at all."

Extracted from: <www.gutenberg.org>. Accessed on January 4, 2011.

1 Did the woman have a disease in her heart?

____

2 What would happen if the doctor failed to cure the woman?

____

B **NOW IT'S YOUR TURN!**

Ask more questions about the tale to a classmate. Use the glossary for help.

WRITING

Now you are the doctor. Rewrite the first paragraph of the tale in your notebook from your point of view.

An old woman became almost totally blind from a disease of the eyes and after consulting me we made...

22 Virtual Idols

Language in Context

A Complete the information. Read the dialogue and check your answers. 44

1 Name of the man: ____________

2 Name of the woman: ____________

A: Hey, I'm Ramona. What's your name?
B: Simon.
A: Hi, Simon. Ask me a question.
B: Do you have a family?
A: Of course I do.
B: What is your favorite thing, Ramona?
A: I like chatting with people online.
B: What was your biggest disappointment?
A: I do not know what a biggest disappointment is.
B: I want to ask you another question.
A: Ask me another question.
B: Do you have problems with words, Ramona?
A: I don't think I have problems with words, Simon.
B: Are you real?
A: What do you think?
B: Well, my friends say that you're virtual.
A: Maybe they are right.
B: What do you mean?
A: I mean I am a real virtual person. What about you, Simon? Are you human?

Send

B Give your opinion.

1 How did you identify the real person?

2 Have you ever chatted with a virtual person?

Vocabulary
chat: conversar
mean: querer dizer

C Think about it. Compare the sentences and answer the questions.

A	B
Ela disse, "Eu gosto de conversar.". Ele disse, "Eu quero fazer uma pergunta.".	Ela disse que (ela) gostava de conversar. Ele disse que (ele) queria fazer uma pergunta.

1 Sublinhe os verbos das frases acima.

2 Observe os verbos e pronomes das frases do grupo **B**.

3 Que mudanças ocorreram em relação às frases do grupo **A**?

4 Write the sentences in groups **A** and **B** in English.

Language Practice

Direct and Indirect Speech (I)

Há duas formas de relatar o que alguém disse:

› Pelo **discurso direto** (*direct speech*) – Quando relatamos o que foi dito usando as mesmas palavras da pessoa, entre aspas: She said, "I love you."

› Pelo **discurso indireto** (*indirect speech*) – Quando contamos o que foi dito com nossas próprias palavras: She said (that) she loved me. (**That** pode ou não ser usado.)

Quando usamos o discurso indireto, geralmente modificamos o tempo verbal, alguns pronomes e advérbios. Observe:

DIRECT SPEECH	INDIRECT SPEECH
She said, **"I am** happy today."	She said **that she was** happy that day.
She said, **"I worked** yesterday."	She said **that she had worked** the day before.
She said, **"I'll study** tomorrow."	She said **that she would study** the next day.
They said, "We **are leaving** now."	They said **that they were leaving** then.
He said, **"I was reading** an hour ago."	He said **that he had been reading** an hour before.
I said, **"I have lived** here."	I said **that I had lived** there.
He said, **"I can go** with you."	He said **that he could go** with me.
He said, **"I must buy** these books."	He said **that he had to buy** those books.

A mudança de tempo não é obrigatória quando:

› a situação relatada ainda existe no presente;

› o verbo usado para relatar (por exemplo, *say*) estiver no *Simple Present*, no *Present Perfect* ou no *Simple Future*.

He says, **"I come** from Brazil."

He says that he comes from Brazil.

A **Rewrite the sentences. Follow the example.**

Example: Vivian said that she had studied the day before.
Vivian said, "I studied yesterday."

1 Tony said that he would study that day.

____

2 Virginia said that it was going to rain.

____

B Complete the information on verb tense changes.

	Direct Speech	Indirect Speech
1	Simple Present	
2	Simple Past	
3	Will	
4	Present Continuous	
5	Past Continuous	Past Perfect Continuous
6	Present Perfect	
7	Can (modal)	
8	Must (modal)	Have to

C Fill in the blanks according to the changes observed in the Language Practice box.

1 today ______________________

2 yesterday ______________________

3 tomorrow ______________________

4 now ______________________

5 ago ______________________

6 here ______________________

7 these ______________________

D Rewrite the sentences. Use indirect speech.

1 Carla said, "I am studying French now."

____

2 She said, "I watch TV every day."

____

3 He said, "I've worked here for a long time."

____

4 I said, "I am going to leave."

____

E Complete the sentences with the correct verb tenses.

1 She said, "I want to go out today."

She said that she ______________________ to go out that day.

2 He said, "The boys are sleeping in their room."

He said that the boys ______________________ in their room.

3 She said, "I will visit my friends next week."

She said she ______________________ her friends the following week.

4 They said, "We've lived here for a long time."

They said they ______________________ there for a long time.

5 I said, "The text is very difficult."

I said that the text ______________________ very difficult.

6 She said, "I was waiting for you."

She said she ______________________ for me.

7 She said, "I made this cake for your birthday."

She said that she ______________________ that cake for my birthday.

8 He said, "I can come tonight."

He said he ______________________ that night.

F Choose the correct alternative.

1 Mary said, "I want to bring my books today."

a ☐ Mary said she wants to bring her books that day.

b ☐ Mary said that she wanted to bring her books that day.

2 The girl said, "I am studying a lot at the moment."

a ☐ The girl said that she had been studying a lot at that moment.

b ☐ The girl said that she was studying a lot at that moment.

3 She said, "You must be tired."

a ☐ She said I had to be tired.

b ☐ She said that I was tired.

4 They said, "We will help you."

a ☐ They said they would help me.

b ☐ They said they were going to help me.

Go to page 306 for Extra Practice.

READING

Before Reading

Approaching the text

Discuss the questions below in Portuguese.

Take a look at the text on page 297. Observe the title, boxes, pictures, etc.

1 What is the subject of the text?

2 Are young people in your country familiar with this subject? What about in other countries? Do you think young people are familiar with and interested in this subject?

Vocabulary

Look up the words below in the glossary.

1 brows ______

2 offspring ______

3 overlook ______

4 release ______

— Then he said that he didn't love me any longer! Then, I said that I didn't love him! Then he said that he was leaving. And I said that I would not miss him. Then...

Virtual Idols

She sings, she dances, she speaks many languages, and she doesn't exist. Surprised? She is Kyoko Date, the first CGC (Computer Generated Character) pop star, created in 1996.

Kyoko is the offspring of HoriPro, a Japanese talent agency. Kyoko's form was pieced together from 40,000 polygons. Her face alone took 10 people to finish. In many of her "publicity shots" it is easy to mistake her for a 16-year-old girl.

Kyoko Date not only looks human, with delicate brows and large eyes, but she also has her own biography with birth date, blood type, hobbies, and a family.

Other CGCs have been created since then, and in some countries they have become an internet fever. Lara Croft, T-Babe, E-Cyas, Ananova, Vandrea, Ramona, and Terai are some of the Virtual Idols, or VIs. They may release videos, CDs and DVDs; appear on TV commercials; and chat online.

Most youngsters are fascinated by CGCs. However, not everybody shares the same opinion.

Why are these images so attractive?

Are people so fascinated with the idea of communicating with machines that they overlook communication with fellow human beings?

"Kyoko is what we think the ideal idol should be: she sings, she is smart, and she is beautiful," says Tori (Japan).

"How can people be so obsessed with a computer generated being? She is not real!," declared Juan (Spain).

"I like chatting with VIs," said Joan (USA). "They are more intelligent than my friends."

"We can still play, but VIs will never replace humans," said Mitie (Japan).

Based on GET WIRED MAGAZINE. March 1997. <www.kurzweilai.net>. Accessed on December 27, 2010.

Vocabulary

alone: só
look: parecer
mistake: confundir
piece together: montar
replace: substituir
share: partilhar
shot: foto
since then: desde então

After Reading

A Look at the text and find the information below:

1 the meaning of the abbreviation CGC: ______

2 the name of the first CGC: ______

3 the name of a Japanese talent agency: ______

B Escolha a alternativa que melhor traduz o sentido das frases abaixo.

1 (lines 6 and 7) "Kyoko's form was pieced together from 40,000 polygons."

a ☐ 40.000 polígonos foram usados para formar Kyoko.

b ☐ Kyoko era uma parte de 40.000 polígonos.

c ☐ Kyoko foi dividida em 40.000 polígonos.

2 (lines 7 and 8) "Her face alone took 10 people to finish."

a ☐ Dez pessoas achavam seu olhar solitário.

b ☐ Seu rosto foi finalizado por mais de 10 pessoas.

c ☐ Foram necessárias dez pessoas para finalizar apenas o seu rosto.

3 (line 10) "Kyoko Date not only looks human [...]"

a ☐ Kyoko Date não parece humana.

b ☐ Ela não só parece humana.

c ☐ Ela tem um olhar humano.

4 (line 14) "Other CGCs have been created since then [...]"

a ☐ Some CGCs were created after that.

b ☐ Some CGCs created many other CGCs.

c ☐ Since the beginning, Kyoko was the best CGC.

C Check True or False according to the text.

		True	False
1	The abbreviation VIs stands for Virtual Idols.		
2	Kyoko doesn't speak any languages other than Japanese.		
3	Kyoko exists only in virtual reality.		
4	Kyoko looks like a 16-year-old boy.		
5	CGCs may chat online.		

D Answer the questions.

1 What is a Computer Generated Character?

______

2 Where did the first VI appear?

______

3 Do all the people share the same opinion about CGCs?

______

4 What is Joan's opinion about them?

______

5 Does Juan agree with Joan?

______

6 Who agrees with Juan?

______

7 Who is Lara Croft?

______

8 Do VIs appear only on the internet?

______

VOCABULARY EXPANSION

A Find words in the text that are synonyms or opposites of the underlined words below.

Synonyms

1 Her <u>shape</u> was pieced together from many polygons. ______

2 Many people worked <u>to complete</u> the project. ______

3 <u>The majority</u> of young people are fascinated by CGCs. ______

4 VIs are <u>intelligent</u> and <u>pretty</u>. ______

5 VIs will never <u>substitute</u> humans. ______

Opposites

1 She was the <u>last</u> Computer Generated Character. ______

2 It took many hours <u>to destroy</u> her face. ______

3 Sometimes my friends and I <u>disagree about something</u>. ______

B Read the box and complete the definitions below.

Prefix over

Descreve uma qualidade, ação ou algo exagerado, além do esperado.
over*act*, ***over****dose*, ***over****populated*

Example: Overact: when someone exaggerates emotions and movement. (act)

1 ____________________: when someone wears clothes that are too formal for the occasion. (dress)

2 ____________________: when there are too many people living in an area. (populated)

3 ____________________: when you sleep longer than you should. (sleep)

4 ____________________: when you do, say, use more of something. (do)

5 ____________________: when a liquid flows over the edges of a container. (flow)

6 ____________________: when someone is more confident than it is sensible to be. (confident)

7 ____________________: when you eat more than is necessary or healthy. (eat)

8 ____________________: when you ask somebody to pay too much money for something. (charge)

C Supply the appropriate preposition.

before: antes
beyond: além; do outro lado

1 My grandpa kept working ____________________ the age of 60. He liked his job.

2 I heard his footsteps ____________________ the front door.

3 She was born a few days ____________________ Christmas.

4 They never come home ____________________ dinner.

5 What you have done is ____________________ my comprehension.

6 We lived in San Martin ____________________ moving to St. Lucia.

7 Go along this street and turn right one block ____________________ the park.

8 He could see ____________________ the mountains and the sea.

LANGUAGE IN USE

A Read the text about a theater play and answer the questions.

www.the-mousetrap.co.uk

St. Martin's Theatre – West Street, Cambridge Circus, WC2H 9NZ

Agatha Christie's

The Mousetrap

The Longest Running Show of any Kind in the World

For the last 34 years the St. Martin's has been the home of *The Mousetrap*, more than half of its record-breaking run!

The Mousetrap has been thrilling audiences from around the world for as long as HRH Queen Elizabeth II has been on the throne. On November 25th, 2002, a Royal Gala Performance was held, attended by Her Majesty the Queen and the Duke of Edinburgh.

During this phenomenal run there have been no fewer than 382 actors and actresses appearing in the play, 116 miles of shirts have been ironed, and over 415 tons of ice cream sold.

Some cast members are in *Guinness World Book of Records*, David Raven as the "Most Durable Actor" for 4,575 performances as Major Metcalf, and the late Nancy Seabrooke for a record-breaking 15 years as an understudy.

The Mousetrap first entered the record books many years ago – on April 12th, 1958 when it became the longest-running show of any kind in the history of British theatre.

In 2000 the set was replaced for the first time during the run at St. Martin's Theater, still to the same design as the original. This task was completed over a weekend without the loss of a performance.

Extracted from <www.the-mousetrap.co.uk>. Accessed on December 20, 2009.

1 Who wrote *The Mousetrap*? ______________________________

2 Who is David Raven? ______________________________

3 When was the set replaced? ______________________________

B NOW IT'S YOUR TURN!

Ask other questions about the play to a classmate. Use the glossary for help.

WRITING

Write one paragraph in your notebook about a theater play or a television show that you liked.

EXTRA PRACTICE 11

A Read the text. Underline all verbs that are in the passive form.

It is estimated that in 1860 there were between 30 and 90 million buffalo on the plains in Washington. The animals had lived on the plains for thousands of years and their stampedes were heard for hundreds of miles.

They were called "Rolling Thunder" by the natives.

By 1870, however, after the railroad had crossed the plains, millions of buffalo had been killed.

The Rolling Thunder was silent.

B Complete the sentences in the passive form. Don't use *by*.

1 They teach Ancient and Medieval History at the university.

Ancient and Medieval History ____________________ at the university.

2 Scientists researched this subject two years ago.

This subject ____________________ two years ago.

3 The surgeon is operating on my friend.

My friend ____________________ on.

4 We will decide everything by tomorrow.

Everything ____________________ by tomorrow.

5 They have rented their house for two years.

Their house ____________________ for two years.

6 I sold my car for $9,000.

My car ____________________ for $9,000.

C Rewrite the sentences in the passive form. Use *by*.

Example: This movie fascinates me.
I am fascinated by this movie.

1 The kids bore Jack.

____

2 The show surprised them.

____

3 They were cleaning the house when I arrived.

____

4 They have produced new car models in the past years.

____

5 I will paint the door tomorrow.

____

6 Mark is drinking a cup of coffee.

____

7 The storm damaged the house.

____

D Underline and correct the mistakes.

Example: Many people are talking about globalization in the meetings.
Globalization is talking about in the meetings.
Globalization is being talked about in the meetings.

1 Fire may destroy forests.
Forests may destroyed by fire.

____

2 That enormous dog licked the baby.
The baby were licked by the enormous dog.

____

3 Brazilian Interpol agents found the American killer in Saquarema, Rio de Janeiro.
The American killer had found by Brazilian Interpol agents in Saquarema, Rio de Janeiro.

____

4 The judge must punish this criminal.
This criminal must be punish by the judge.

____

E Choose the correct alternative in the passive form.

1 I am going to prepare some sandwiches.
Some sandwiches ________ prepared.

a ☐ will be to b ☐ are going to be

2 They will speak Chinese at the meeting.
Chinese ________ at the meeting.

a ☐ will be spoken b ☐ would speak

3 They make this product in Japan.
This product ________ in Japan.

a ☐ is made b ☐ is make

4 She had finished dinner when I arrived.
Dinner ________ when I arrived.

a ☐ was finished b ☐ had been finished

5 The plan interests me.
I ________ in the plan.

a ☐ was interested b ☐ am interested

6 Someone was repairing the street this morning.
The street ________ this morning.

a ☐ was being repaired b ☐ did repair

7 Susan will finish her course in July.
Her course ________ in July.

a ☐ is going to finish b ☐ will be finished

8 They built this bridge in 1890.
This bridge ________ in 1890.

a ☐ is built b ☐ was built

9 People have dumped contaminants into the river.
Contaminants ________ into the river.

a ☐ have been dumped b ☐ were dumped

10 Jorge Amado wrote *Capitães da Areia*.
Capitães da Areia ________ by Jorge Amado.

a ☐ was written b ☐ is written

11 They were painting the room when I left.
The room ________ when I left.

a ☐ has being painted b ☐ was being painted

F Indique duas formas passivas corretas para cada sentença.

1 I'll give Paul new shoes.

a ☐ Paul will be given new shoes.

b ☐ Paul will give me new shoes.

c ☐ New shoes will be given to Paul.

d ☐ I will be given new shoes by Paul.

2 She is going to buy Grandma some books.

a ☐ Grandma will buy her some books.

b ☐ Grandma is going to be bought some books.

c ☐ Some books are going to be bought for grandma.

d ☐ Books are going to be bought by her.

3 They sang a song for us.

a ☐ We were sung a song.

b ☐ A song was sung for us.

c ☐ We sang them a song.

d ☐ They had sung a song.

4 We must send letters to Mary.

a ☐ Letters must send us to Mary.

b ☐ Mary must be sent letters.

c ☐ Letters will be sent by us.

d ☐ Letters must be sent to Mary.

5 We sent flowers to Jessica.

a ☐ Flowers were sent to us.

b ☐ Jessica has sent us flowers.

c ☐ Jessica was sent flowers.

d ☐ Flowers were sent to Jessica.

6 He baked a cake to Carol.

a ☐ A cake were baked to her.

b ☐ Carol was baked a cake.

c ☐ He has baked a cake.

d ☐ A cake was baked to Carol.

G Complete the sentences using the reported speech.

1 My friend said, "I will receive a postcard from my boyfriend."

My friend said that she ______________________________.

2 Mom said, "I can't do that."

Mom said that she ______________________________.

3 Ted said, "I have studied here for two years."

Ted said that he ______________________________.

4 I said, "I am going to arrive late."

I said that I ______________________________.

5 Tim said, "I didn't work yesterday."

Tim said that he ______________________________.

6 Paul said, "Sally doesn't like vegetables."

Paul said that Sally ______________________________.

7 I said, "I will think about it."

I said that I ______________________________.

8 He said, "I have been cleaning these windows for two hours."

He said that he ______________________________.

H Choose the correct transformation.

1 Tom said, "I have already eaten."

a ☐ Tom sad he had had eaten.

b ☐ Tom said that he had already eaten.

2 He said, "I may bring someone with me to the party."

a ☐ He said that he might bring someone with him to the party.

b ☐ He said that I may bring someone with me to the party.

3 She said, "I bought these shoes in a garage sale."

a ☐ She said that she had bought those shoes in a garage sale.

b ☐ She said that I have bought those shoes in a garage sale.

4 I said, "These flowers are for you."

a ☐ He said that these flowers were for you.

b ☐ I said that those flowers were for you.

Job Corner 11

BIOTECHNOLOGY

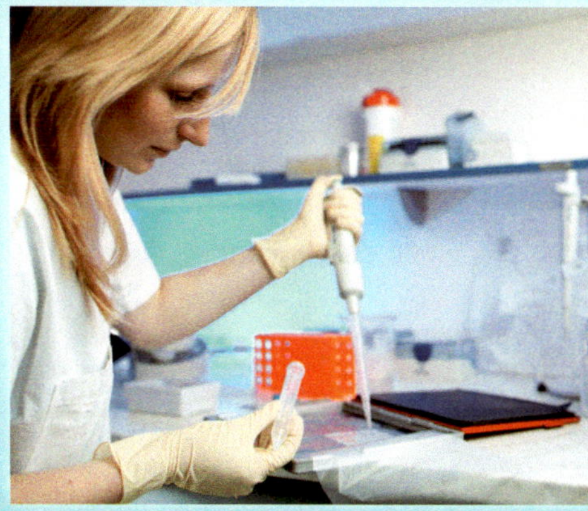

Biotechnology is one of the new professional courses of study offered by universities. Biotechnology uses chemical and biological knowledge and the knowledge of new technologies in the areas of healthcare, food, chemistry, and the environment. Biotechnology graduates are multidisciplinary professionals. They study biology, chemistry, physics, statistics, and information technology.

In the area of microbiology, these professionals study fungi, bacteria, viruses, and protozoa and the diseases that such microorganisms cause in plants, animals, and human beings. They also research the methods of using such microorganisms in the production of foods and beverages – such as dairy products, beer, and wine.

Biotechnologists specializing in immunology use microorganisms in the production of vaccines and kits for diagnosis. In the food and pharmaceutical industries, they improve safety and hygiene at the workplace by controlling microbial growth. They also research the development of new pharmaceutical drugs.

They also work in the environmental area, to evaluate and prevent water and soil contamination.

Based on
GUIA DO ESTUDANTE. São Paulo: Abril, 2008.
<www.guiadasprofissoes.com.br>;
<www.vestibular.brasilescola.com>;
<http://guiadoestudante.abril.com.br>;
<www.portaldeensino.com.br>.
Accessed on January 5, 2011.

Vocabulary

beer: cerveja
beverages: bebidas
dairy: laticínios
diseases: doenças
food: alimentos
graduate: formado(a)
growth: crescimento
healthcare: cuidados com a saúde
information technology: tecnologia da informação
knowledge: conhecimento
research: pesquisar
safety: segurança
wine: vinho

23 The Old Man and the Sea

Language in Context

A **Complete the information. Read the dialogue and check your answers:** 46

1 Subject: ____________________

2 Who is away on a trip? __________

B **Give your opinion.**

1 Has the mother been away for a long time? How do you know?

2 Why does the daughter say, "That's Mom!"?

C **Think about it. Compare the sentences and answer the questions.**

1 Que mudanças você percebe na frase abaixo na passagem para o discurso indireto?
Ela disse: "Você levou o cão para passear?" (discurso direto)
Ela perguntou se eu tinha levado o cão para passear. (discurso indireto)

2 Verifique se as mesmas mudanças ocorrem na língua inglesa.
She said, "Did you walk the dog?" (discurso direto)
She asked if I had walked the dog. (discurso indireto)

Vocabulary

every other day: dia sim, dia não
guess: achar; supor

Father: Mom called from London last night.
Daughter: Is she enjoying her trip?
Father: I guess so…
Daughter: You guess so? Didn't she say if she's having a good time?
Father: No, she didn't.
Daughter: What did she say, then?
Father: She told me not to forget to lock the doors at night. And she told you to visit Grandma every other day.
Daughter: Was that all?
Father: No, she asked if you were studying. She asked if your brother had gone to his piano lesson. She also asked me if I had taken the dog for a walk, if I had phoned the dentist, and if you had talked to Aunt Julia.
Daughter: That's Mom!

Language Practice

Direct and Indirect Speech (II)

Uso

Para relatar uma pergunta, colocamos a frase na forma afirmativa.

He said, "Does she study?" **He asked if she studied.**

He said, "Where does she live?" **He asked where she lived.**

Para relatar ordens e pedidos, geralmente usamos **tell**, **ask** e **order**.

He said, "Open the door." **He told me to open the door.**

He said, "Don't go." **He asked me not to go.**

He said, "Don't call me later." **He ordered me not to call him later.**

Say/tell – O uso do objeto indireto é obrigatório quando usamos **tell**.

He **told me** that he was sick.

He **said** that he was sick.

Os modais **would**, **could**, **should**, **might** e **ought to** não mudam de forma.

He said, "I could help you." **He said that he could help me.**

A Rewrite the sentences using indirect speech.

1 Mary said to me, "Don't speak to me."

Mary asked me ______________________.

2 Mom said to me, "Turn on the TV."

Mom told me ______________________.

3 She said to Jane, "What time is it?"

She asked Jane ______________________.

4 The woman said, "Are you a student?"

The woman asked ______________________.

5 She said, "Did you make the cake?"

She asked ______________________.

Go to page 330 for Extra Practice.

B Put the sentences into direct speech.

1 He asked me if I was reading the book.

He said, ____________________

2 He told me not to smoke.

He said, ____________________

3 He asked when I would leave.

He said, ____________________

4 He told me to go home.

He said, ____________________

5 He asked me where I studied.

He said, ____________________

C Underline the appropriate form of the verbs in indirect speech.

1 "Open the window, please."
She told me (open – to open) the window.

2 "Do you know the answer?"
He asked me if I (knew – to know) the answer.

3 "Will you help me?"
He asked me if I (will to – would) help him.

4 "Don't touch the dog."
He told me (not to touch – touch) the dog.

5 "Where did you meet her?"
He asked me where I (had met – met) her.

6 "What are they saying?"
He asked me what they (said – were saying).

7 "Stand up, please."
He told us (to stand – stand) up.

8 "When do you want to leave?"
He asked me when I (had wanted – wanted) to leave.

9 "Have you seen this film?"
He asked if we (saw – had seen) that film.

10 "Could you give the money to her?"
He asked if I (could – can) give the money to her.

Would rather, Had better, It takes

Would rather ('d rather) – Expressa preferência.

I **would rather walk** to school. (Prefiro andar até a escola.)

Had better ('d better) – Expressa conselho ou recomendação.

You **had better go** home. (É melhor você ir para casa.)

It takes... – Expressa o tempo que alguém leva para praticar uma ação.

It takes me **10 minutes** to get ready. [Levo 10 minutos para ficar pronto(a).]

It took us **one day** to get there. (Levamos um dia para chegar lá.)

It will take him **one hour** to have lunch. (Ele levará uma hora para almoçar.)

O pronome pessoal objeto pode ser eliminado se não for essencial para a compreensão da frase.

It **took 45 minutes** to bake the cake.

D Complete the sentences. Use *would rather* or *had better*.

1 I love blue. I ________________ wear the blue dress.

2 It is raining. You ________________ take an umbrella.

3 The day is beautiful. I ________________ walk home.

4 I have a headache. I ________________ take an aspirin.

E Answer the questions.

Example: How long did it take you to go home yesterday?
(30 minutes) It took me 30 minutes.

1 How long will it take us to get there by train?
(one day) ________________

2 How long does it take Jane to wash the dog?
(one hour) ________________

3 How long does it take you to water the flowers?
(a few minutes) ________________

4 How long did it take Hemingway to win the Nobel Prize for Literature?
(55 years) ________________

5 How long did it take to cook the meat?
(2 hours) ________________

Go to page 332 for Extra Practice.

READING

Before Reading

Approaching the text

Learning about the author.

Ernest (Miller) Hemingway (1899-1961)
American novelist

Ernest (Miller) Hemingway

He used to accompany his father on hunting and fishing trips. His love for adventure was reflected in many of his stories. He participated in World War I as an ambulance driver and in World War II as a war correspondent. Although his work received good critical acclaim, it took him 55 years to receive the Nobel Prize for Literature (1954).

The Old Man and the Sea

Summary

This is the story of Santiago, an aging fisherman. One day, after 84 days of bad luck, Santiago decides to sail far out to sea in search of a big fish. This time, he goes to sea alone. A boy who is his best friend can't go with him.

Later that day his luck turns and he hooks a giant Marlin.

For two days and two nights the fish pulls the old man further out to sea.

47

[1] The fish never changed his course all that day. Santiago looked behind him and saw that no land was visible. I have no cramps and I feel strong, he thought. I wish I could see him once to know what I have against me.

[2] It was cold after the sun went down. He could feel the strength of the fish through the line he held across his shoulders. They were moving more slowly now and the glow of Havana was not so strong. We must be going to the eastward, he thought.

[3] Then, he said aloud, "I wish I had the boy here. To help me and to see this." Then he began to think about the great fish that he had hooked. "He is wonderful and strange and who knows how old he is," he told himself. "But, he cannot know that it is only one man against him, nor that it is an old man. Oh, I must remember to eat the tuna in order to keep strong. I must remember," he said to himself. No one should be alone in their old age, he thought. But it is unavoidable.

[4] It was very cold now in the time before daylight and the old man pushed against the wood to be warm. "Fish", he said softly, aloud, "I'll stay with you until I am dead." He'll stay with me too, I suppose, the old man thought, and he waited for it to be light.

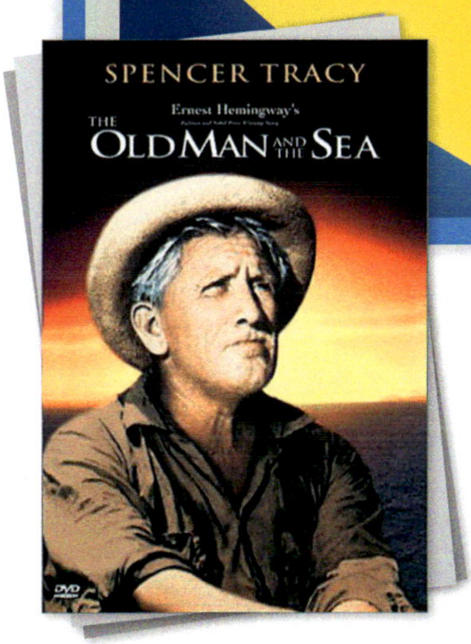

Extracted from HEMINGWAY, Ernest. *The Old Man and the Sea*. New York: Charles Scribner's Sons, 1952.

Vocabulary

aged: idoso
cramp: câimbra
further: mais longe
glow: brilho
hook: fisgar
sail: navegar
search: procurar
tuna: atum
unavoidable: inevitável

After Reading

A **Read the first paragraph of the text and do the exercises.**

1 Hemingway usa algum recurso para separar os pensamentos de Santiago das demais frases do texto? ______________________

2 Transcreva a frase que descreve como Santiago se sente.

____

3 In the sentence "I wish I could see him once to know what I have against me." the word "him" refers to:

a ☐ the old man.

b ☐ the fish.

We can infer that Santiago:

a ☐ had already seen the fish.

b ☐ had not seen the fish yet.

B **Read the second paragraph.**

1 Find the name of:

a a direction ______________________

b the English word for "força" ______________________

2 Answer the questions.

2.1 Como Santiago sabia sua localização aproximada?

____

2.2 The strength of the fish could be felt:

a ☐ through the tension in the line.

b ☐ because they were moving slowly.

C Read the third paragraph.

1 Write T (true) or F (false).

a ☐ Santiago's wish was to have the boy there.

b ☐ Santiago imagined the fish was wonderful.

c ☐ He knew how old the fish was.

2 Answer the questions in Portuguese.

2.1 What was Santiago probably feeling when he thought "no one should be alone in their old age [...]"?

____

2.2 Por que, provavelmente, ele disse a si mesmo: "Oh, I must remember to eat the tuna [...]"?

____

____

D Read the fourth paragraph.

Transcreva a frase que mostra a determinação do velho para pegar o peixe.

____

Vocabulary Expansion

A Read the box. Then supply the adequate prepositions.

behind: atrás
down: para baixo, movimento descendente
out: fora
through: através
until: até
with: com

1 He waited ______________ daylight to see the fish.

2 He wanted the boy to be ______________ him.

3 Santiago could feel the strength of the fish ______________ the line.

4 Havana was somewhere ______________ him.

5 One day, he decided to sail far ______________ to sea.

6 When the sun went ______________, the glow of Havana was visible.

7 The subway runs ______________ a tunnel.

8 The famous actor is expected to be in Brazil ______________ the end of the month.

9 My father is ______________ right now. Can I take a message?

B Write out the meanings of the phrasal verbs formed with *to go.*

approach | pursue | proceed | leave | pass | examine

1 "Time **goes by** so slowly," says a famous old song. ____________________

2 I'll **go over** the books to determine our real situation. ____________________

3 I don't know how to **go about** this problem. ____________________

4 They have decided to **go ahead** with the plan. ____________________

5 Don't give up. You must **go after** your goals! ____________________

6 Can we **go away** to the beach next weekend? ____________________

C Complete the sentences. Use the words and phrases in the boxes.

sick | unhappy | isn't working | to a lower level | take them off and put them on a surface

1 If you are **feeling down**, you are ____________________.

2 If the computer **is down**, it ____________________.

3 If you **are down** with the flu, you are ____________________.

4 If you **put down** your glasses, you ____________________.

5 If you are **going down** a hill, you go ____________________.

D Read the box and complete the chart. Then, fill in the blanks with words from the chart.

Verb	Adjective	Translation
to avoid	avoid**able**	evitável
to admire	admir**able**	admirável
to love	____________	____________
to accept	____________	____________
to reason	____________	____________
to eat	____________	____________

Suffix able
Acrescentado a verbos, forma adjetivos.

1 He made ____________ efforts to achieve his goals.

2 The teacher did not ____________ her answer.

3 His courage is ____________.

4 If you don't like potatoes, don't ____________ them.

5 Little Emily is a ____________ girl.

LANGUAGE IN USE

A Read the news article. Then match the columns.

www.news.com.au

Chemicals Stolen from Redeemer Lutheran College Rochedale Lab

September 20, 2009 08:22 a.m.

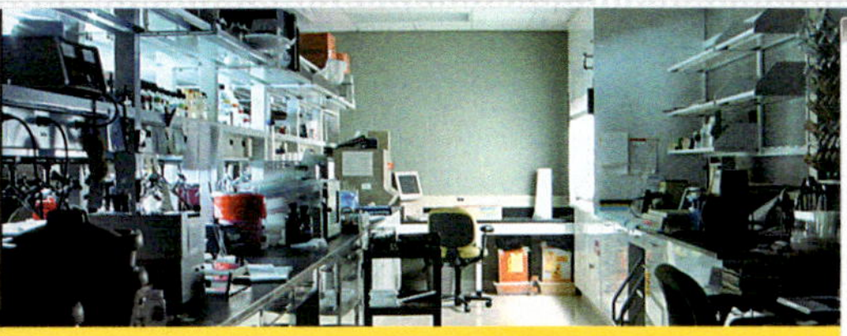

A school employee who disturbed two men who broke into a classroom science lab in Brisbane was hit with a screwdriver before the intruders fled with chemicals and equipment.

The employee received minor injuries when he was struck by one of the thieves during last night's break and enter, police said.

At around 10:45 a.m. (AEST) an alarm alerted the school employee to a possible break-in at Redeemer Lutheran College in the suburb of Rochedale.

When the 53-year-old male employee arrived at the science laboratory he was struck on the head with the handle of a screwdriver, police said.

Two men ran off along Rochedale Road with an unknown amount of lab equipment and chemicals.

The employee was taken to the QEII Hospital, where he was treated for a minor laceration to his forehead.

The two intruders are described as being Caucasian and around 183 cm tall.

One of the men had a slim build and brown hair and was wearing a baseball cap.

The second man had a solid build and brown hair.

Police have appealed for anyone with information to contact Crime Stoppers at 1-800-333-000.

Extracted from <www.news.com.au>. Accessed on January 7, 2011.

1	What is the race of the intruders?	a	☐	They ran off.
2	How old is the school employee?	b	☐	It is in Brisbane.
3	Where is Redeemer Lutheran College?	c	☐	They are Caucasian.
4	Where was the employee hit?	d	☐	He is fifty-three.
5	How did the intruders escape?	e	☐	He was hit on the forehead.

B NOW IT'S YOUR TURN!

Ask more questions about the news article to a classmate. Use the glossary for help.

WRITING

You are the school employee. Write in your notebook your statement for the police.

24 The Millennium Development Goals

Language in Context

A **Luís Carlos Rodrigues is going to study abroad. Listen to the dialogue, and answer the questions in Portuguese.** 48

1. Where is Luís Carlos?

____

2. How long is he going to stay?

____

3. Where is he going to live?

____

B **Give your opinion.**

1. Did Luís Carlos enter the country?
2. Why did the official ask if Luís Carlos had left his luggage unattended?

C **Think about it. Compare the sentences and do the exercises.**

a I want **to study** here.

b Do you **intend to work**?

c Did you **leave** your luggage unattended after **landing**?

1. Relacione cada palavra em destaque à sua possível denominação.

   infinitivo **com to** ______________

   infinitivo **sem to** ______________

   gerúndio ______________

2. Sublinhe as palavras que podem ter "atraído" o infinitivo ou o gerúndio.

Interviewer: Mr. Rodrigues? Why are you coming to this country?
Mr. Rodrigues: I want to study here.
Interviewer: Do you intend to work, too?
Mr. Rodrigues: No. I want to study and surf.
Interviewer: Where are you going to stay?
Mr. Rodrigues: At the university dormitory.
Interviewer: How long do you want to stay?
Mr. Rodrigues: Four years.
Interviewer: Did you bring enough money?
Mr. Rodrigues: Yes, I did.
Interviewer: Did you leave your luggage unattended after landing?
Mr. Rodrigues: No, sir. I've kept my luggage near me all the time.
Interviewer: Did anybody give you anything to carry after landing?
Mr. Rodrigues: No, sir.
Interviewer: Welcome, Mr. Rodrigues. Here is your passport. Enjoy your stay.

Vocabulary

landing: aterrissagem
unnatended: desacompanhado(a), largado(a)

Language Practice

Infinitive: to go, to talk, to eat
(to) + verb

O infinitivo é uma forma do verbo e pode aparecer com ou sem **to.**

Uso

Usa-se o infinitivo com **to** na maioria dos casos.

She wants **to leave.**
We decided not **to go.**
He was the first **to arrive.**
You are too young **to drive.**
What a nice thing **to say!**
It's time **to leave.**
I am pleased **to meet** you.
It took us one hour **to get** there.

Usa-se o infinitivo sem **to:**

- após os verbos modais (**can, may,** etc.), os verbos auxiliares (**do** e **will**) e os verbos **make** e **let;**
  Do you **like** tea?
  She **can dance.**
  Let me **go.**
  He **made** me **cry.**
- após **but** e **except.**
  We did nothing **but cry.**
  You should do nothing **except wait.**

Nota

- **To help** pode ser seguido de infinitivo **com** ou **sem to:**
  Help me ***push /*** ***to push*** *the car.*

A Answer the questions. Use *not* and the expressions in parentheses.

Example: What did he decide?

(go to the beach) He decided not to go to the beach.

1 What did she promise?

(arrive late) ______________________________

2 What do they expect?

(fail the examination) ______________________________

3 Why did they hurry?

(miss the train) ______________________________

Go to page 334 for Extra Practice.

B Underline the adequate infinitive form.

1 Does he (to like – like) to paint in the morning?

2 Can I (offer – to offer) you something to drink?

3 He made me (to laugh – laugh) at the party.

4 Grandma was the first woman (to drive – drive) a bus in her town.

5 It is bad luck (break – to break) a mirror.

6 Let's (to talk – talk) to Mr. Johnson.

7 They decided not (to arrive – arrive) early.

8 Last Sunday we did nothing but (work – to work).

9 She's too young (to drive – drive).

10 It's time (go – to go) back home.

C Match the parts to form complete sentences.

1	There's nothing they can do except...	a	[ ]	hope for the best.
2	What time do you...	b	[ ]	the control of the car.
3	We must...	c	[ ]	leave for school?
4	It's very difficult to...	d	[ ]	answer this question.
5	The kids made me lose...	e	[ ]	arrive at 6:00 tomorrow.

Gerund: going, talking, eating
Verb + ing

O gerúndio é uma forma verbal caracterizada pela terminação **ing** e que pode funcionar como **substantivo**.

Uso

Pode ser usado:

- como sujeito;
  Painting is a good hobby.
- como objeto;
  I enjoy **dancing**.
- após preposição;
  He is tired **of working**.
- após os verbos **come** e **go** (indicando atividade física);
  I **went skiing**.
- após expressões como *can't help* e *no use*;
  I **can't help looking** at him.
  It's **no use going** there in the morning.
- após verbos como *avoid*, *appreciate*, *consider*, *enjoy*, *finish*, *mind*, etc.
  I **avoid sleeping** late.
  They **enjoy eating** pizza.

can't help: não conseguir evitar
it's no use: não adianta

D **Supply the gerund form of the verbs in parentheses.**

1 I don't mind __________ (wait) a little longer.

2 She dedicates her time to __________ (dance).

3 Go home when you finish __________ (write) the letter.

4 __________ (fly) makes me nervous.

5 __________ (hunt) crocodiles is dangerous.

6 I can't help __________ (feel) worried about you.

7 We will appreciate __________ (hear) from you.

8 The baby enjoys __________ (listen) to your voice.

9 I couldn't avoid __________ (buy) these shoes.

10 She loves __________ (run) in the park.

Infinitive and Gerund: I like to study / I like studying

Alguns verbos podem ser seguidos por gerúndio ou infinitivo sem **to**: *feel*, *hear*, *notice*, *see*, *observe* e *watch*.

I **heard** him **crying/cry**.

I **saw** it **falling/fall**.

Outros podem ser seguidos por gerúndio ou infinitivo com **to**:

advise, *allow*, *attempt*, *begin*, *continue*, *dislike*, *forget*, *hate*, *intend*, *like*, *love*, *neglect*, *permit*, *prefer*, *remember*, *start*, *stop* e *try*.

He **likes studying/to study**.

He **started eating/to eat**.

Nota

- Alguns verbos mudam de significado:

  *He **stopped talking**. (parou de falar)*

  *He stopped **to talk**. (parou para conversar)*

E Underline the appropriate form.

1 Don't keep on (shout – shouting). The baby is sleeping.

2 We intend (to go – go) out after dinner.

3 I asked the boys to stop (talk – talking).

4 I can't think of (to buy – buying) a new car before (sell – selling) the old one.

5 I can't imagine Grandpa (to go – going) to work by bike.

6 He saw the little girl (crossing – to cross) the street.

7 The man asked me how (get – to get) to the airport.

8 Carol loves (working – work) in Hawaii.

F Supply the correct form of the verbs in parentheses.

1 I like ______________________ (swim) in the lake.

2 ______________________ (read) is her favorite pastime.

3 Are you thinking of ______________________ (go) out now?

4 The teacher allowed (us) ______________________ (leave) earlier.

5 I hate ______________________ (take) this medicine.

6 We went ______________________ (fish) last vacations.

7 Before ______________________ (go) to bed she turned off the lights.

8 In the end we decided ______________________ (stay).

READING

Before Reading

Approaching the text

Discuss the questions below in Portuguese.

1 Do you know what the United Nations is?

2 What is the Brazilian level of participation in UN efforts?

3 Is there a UN organization that cares for children?

Vocabulary

Match the synonyms.

1	eradicate	a ☐	establish
2	disease	b ☐	obtain
3	draw up	c ☐	stop
4	gender	d ☐	sex
5	halt	e ☐	eliminate
6	achieve	f ☐	illness
7	ratio	g ☐	fifty percent
8	half	h ☐	proportion

Group task

Look at the pictures. Label them. Use the expressions in the boxes.

Global Partnership | Maternal Health | Universal Education | Combat HIV/AIDS

End Poverty and Hunger | Gender Equality | Environmental Sustainability | Child Health

The Millennium Development Goals

The United Nations Millennium Declaration was adopted by UN member states in September 2000. This declaration contains eight Millennium Development Goals, ranging from eradicating extreme poverty to combating HIV/AIDS and other diseases.

The Millennium Development Goals (MDGs) were introduced as part of an attempt to encourage the international community to stop talking about making a difference in the developing world and join forces to start doing something about it.

A series of targets were drawn up to make it easier for the international community to measure their progress over time and to give them a number of improvements to be reached within a fixed period of time.

The intention is that most of these targets will be achieved by 2015.

The Eight Millennium Development Goals

1. **Eradicate extreme poverty and hunger.** Reduce by half the proportion of people living on less than a dollar a day. Reduce by half the proportion of people who suffer from hunger.
2. **Achieve universal primary education.** Ensure that all boys and girls complete a full course of primary schooling.
3. **Promote gender equality and empower women.** Eliminate gender disparity in primary and secondary education, preferably by 2005, and at all levels by 2015.
4. **Reduce child mortality.** Reduce by two thirds the mortality rate among children under five.
5. **Improve maternal health.** Reduce by three quarters the maternal mortality ratio.
6. **Combat HIV/AIDS, malaria, and other diseases.** Halt and begin to reverse the spread of HIV/AIDS. Halt and begin to reverse the incidence of malaria and other major diseases.
7. **Ensure environmental sustainability.** Reverse loss of environmental resources. Reduce by half the proportion of people without sustainable access to safe drinking water. Achieve significant improvement in the lives of at least 100 million slum dwellers by 2020.
8. **Develop a global partnership for development.** In cooperation with the developing countries, develop decent and productive work for youth. In cooperation with pharmaceutical companies, provide access to affordable essential drugs in developing countries. In cooperation with the private sector, make available the benefits of new technologies – especially information and communications technologies.

Based on the Millennium Development Goals. <www.un.org>. Accessed on January 6, 2011.

Vocabulary

development: desenvolvimento
draw up: delinear
goal: meta
improvement: melhoria
join: unir
measure: medir
poverty: pobreza
ranging: abrangendo
target: objetivo
within: dentro de

After Reading

A Complete the information.

1 MDG stands for ______________________.

2 Ao ler o 1º parágrafo, podemos inferir que as 8 metas para o desenvolvimento do milênio adotadas pelos países-membros das Nações Unidas (United Nations):

a ☐ estão dirigidas para a área da saúde.

b ☐ estão focadas na extrema pobreza.

c ☐ abrangem uma vasta área de necessidades humanas.

3 The 2nd paragraph talks about the importance of creating:

a ☐ a global alliance for development.

b ☐ an international community.

c ☐ a developing world.

B Transcreva do texto.

1 A frase que indica quando se espera que a maioria dos objetivos sejam alcançados:

____

2 A frase que indica que é preciso disponibilizar o benefício das novas tecnologias, em cooperação com o setor privado:

____

3 A frase que indica que é preciso eliminar a diferença entre os sexos na educação:

____

C Answer the questions.

What is the reduction intended...

1 in the first Millennium Development Goal?

____

2 in the fourth Millennium Development Goal?

____

3 in the fifth Millennium Development Goal?

____

4 in the seventh Millennium Development Goal?

____

Vocabulary Expansion

A **Read the box. Match the expressions to their meanings.**

> **To make**
> É usado no sentido de "criar", "construir", "produzir".
> *Mom is **making** dinner early today.*

1	to make the bed	a ( )	cometer um erro, engano
2	to make a decision	b ( )	fazer uma experiência
3	to make an experiment	c ( )	fazer chá, café, almoço
4	to make fun (of)	d ( )	arrumar a cama
5	to make love (to)	e ( )	tomar uma decisão
6	to make a mess	f ( )	fazer amor
7	to make a mistake	g ( )	caçoar de alguém
8	to make tea, coffee, lunch	h ( )	fazer bagunça
9	to make a speech	i ( )	fazer uma reserva
10	to make a journey	j ( )	fazer um discurso
11	to make a reservation	k ( )	fazer uma viagem

B **Read the box. Match the expressions to their meanings.**

> **To do**
> É usado em ações mais abstratas, com o sentido de "realizar".
> *I **did** everything I could to help her.*

1	to do the best	a ( )	lavar a louça
2	to do the duty	b ( )	fazer a tarefa de casa
3	to do the cleaning	c ( )	arrumar a casa
4	to do the dishes	d ( )	fazer a obrigação
5	to do the cooking	e ( )	ir bem nos estudos
6	to do the housework	f ( )	fazer o melhor possível
7	to do the homework	g ( )	fazer a limpeza
8	to do well at school	h ( )	fazer a comida
9	to do the shopping	i ( )	fazer um bom trabalho
10	to do an exercise	j ( )	fazer compras
11	to do a good job	k ( )	fazer um exercício

C Complete the sentences. Use *do* or *make*.

1 She is in trouble. She can't ______________ anything right.

2 I always ______________ my best to organize everything here.

3 Hey, young lady! Don't leave without ______________ your bed.

4 Don't worry, from now on I will ______________ all my duties.

5 Last weekend he made lunch and I ______________ the dishes.

6 The teacher told us not to ______________ the experiment at home.

7 I don't know why they keep ______________ fun of the others.

8 Children, don't ______________ a mess around the house.
______________ your homework instead!

D Fill in the blanks with words from exercise "Vocabulary" on page 323.

1 All countries should ______________ polio and other diseases.

2 A: What is the ______________ of women in this factory?

B: It is only 10%.

3 Congressmen ______________ the laws of the country.

4 We have to ______________ gender/sex disparity. Men and women are equal.

5 We must ______________ the spread of hunger.

6 You have to study hard to ______________ good grades at university.

7 Alzheimer is a ______________ described only recently.

8 Women are more than ______________ of the world.

Language in Use

A **Read the film review. Then answer the questions.**

www.film.com

HOME | MOVIES | TV | DVDs | CELEBRITIES | PHOTOS

Home > Movies

Fame (2009, Remake)

Rate this Movie | User Average

Watch Video

Details

Studio: Metro-Goldwyn-Mayer Studios Inc. (MGM)

Release date: Sep 25, 2009

Country of origin: United States

Starring: Paul Iacono, Naturi Naughton, Kay Panabaker, Kherington Payne, Collins Pennie, Walter Perez, Anne Marie Perez de Tagle, Johanna Braddy, Megan Mullally

Director: Kevin Tancharoen

Synopsis

A talented group of dancers, singers, actors, and artists attending New York City High School of Performing Arts are given a chance to live out their dreams and achieve real and lasting fame... the kind that comes only from talent, dedication, and hard work.

As each student strives for his or her moment in the spotlight, they'll discover who among them has the innate talent and necessary discipline to succeed. With the love and support of their friends and fellow artists, they'll find out who amongst them will achieve Fame.

Extracted from <www.film.com>.
Accessed on January 4, 2011.

1 Who is Kevin Tancharoen?

2 Is the film about famous people?

3 What is a synopsis?

B NOW IT'S YOUR TURN!

Ask more questions about the film review to a classmate. Use the glossary for help.

WRITING

Choose a review of a film that you liked. Give the details and write a synopsis.

EXTRA PRACTICE 12

A Rewrite the sentences using reported speech.

1 Tess said, "My teacher will go to China tomorrow."

Tess said that ______________________________.

2 I said to the officer, "I was reading a book in my room yesterday."

I told the officer (that) ______________________________.

3 She said, "My friend flew to Paris last night."

She said that ______________________________.

4 He said to me, "We didn't see you at school two days ago."

He told me that ______________________________.

5 Leo said, "She has already been there."

Leo said that ______________________________.

6 I said to them, "I often read this book."

I told them that ______________________________.

7 She said to me, "You should sign this letter."

She told me that ______________________________.

8 He said, "I'm working now."

He said that ______________________________.

9 Linda said, "Bob was ill."

Linda said that ______________________________.

10 We said to Karen, "We have cleaned your room."

We told Karen (that) ______________________________.

B Choose the best alternative to complete each sentence.

1 He asked ________.

a ☐ where is the bus stop

b ☐ where the bus stop was

c ☐ where stops the bus

2 He asked ________.

a ☐ that we liked the movie

b ☐ that we to like the movie

c ☐ if we had liked the movie

3 She said ________.

a ☐ that she was tired

b ☐ that she tired

c ☐ she to be tired

4 He said ________.

a ☐ the plane will been on time

b ☐ the plane to be on time

c ☐ the plane would be on time

5 He said ________.

a ☐ he had gone downtown the day before

b ☐ he went downtown yesterday

c ☐ he goes downtown the day before

6 Mom told me ________.

a ☐ clean the kitchen

b ☐ not clean the kitchen

c ☐ to clean the kitchen

7 She asked me ________.

a ☐ to do my homework

b ☐ did my homework

c ☐ had done my homework

8 She said ________.

a ☐ she visited her relatives in the afternoon

b ☐ she had visited her relatives two days before

c ☐ she visits her relatives one hour before

C Write sentences. Follow the examples.

Examples: She / arrive early (advice) — She'd better arrive early.
They / go on foot (preference) — They'd rather go on foot.

1 I / go by plane (preference)

2 You / work tomorrow morning (advice)

3 She / take a taxi (advice)

4 We / walk in the park (preference)

5 He / wake up early (preference)

D Que conselhos você daria a alguém que...

1 feels sick? (see a doctor)

2 feels stressed? (go for a walk)

3 is hungry? (eat something)

4 feels sad? (talk to a friend)

5 feels happy? (sing)

E Answer the questions.

1 How long does it take you to go from home to school?

2 How long did it take you to shower yesterday?

3 How long will it take you to finish high school?

F Rewrite the sentences according to the information in parentheses.

1 It took me an hour to do my homework.

(present) ______

2 It will take them 10 months to build a new house.

(past) ______

3 It took us three years to write a book.

(future) ______

4 It will take her 20 minutes to make a cake.

(present) ______

G Answer the questions. Use one of the forms below.

Example: Why does she want the money? (buy a car)

She wants the money to buy a car.

She wants the money in order to buy a car.

1 Why is he working hard? (get a promotion)

______

2 Why are you saving money? (buy a new house)

______

3 Why does she study in the evening? (work in the afternoon)

______

H Combine the sentences. Use *and*.

Example: He decided to go. He decided to study.

He decided to go and to study.

1 She could come. She could see her new room.

______

2 I stopped to talk. I stopped to laugh.

______

3 We like to run. We like to swim.

______

I Supply the adequate infinitive form of the verbs in parentheses.

1 It's difficult ________________ (learn) Greek.

2 Jennifer may ________________ (visit) us next month.

3 He'll do anything except ________________ (wash) the dog.

4 Can you ________________ (teach) me how ________________ (play) baseball?

5 I was the last one ________________ (arrive) yesterday.

6 He will ________________ (tell) us where ________________ (go) after the show.

7 I want ________________ (talk) to you before the end of the week.

8 They helped me ________________ (do) my homework.

9 Are you planning ________________ (go) to the party?

10 We are planning ________________ (see) a movie.

11 They hope ________________ (go) to a restaurant for dinner.

12 She expects ________________ (pass) the test tomorrow.

13 There is nothing you can ________________ (do) but ________________ (hope) for the best.

14 He was the first ________________ (answer) the question.

15 You should ________________ (go) to the dentist before lunch.

J Supply the gerund form of the verbs in parentheses.

1 My brother's passion is ________________ (swim).

2 She couldn't stand ________________ (look) at those bright lights.

3 Go home when you finish ________________ (do) homework.

4 They stopped ________________ (to talk) at 10 p.m.

5 He's bored with ________________ (to live) here.

6 ________________ (to paint) is a terrific pastime.

7 I really enjoy ________________ (to meet) people.

8 ________________ (to work) hard is something we all have to do.

9 My father is interested in ________________ (to learn) another language.

10 We both stopped ________________ (to smoke) about 5 years ago.

11 I am considering ________________ (travel) by plane.

12 She is good at ________________ (surf).

JOB CORNER 12

Professions in the Media

If you decide to work in the media, you can choose among many courses of study: social communications, news coverage, investigative journalism, news editing, cinema and video, photography, multimedia, editorial production, radio and TV, public relations, and many others.

You can also work as a press assistant, to make the link between a company and the media. This is the area that offers the most job opportunities, since companies are always looking for more visibility for their names and their products. A press assistant can also prepare publications for employees, customers, and suppliers.

If you work as an editor, you can define focus and length of the news, and you can write or approve the final text. In the printed media and on the internet, you choose the photos and illustrations that will accompany a text. On the radio and TV, you choose soundtracks and images that will be presented in news shows.

As a reporter, you can collect information and write texts to be presented on radio, television, and internet – or published in newspapers and magazines.

professional guide 20

Based on
GUIA DO ESTUDANTE. São Paulo: Abril, 2008;
<www.guiadasprofissoes.com.br>;
<www.vestibular.brasilescola.com>;
<http://guiadoestudante.abril.com.br>;
<www.portaldeensino.com.br>.
Accessed on December 20, 2010.

Vocabulary

coverage: cobertura
customer: cliente
focus: foco, enfoque
length: comprimento
link: ligação
look for: procurar
media: mídia
news: notícia
news show: noticiário
press: imprensa
printed: impresso
supplier: fornecedor(a)

READING

Before Reading

Discuss the questions below.

1 What are rainforests?

2 Are they respected and preserved?

Rainforests are the Earth's oldest living ecosystems

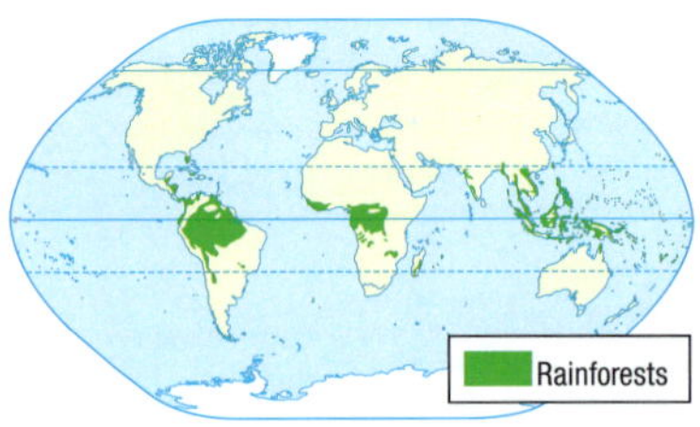

Source: IBGE – Instituto Brasileiro de Geografia e Estatística, 2006.

A rainforest can be described as a tall, dense jungle that gets a high amount of rainfall per year. Rainforests cover only 6% of the Earth's surface but yet they **contain MORE THAN ½ of the world's plant and animal species!** They are all part of a complex system, each depending on the others to survive. The destruction of one can result in the extinction of the other.

Animals of the rainforest occupy specific micro-environments:

Emergent layer

The tallest trees (45-55 m tall) are the emergents. Sunlight is plentiful up here. Animals found are eagles, monkeys, bats and butterflies.

Canopy layer

The canopy layer contains the majority of the largest trees (30-45 m tall). Many animals – snakes, toucans and tree frogs – live in this area since food is abundant.

Understory layer

Only about 5% of the sunlight reaches this area so the plants have to grow larger leaves to reach the sunlight. Many animals live here including birds, snakes, lizards as well as jaguars, and leopards.

Forest floor

The forest floor receives only 2% of sunlight. Almost no plants grow in this area, as a result giant anteaters and tapirs live in this layer.

About *2,000 trees per minute* are cut down in the rainforests.

Based on <www.srl.caltech.edu>. Accessed on January 3, 2011.

Vocabulary

anteater: tamanduá
bat: morcego
bird: pássaro
butterfly: borboleta
canopy: cobertura
eagle: águia
environment: meio ambiente
grow: crescer
jaguar: jaguar
jungle: floresta; selva
layer: camada
leopard: leopardo
living: vivo
lizard: lagarto
monkey: macaco
snake: cobra
surface: superfície
tapir: anta
toucan: tucano
tree frog: perereca

After Reading

A Check the correct alternatives.

Rainforests...

1 ☐ cover less than 10% of the Earth's surface.

2 ☐ contain more than 50% of the world's plant and animal species.

3 ☐ are dense jungles.

4 ☐ have tall trees only.

5 ☐ have just large animals.

6 ☐ house specific micro-environments.

B Choose the correct alternative.

1 The tallest trees...

a ☐ are in the understory layer.

b ☐ are in the emergent layer.

2 The canopy layer...

a ☐ houses bats and monkeys.

b ☐ contains most of the largest trees.

3 Almost no plants...

a ☐ grow on the forest floor.

b ☐ grow where sunlight is plentiful.

4 Jaguars don't live...

a ☐ in the highest layers.

b ☐ in the understory layers.

C Answer the questions.

1 Why are rainforests called so?

____

2 Why do many animals live in the canopy layer?

____

3 Why do almost no plants grow on the forest floor?

____

D Give the meaning of the underlined words in the sentences below.

1 Sunlight is <u>plentiful</u> up here. ______________

2 About 2,000 trees per minute are <u>cut down</u> in the rainforests. ______________

READING

Before Reading

Discuss the questions below.

1 Do you practice any sports or physical exercises?

2 Do you stretch when you feel tired or tense?

STRETCHING

Stretching is an important part of any workout routine. It helps increase your flexibility and reduces your chances of injury.

Do the following exercises when you are tired or before you start your routine.

1. **Neck** Turn your head to the right, then to the left. Do this 12 times. Tilt your head backwards, then bend it forward. Do this 12 times.
2. **Arms** Extend your arms in front of you. Swing them upward over your shoulders and rotate them towards the back, returning to the original position (12 times). Do the same in the reverse direction (12 times).
3. **Upper Body** Twist only your upper body to the left, then to the right (12 times).
4. **Hips** With your hands on your hips, rotate your hips 12 times to the right, then 12 times to the left.
5. **Body** Raise your arms over your head. Bend your body forward. Simultaneously, bend your knees slightly, and touch the floor with your fingers. Do this 12 times.
6. **Feet** Rotate your right foot clockwise (12 times) and then, counter-clockwise (12 times). Do the same with the left foot.

Based on <http://exercise.about.com>. Accessed on January 5, 2011.

Vocabulary

bend: curvar(-se) **stretching:** alongamento **tilt:** inclinar(-se)
slightly: levemente **swing:** girar **twist:** torcer; girar

After Reading

A Check the meaning of the words in bold.

1 "Twist only your **upper** body to the left [...]"

a ☐ parte superior   b ☐ parte inferior   c ☐ parte do meio

2 "**Simultaneously**, bend your knees slightly [...]"

a ☐ after   b ☐ before   c ☐ at the same time

3 "Rotate your right foot **clockwise** [...]"

a ☐ em semicírculo   b ☐ na hora certa   c ☐ no sentido horário

B Check the correct alternative.

1 Clockwise is a movement...

a ☐ to the right.

b ☐ to the left.

2 Counter-clockwise is a movement...

a ☐ to the right.

b ☐ to the left.

3 Os exercícios apresentados devem ser feitos...

a ☐ quando não se está cansado.

b ☐ após exercícios físicos.

c ☐ após as refeições.

d ☐ antes de iniciar as tarefas do dia.

4 A sequência apresenta exercícios para as seguintes partes:

a ☐ corpo   f ☐ parte superior do corpo

b ☐ pernas   g ☐ quadris

c ☐ pescoço   h ☐ cintura

d ☐ braços   i ☐ dedos

e ☐ pés

5 Deve-se fazer cada sequência de exercícios...

a ☐ três vezes.

b ☐ seis vezes.

c ☐ doze vezes.

READING

Before Reading

Discuss the questions below.

1 Do people usually help people they don't know?

2 Have you ever helped a person you didn't know?

AN ACT OF KINDNESS

She was just 14 and she was very angry.

She had many dreams. She wanted to know the world.

So, she decided to run away from Cleveland and took a bus to New York.

It was winter time. It was very cold in NY. A man noticed that 14-year-old girl wandering in the cold streets. After hearing her story, he took the teenager to the bus station and bought her a ticket back home.

He gave her 20 dollars and wrote his address on a small piece of paper. He then told her, "Whatever you desire, you can make it happen."

The girl went back home.

Time went by; the girl went to high school, to college, then to medical school and became a surgeon. She got married and had two children. She always thought about the man, but she couldn't find the small piece of paper with his address.

One day, when her daughter was 14, they decided to clean the attic. An old box attracted their attention. Inside it, among old school things, they found the small piece of paper.

The surgeon located her benefactor and sent him a letter with 500 dollars. "Your kindness has no price," she wrote. "I just hope that you come meet my family. Clara."

Ralph Burke accepted the invitation and was welcomed as a long-lost uncle.

Based on <www.lifeway.com>. Accessed on September 29, 2009.

Vocabulary

angry: zangado(a)
attic: sótão
benefactor: benfeitor(a)
kindness: bondade
run away: fugir
wander: perambular
whatever: o que quer que seja

After Reading

A **Find in the text words and expressions with the following meanings.**

1 o tempo passou: ______________________

2 casou-se: ______________________

3 um tio perdido há muito tempo: ______________________

B **The text states that...**

1 [ ] the girl lived in New York.

2 [ ] Ralph Burke helped the girl on a cold night.

3 [ ] her benefactor was a surgeon.

4 [ ] the girl became a surgeon.

5 [ ] the surgeon had a daughter.

C **Express your opinion in Portuguese.**

What did the man mean with the proverb "Whatever you desire, you can make it happen"?

____

____

____

D **Read the information in the box. Then, write new words and translate them.**

1	kind	kindness	bondade
2	white	________	________
3	sad	________	________
4	glad	________	________
5	empty	________	________

Suffix ness

O sufixo **ness** forma substantivos e indica qualidade, estado ou condição.

E **Complete the sentences. Use words ending in *ness*.**

1 ______________ is the quality of being polite.

2 ______________ is the quality of being good.

3 ______________ is the state of being nervous.

4 ______________ is the state of being happy.

Reading

Before Reading

A Discuss the questions below.

1 What do you know about human trafficking?

2 Who are the greatest victims?

B Look for the following words in the glossary.

1 support ______________________

2 majority ______________________

3 slavery ______________________

SLAVES FROM BRAZIL

Brazil is responsible for 15 percent of women trafficked in South America. Most of them are from the North and the Northeast.

Although slavery officially ended in Brazil at the end of the 19th century, it is still in practice into the 21st century in Brazil and in other parts of the world. One modern form of slavery is "human trafficking". There are more than 4 million victims of this type of slavery all over the world. Most of these victims are women and children.

Brazil is considered to be one of the main sources of human trafficking domestically and internationally. The majority of the women who are exported to other countries are lured in by false promises. Most of the women are young – between 12 and 18 years old – and have little schooling. Many are trying to support a child, and have suffered some sort of sexual violence.

Read the testimony of L.A.S., a young woman ensnared in the traps of human trafficking:

"At age 14, my father kicked me out of the house because of a boy I was dating. One day, a taxi driver talked to me and invited me to go to Europe. He said that I was pretty, and I could work as a model. I traveled on August 18, 2002, to Spain. I was 17 at that time. Three other girls went with me.

When we arrived at the place, we saw that it was in fact a house of prostitution. At the house, we were slaves.

I fled when I met a Brazilian customer to whom I told my story. I escaped, but even today I think of my friends there who are being held prisoners, like animals in a zoo."

Based on <www.brazzil.com>. Accessed on January 2, 2011.

Vocabulary

ensnare: ser pego(a) em uma armadilha
flee: escapar
lured in: atraído(a)
promise: promessa
schooling: escolaridade
slave: escravo(a)
source: fonte
trap: armadilha

After Reading

A Find a synonym for the words in bold.

1 "The majority of the women who are exported to other countries are **lured in** by false promises."

a ☐ convinced

b ☐ saved

c ☐ attracted

2 "Read the testimony of L.A.S., a young woman **ensnared** in the traps of human trafficking."

a ☐ learned

b ☐ captured

c ☐ taught

3 "Most of the women are young – between 12 and 18 years old – and have little **schooling**."

a ☐ education

b ☐ teachers

c ☐ choice

B Check the statements and rewrite the incorrect ones.

		correct	incorrect
1	The majority of the women are not young. ____		
2	There are victims of slavery in Brazil only. ____		
3	Some of the women are supported by their children. ____		
4	Most women are attracted by false promises. ____		

C Answer the questions.

1 Why are women one of the greatest victims of human trafficking?

____

2 Why do they believe in promises?

____

READING

Before Reading

Discuss the questions below.

1 What does "social inclusion" mean?

2 Can arts and sports promote social inclusion? Why/Why not?

Brazil: Awakening the Dreams of Young Slum Dwellers

By Mario Osava

RECIFE, Brazil, Aug 18 (IPS) – Left blind in one eye by a bullet wound, 18-year-old Rosinaldo Inaldo admits that he used to be violent, but says he now dreams of becoming a singer of traditional songs from northeastern Brazil like the *axé* and *frevo*.

He attributes the change to the Art and Life Association, which he says, "made me a better person and improved my life."

Thanks to his five years of involvement in the programme, he now enjoys going to school, where he is trying to complete his primary education, while dreaming about making money as a singer, actor, or computer operator, "to help my family and to help out other people as well," he tells IPS.

[...]

In a three-story building in the city's historic centre, the youngsters take drumming, music, dance, art, and literature classes.

[...]

Art as a tool for transformation was the method chosen by the firm, following the example of a number of Brazilian programmes in which art and sports have been successfully used to promote social inclusion and prevent juvenile delinquency among young slum dwellers.

[...]

Danuzia Pereira, 18, was until recently a participant in the programme and now works as an assistant to the teachers who provide tutoring.

The children's academic performance improves after they join Art and Life because the project "awakens their interest and enthusiasm for learning," says Pereira.

[...]

Source: IPS Inter PressService. Extracted from <www.ipsterraviva.net>. Accessed on January 9, 2011.

Vocabulary

awaken: despertar
blind: cego(a)
bullet: bala
dweller: morador(a)
improve: melhorar
make money: ganhar dinheiro
slum: favela
tool: ferramenta
wound: ferimento

After Reading

A According to the text, Rosinaldo Inaldo...

1 a ☐ was born blind due to a bullet wound.
  b ☐ was left blind in one eye by a bullet wound.

2 a ☐ is completing his primary education.
  b ☐ is an assistant to teachers at Art and Life Association.

3 a ☐ wants to help other people nowadays.
  b ☐ is a violent person because of a bullet wound.

B According to the text, the Art and Life Association...

1 a ☐ is an Arts school.
  b ☐ is in Recife's historic center.

2 a ☐ is trying to transform youngsters through arts and sports.
  b ☐ is trying to buy a three-story building in the city's historic center.

3 a ☐ supports juvenile delinquency through its programes.
  b ☐ prevents juvenile delinquency among slum dwellers.

C Write T (true) or F (false).

1 ☐ Rosinaldo Inaldo attributes the change in his life to the Art and Life Association.

2 ☐ Participants can't work as assistants to the teachers.

3 ☐ The youngsters take drumming, music, dance, art, and literature classes.

D Check the appropriate meaning of the sentences.

1 The children's academic performance improves after they join Art and Life.
  a ☐ The children do better in their studies after they join the association.
  b ☐ The children want to take tests as they enter the association.

2 The project awakens their interest and enthusiasm for learning.
  a ☐ The people in the association don't care about the student's enthusiasm.
  b ☐ The project promotes positive transformations in the youngsters.

READING

Before Reading

Discuss the questions below.

1 Do you use batteries? Where?

2 Are they expensive or cheap?

www.instructables.com

Battery life

> Identification

An alkaline battery is defined by the chemical reaction that serves as its power source, namely the reaction between manganese dioxide and zinc. The battery derives its name from the alkaline electrolyte involved in the reaction, in contrast to the acidic electrolyte used in previous battery designs.

> Increasing alkaline battery storage life

If you want to increase the storage life of alkaline batteries, you should store them in a cool, dry, and non-corrosive place, like in a closet or other places like that.

Storing alkaline batteries in a cool place will slow down chemical reaction activity, thus increasing alkaline battery life.

Storing alkaline batteries in a warm or hot place will dramatically decrease alkaline battery life because chemical reaction activity speeds up. However, there is an advantage of having fast chemical reaction activity in alkaline batteries: it gives much better performance in electronic devices like digital cameras.

You should never try to recharge normal alkaline batteries. They will heat up so dramatically that they can melt the charger and catch on fire.

You can only recharge rechargeable alkaline batteries.

Extracted from <www.instructables.com>. Accessed on January 13, 2011.

Vocabulary

closet: guarda-roupa, armário
heat up: aquecer-se
increase: aumentar
melt: derreter
powder: pó
power: força
recharge: recarregar
slow down: diminuir a velocidade
source: fonte
storage: armazenamento
store: armazenar
thus: assim

www.ehow.com

> The Chemistry

In this battery design, the anode (negative) is made of a zinc powder, which offers a greater surface area and thus increases the flow of electrons. The cathode (positive) is composed of manganese dioxide. Electricity is generated by the chemical reaction between the two substances.

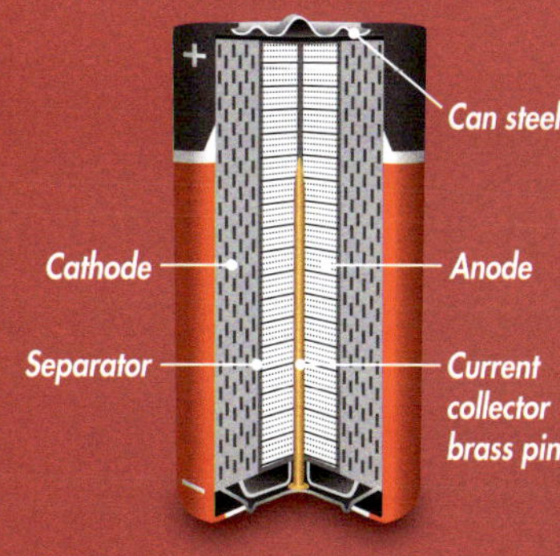

Extracted from <www.ehow.com>. Accessed on January 13, 2011.

After Reading

A Match according to the text.

1 a cool place
2 a hot place
3 normal alkaline batteries
4 rechargeable alkaline batteries
5 the name of the battery

a [ ] cannot be recharged
b [ ] slows down reaction activity of the chemicals
c [ ] speeds up reaction activity of the chemicals
d [ ] comes from a substance used in the reaction
e [ ] can be recharged

B Find the opposites in the text.

1 increase ______________________
2 slow down ______________________
3 warm ______________________
4 smaller ______________________

C Answer the questions.

1 What happens if you try to recharge a normal alkaline battery?

____

____

2 How do alkaline batteries generate electricity?

____

____

READING

Before Reading

Discuss the questions below.

1 What is the smallest thing your eyes can see?

2 How small a sculpture do you believe a person can create?

Nanotechnology

MICRO BULL

Though it may not be as dangerous as the Running of the Bulls in Spain, scientists in Japan have fashioned their own, tiny version of the huge beast.

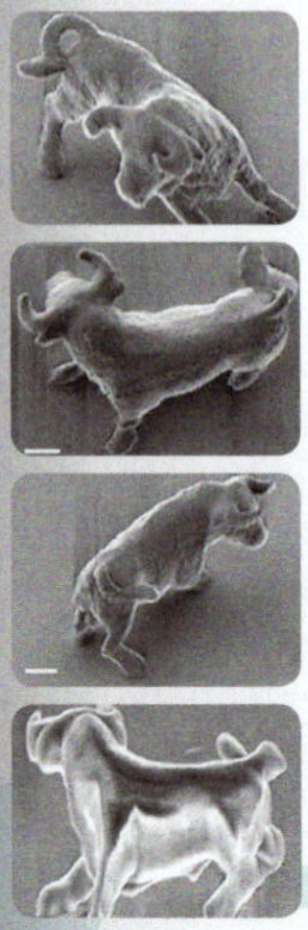

The smallest sculpture ever created looks like an angry fighting bull turning to charge at some unknown threat.

This tiny figurine is no larger than a red blood cell. The "micro bull" measures ten micrometers long by seven micrometers high. It was constructed from plastic resin by two infra-red laser beams tracing its outlines, solidifying the resin only at the focus point of the lasers. A computer controlled the lasers to create the shape with pinpoint accuracy.

Professor Satoshi Kawata, who led the team at Osaka University, said "You only get polymerization at the position of interest. The result is that you can fabricate real 3D structures rather than two dimensional layer patterns, as in traditional lithography. One possible application of the technology could be in the construction of tiny machines to deliver drugs inside the body. It could be used to make micro machines small enough to run inside blood vessels."

Extracted from <www.nanopicoftheday.org>. Accessed on August 10, 2009.

SATOSHI KAWATA

[...] Satoshi Kawata was born in 1951 in Osaka, Japan. He received his BSc, Msc, and PhD all in Applied Physics in 1974, '76, and '79, respectively, from Osaka University. After the experience of postdoctoral fellow of JSPS, he spent two years in University of California, at Irvine, as a Research Associate. He joined Osaka University as a faculty member in 1981 and was promoted to a full Professor of Applied Physics in 1993. [...]

BSc – Bacharel em Ciências
MSc – Mestre em Ciências
PhD – Doutor (título acadêmico)
JSPS – Japan Society for Promotion of Science (Sociedade Japonesa para a Promoção da Ciência)

Extracted from <www.skawata.com>. Accessed on August 10, 2009.

Vocabulary

accuracy: precisão
charge: atacar
ever: jamais
faculty: corpo docente
fashion: amoldar
look like: parecer
measure: medida
outline: contorno
though: embora
threat: ameaça
tiny: minúsculo(a)
vessel: vaso (sanguíneo)

After Reading

A Match the columns according to Professor Kawata's biography.

1 1974 a ☐ He started working at Osaka University.

2 1951 b ☐ He received his doctoral degree at Osaka University.

3 1981 c ☐ He graduated from Osaka University and received his BSc degree.

4 1976 d ☐ Satoshi Kawata was born in Osaka, Japan.

5 1993 e ☐ He received his Master's degree.

6 1979 f ☐ He was promoted and became a full professor at Osaka University.

B Choose the correct alternative according to the text.

1 The micro bull was created in ________.

a ☐ Spain

b ☐ Japan

c ☐ the University of California

2 The sculpture created by Professor Kawata and his team is ________.

a ☐ tiny

b ☐ dangerous

c ☐ huge

C Find words in the text that correspond to the ones below.

1 resemble ______________________

2 get ______________________

3 enormous ______________________

4 attack ______________________

D Answer the questions.

1 What is the size of the micro bull?

____

2 What is the micro bull made of?

____

3 Where can the technology of the micro bull be used?

____

READING

Before Reading

Discuss the questions below.

1 Is it possible to make music without musical instruments or the human voice?

2 How would you define a musical instrument?

STOMP

Members of Stomp Perform at the Food Bank

By Stephen Hunt, *Calgary Herald*

Take a mixing bowl. A box of Grape Nuts. A shopping cart. An empty water jug. A biscuit tin, two coffee cups, one bell, one stool, one cake tray, a mixing bowl, a green plastic garbage bin, a milk crate and a Calgary Food Bank donation bucket, add a few members of the cast of Stomp and what have you got?

A lunch-hour concert like no other.

Those were the instruments played Tuesday at the Calgary Inter-Faith Food Bank's 11th Street warehouse, where a few members of the cast of Stomp dropped by to perform an impromptu concert on a bunch of stuff they found lying around in the break room.

The result was a brief, brilliant glimpse into the world of Stomp, where everyday objects become musical instruments.

[...]

What Is Stomp?

[...]

Stomp is performed in theaters, but it is not a play, musical, or opera. It is not theater in the traditional sense of the word. There is no speech, dialogue, or plot. However, it does have two characteristics of traditional theater: mime and characterization. Each performer has an individual character which is distinct from the others. These characters are brought out through the mime and dance in the show.

[...]

"People drum their fingers on table tops when they are waiting for something to happen. They tap their feet when they are bored. They walk in rhythm quite naturally when they walk down the street... and jangle keys in their pockets... Yes, everything has a rhythm to it. Everything has music to it."

Luke Cresswell and Steve McNicholas – creators of Stomp.

Extracted from <www.stomponline.com>. Accessed on January 20, 2011.

Vocabulary

bowl: tigela
brief: breve, curto
cast: elenco
crate: engradado (de garrafas)
garbage bin: lata de lixo
jangle: chacoalhar
jug: jarra
plot: trama
stool: banquinho
tin: lata
tray: bandeja

After Reading

A Check the correct alternative.

1 The piece of text is...

a ☐ a letter. b ☐ a newspaper article. c ☐ an advertisement.

2 A shopping cart, an empty water jug, a biscuit tin, two coffee cups, one bell, one stool, one cake tray, a mixing bowl, a green plastic garbage bin, a milk crate, and a Calgary Food Bank donation bucket are...

a ☐ considered musical instruments by the members of Stomp.

b ☐ not part of a Stomp show.

c ☐ everyday objects but not musical instruments.

3 Stephen Hunt is...

a ☐ a member of the cast of Stomp.

b ☐ the author of the first piece of text.

c ☐ one of the creators of Stomp.

B Match the corresponding words.

1	many things	a	☐	tap
2	interval	b	☐	impromptu
3	strike gently	c	☐	break
4	by means of	d	☐	a bunch of stuff
5	improvised	e	☐	through

C Find the words in the text that match these definitions.

1 a person portrayed in a theater play, a movie, or a novel ______________

2 the articulation of words ______________

3 a quick and brief view ______________

D Answer the questions.

1 Where did the Stomp performance take place?

____

2 According to the text, when do people make music?

____

READING

Before Reading

Discuss the questions below.

1 Do you know anyone who is a drug addict?

2 What are the signs of drug addiction?

SIGNS OF DRUG ADDICTION

It is important to stress the fact that drug addicts regularly try to deny their drug-related problems while they hide the symptoms of their addiction. There are, however, many well-known and predictable "warning" signs of drug addiction that strongly suggest drug dependency. The following list represents some of the more common and recognizable warning signs of drug addiction:

- The inability to limit one's drug use over time or during any given situation.
- Talking incoherently or making inappropriate remarks.
- Inappropriately and frequently wearing long sleeve shirts and/or sunglasses.
- Engaging in secretive or suspicious behaviors, such as making numerous trips to the restroom, basement, garage, or other isolated areas where drug usage can take place.
- Withdrawal symptoms that take place when an individual suddenly quits taking drugs. Such symptoms include "the shakes", sweating, headaches, and nausea.
- Noticeable degradation regarding one's grooming and physical appearance.
- Sudden increase in school absences or work problems, while grades or quality of work diminish.

[...]

Extracted from <www.drug-addiction-facts.com>. Accessed on January 8, 2011.

Vocabulary

behavior: comportamento
deny: negar
hide: esconder
quit: parar
remark: comentário
the shakes: tremores
warning: alerta
withdrawal: abstinência

After Reading

A Complete the sentences with the verbs given. Put the verbs in the correct tense.

limit | deny | shake | stress | hide

1 It is good to ______________________ that you are not ill.

2 This is evident. Don't ______________________ it.

3 The boy is ______________________ the ball from his brother.

4 Only ignorance ______________________ my understanding.

5 A high fever makes her ______________________.

B Write T (true) or F (false) according to the text.

1 ☐ There are no signs of drug addiction.

2 ☐ When a person stops using drugs, withdrawal signs will appear.

3 ☐ Drug addicts take good care of their appearance.

4 ☐ Restrooms, basements, and garages are the only places where people take drugs.

5 ☐ Drug addiction leads to better grades at school.

6 ☐ Talking incoherently is a sign of drug addiction.

7 ☐ Drug addicts never make inappropriate remarks.

8 ☐ Sweating, headaches, and nausea are drug addiction signs.

C Match the synonyms.

1	limit	a ☐	visible
2	inappropriate	b ☐	usual
3	quit	c ☐	improper
4	take place	d ☐	comment
5	noticeable	e ☐	restrict
6	remark	f ☐	stop
7	diminish	g ☐	occur
8	common	h ☐	decrease
9	predictable	i ☐	renowned
10	well-known	j ☐	unsurprising

Reading

Before Reading

Discuss the questions below.

1 Are there gangs in your school or neighborhood?

2 What makes a teenager join a gang?

www.gangsorus.com

The Business of Gangs, Gang Members, and Gang Identification

STUDENTS
Do you want information and help to stay away from gangs?
Join our website – Students Against Gangs

[...]

On this site you will find many pages and over 1200 external gang videos and text links about street gangs and prison gangs. The site is designed to teach you about clothing, colors, graffiti, marks, and tattoos. Investigations, prosecutions, rivalries, and alliances.

[...]

Where Do We Find Gangs?

Odds are that you have street gangs in your community. Gangs are no longer confined to the large urban communities. They are now found in many of the smallest towns across America and are no longer limited to low income, poorly educated, drop-outs from society. Gang members are now found to be a mixture of ALL races, cultures, and ethnicities. No longer do the members come from a family of one parent who is never available to show love and guidance to the child. Our youth of today are sometimes joining gangs even though they live with both parents who are in the middle income or even the upper income segments of society.

[...]

It is easy to understand why any community, large or small, might deny the existence of gangs within the community – no community wants the stigma of having gangs. However, by denying the existence of gang activity, the community is doing the gangs a favor – they are allowing the gangs to develop, grow stronger in numbers, and develop a power base.

A New Hotline to Gang News

As we have indicated, gangs are everywhere. To give you a better perspective of the gang problem, Gangs OR Us has created a Hotline to Gang News blog that contains news articles from around the country. The blog also offers videos about gangs in the streets and the prisons.

[...]

Extracted from <www.gangsorus.com>. Accessed on January 18, 2011.

Vocabulary

drop-out: aluno que abandona os estudos
income: renda
join: entrar, juntar(-se)
odds are: é provável
parent: pai ou mãe
rivalry: rivalidade

After Reading

A Match the columns. Use the glossary to help you.

1	stay away	a ( )	alta renda
2	design	b ( )	juventude
3	clothing	c ( )	roupas; vestuário
4	prosecution	d ( )	ficar longe
5	no longer	e ( )	não mais
6	available	f ( )	permitir
7	youth	g ( )	negar
8	upper income	h ( )	disponível
9	deny	i ( )	acusação; instauração de processo
10	allow	j ( )	projetar

B Answer the questions according to the text.

1 Who is the site www.gangsorus.com directed to?

____

2 What types of gangs are mentioned?

____

3 Do gang members come only from low income families?

____

4 Why do communities deny the existence of gangs?

____

5 What does *Gangs OR Us* offer to young people?

____

6 Are gang members limited by race or culture?

____

7 What are some elements that identify gangs?

____

8 What kind of internet site is *Gangs OR Us*?

____

READING

Before Reading

Discuss the questions below.

1 What is music piracy?

2 Who is harmed by music piracy?

How to Fight Music Industry Piracy

Fighting music industry piracy is the goal of many different groups of people who are affected by music and the musical arts. For example, music industry piracy fighters could include music industry professionals, record labels, major label artists, and even independent bands and artists. Read on to learn how to fight music industry piracy.

Step 1

The first step in fighting and stopping music industry piracy is to start at home with your family and friends. You should refrain from downloading free music and free ringtones unless the artist is giving the track away for free, and you should encourage your family and friends to do the same.

Step 2

Next, you should research and raise awareness concerning music piracy. While some music listeners believe only major labels are harmed by music piracy, independent bands and independent artists can be harmed by MP3 pirating as well – in the form of diminished CD sales on the road.

Step 3

Finally, contact your lawmakers to enforce stricter piracy limitations. The choice of whether to give music away for free is the choice of an artist. And while free music may be the business model of the future, music fans still need to abide by the laws and wait for their favorite artists to give their music away for free and find new music business models to profit from.

Extracted from <www.ehow.com>.
Accessed on January 16, 2011.

Vocabulary

abide by: cumprir
choice: escolha
fight: combater
free: grátis
harm: prejudicar
lawmaker: legislador
piracy: pirataria
record labels: gravadoras
refrain from: abster-se de
research: pesquisar

After Reading

A Complete the sentences with the words and expressions given. Make changes, if necessary.

goal | step | give away | wait for | awareness | profit | listener | strict

1 The author is ______________ his books ______________ for free.

2 They are very ______________ with the students in this school.

3 Why are you doing that? What is your ______________?

4 Sylvia is a good ______________. She has a lot of patience.

5 Go slowly — one ______________ at a time.

6 There is a good ______________ in selling high-quality products.

7 People's ______________ of the dangers of smoking tobacco is increasing.

8 They are ______________ your letter, but you did not write to them.

B Answer the questions according to the text.

1 Who fights against music industry piracy?

____

2 Is it easy for you to download music and ringtones?

____

3 Where should you start to fight against music piracy?

____

4 When can you download free music?

____

5 What is the method of raising awareness mentioned in the text?

____

6 Who is harmed by music piracy?

____

7 What can lawmakers do?

____

8 What do music fans have to do?

____

READING

Before Reading

Discuss the questions below.

1 Have you ever gone to a music festival?

2 Is it comfortable to be in a crowded audience?

WOODSTOCK

The 1960s were a time of revolution. Young people were breaking out of the molds that were cast by their parents' era. This revolution of the anti-war protests and the Baby Boomer generation found that one effective outlet for their ideas was music. The Woodstock Music and Art Fair in 1969 drew more than 450,000 people to a pasture in Sullivan County.

The music began on Friday August 15 at 5:07 p.m., and continued until mid-morning Monday, August 18. The weekend was rainy, the facilities were overcrowded, and attendees shared food, alcoholic beverages, and drugs. However, no violence was reported. The festival closed the New York State Thruway and created one of the nation's worst traffic jams. It also inspired a slew of local and state laws to ensure that nothing like it would ever happen again!

The Days of Peace and Music

Friday – The performers were Richie Havens, Joan Baez, Arlo Guthrie, Melanie, Tim Harden, Ravi Shankar, John Sebastian, Country Joe McDonald, Sweetwater, The Incredible String Band & Bert Sommer.

Saturday – The performers were Santana, Canned Heat, Mountain, Janis Joplin, Sly & The Family Stone, The Grateful Dead, Creedence Clearwater Revival, The Who, Quill and Keef Hartley.

Sunday – The performers were Jefferson Airplane, Joe Cocker, Country Joe & The Fish, Ten Years After, The Band, Johnny Winter, Blood, Sweat & Tears and Cosby, Stills, Nash & Young. *(Performing after Midnight or on Monday morning were the Paul Butterfield Blues Band, Sha-Na-Na and Jimi Hendrix.)*

Memorabilia for Sale

Woodstock 1969 Single Day Ticket – Woodstock tickets were originally meant to be sold for the festival, but once the event was declared a "free" concert, all sales stopped. This $8 ticket for Saturday August 16th is in excellent condition. $199.95 – SOLD

Original Woodstock '69 Program

RARE and hard To Find
"3 days of peace & music" – Original concert program from the Woodstock Aquarian Exposition in Bethel, NY, August 15th-17th of 1969. Because of the rain and mud so few survived. This is in excellent condition. Great memorabilia of Woodstock '69 and a special time in history.
$499.95 – SOLD

Extracted from <www.irocknroll.com>. Accessed on January 18, 2011.

Vocabulary

cast: estabelecer
draw: atrair
facilities: instalações
overcrowded: superlotado
share: compartilhar
slew: muitos
thruway: estrada, rodovia
traffic jam: engarrafamento

After Reading

A Answer the questions according to the text.

1 How many days did the Woodstock Festival last?

2 What was the weather like?

3 When did Janis Joplin sing?

4 Was it a violent festival?

5 How many people went to Woodstock?

6 Where were the concerts?

7 Why were most of the festival programs destroyed?

8 How much was the ticket for one day at the festival?

9 Were all the tickets sold? Why? / Why not?

10 How much was the program sold for on the internet?

B Give the correct meaning of the words in bold.

1 They found an effective **outlet** for their ideas.

a ☐ loja de desconto b ☐ terceiro c ☐ saída

2 **Attendees** shared food, alcoholic beverages and drugs.

a ☐ participantes b ☐ desocupados c ☐ atendentes

3 Few survived because of the rain and **mud**.

a ☐ muda b ☐ trovoada c ☐ lama

READING

Before Reading

Discuss the questions below.

1 What can you say about Barack Obama?

2 Do you think his attitudes have an impact on Latin America? Why? / Why not?

http://edition.cnn.com

The 44th president **Inauguration** January 20, 2009 -- Updated 1728 GMT (0128 HKT)

Obama's Inaugural Speech

(CNN) – Barack Obama was sworn in as the 44th president of the United States and the nation's first African-American president. This is a transcript of his prepared speech.

In his speech, President Obama said America must play its role in ushering in a new era of peace.

My fellow citizens:

I stand here today humbled by the task before us, grateful for the trust you have bestowed, mindful of the sacrifices borne by our ancestors. I thank President Bush for his service to our nation, as well as the generosity and cooperation he has shown throughout this transition.

Forty-four Americans have now taken the presidential oath. The words have been spoken during rising tides of prosperity and the still waters of peace. Yet, every so often, the oath is taken amidst gathering clouds and raging storms. At these moments, America has carried on not simply because of the skill or vision of those in high office, but because We the People have remained faithful to the ideals of our forbearers, and true to our founding documents.

So it has been. So it must be with this generation of Americans.

[...]

Today I say to you that the challenges we face are real. They are serious and they are many. They will not be met easily or in a short span of time. But know this, America: They will be met.

On this day, we gather because we have chosen hope over fear, unity of purpose over conflict and discord.

On this day, we come to proclaim an end to the petty grievances and false promises, the recriminations and worn-out dogmas, that for far too long have strangled our politics.

We remain a young nation, but in the words of Scripture, the time has come to set aside childish things. The time has come to reaffirm our enduring spirit; to choose our better history; to carry forward that precious gift, that noble idea, passed on from generation to generation: the God-given promise that all are equal, all are free, and all deserve a chance to pursue their full measure of happiness.

[...]

Extracted from <http://edition.cnn.com>. Accessed on January 17, 2011.

Vocabulary

faithful: fiel
gathering clouds: nuvens acumuladas
humbled: com humildade
inaugural speech: discurso de posse
mindful: consciente
over: em vez de
raging storms: tempestades violentas
rising tide: maré alta
span of time: período
worn-out: desgastado

After Reading

A Find in the text the English translations for the expressions below.

1 confiança depositada ____________________

2 prestaram juramento ____________________

3 de vez em quando ____________________

4 alto escalão ____________________

5 queixas insignificantes ____________________

6 pôr de lado ____________________

7 levar adiante ____________________

8 todos são iguais ____________________

B Write T (true) or F (false).

1 ☐ Mr. Obama is grateful because his task is easy.

2 ☐ There are true challenges before the American people.

3 ☐ Mr. Obama is the 44th president of the United States.

4 ☐ The problems of America will be solved quickly.

5 ☐ Americans must stop fighting because of unimportant things.

6 ☐ They must abandon old dogmas.

7 ☐ Americans believe that they have to change their history.

8 ☐ Their ancestors experienced only times of peace and prosperity.

9 ☐ President Bush did not help in the transition.

10 ☐ Americans chose hope over fear.

C Answer the questions according to the text.

1 Why does Barack Obama thank President Bush?

____

2 How many presidents took the presidential oath before Barack Obama?

____

3 How does Obama describe the challenges they face?

____

12th-grader: aluno do 3º ano do Ensino Médio
24/7: 24 horas por dia, 7 dias por semana

A

a bit: um pouco
a few: alguns, algumas
a little: um pouco
a lot (of): muito(a), muitos(as)
abide by: cumprir; acatar
ability: capacidade, habilidade
able: hábil, capaz
aboard: a bordo
about: sobre, a respeito de
above: acima
abroad: fora do país, no exterior
absence: ausência, falta
abuse: abuso
abusive: abusivo(a)
accept: aceitar
acceptable: aceitável
access: acesso
accommodations: acomodação
accompany: acompanhar
accomplish: realizar
according to: de acordo com
accordingly: de acordo, dessa maneira; portanto
accountant: contador(a)
accuracy: precisão
accuse: acusar
achieve: alcançar, atingir; realizar
acidic: acidífero
acquire: adquirir
across: através
act: agir; ato; atuar
action: ação
active: ativo(a)
activity: atividade
actor: ator
actress: atriz
actually: de fato, realmente, na verdade
acute: preciso(a), exato(a)
ad: anúncio, propaganda
adapt: adaptar(-se)
add: acrescentar, adicionar
addict: viciado(a)
addiction: vício
addressee: destinatário(a)
adjust: adaptar-se
adjustment: ajuste
admirable: admirável
admire: admirar
adopt: adotar
adoption: adoção
adult: adulto(a)
advantage: vantagem
advertise: anunciar, promover
advertisement: anúncio, propaganda
advertising: publicidade
advice: conselho
advise: aconselhar
Aesop: Esopo
affordable: acessível (que pode ser comprado)
afraid: ter medo; temeroso(a)
after: após, depois
after all: afinal
afterwards: depois, mais tarde
again: de novo, novamente
against: contra
age: idade; relativo a idade, era, época, século
aged: idoso(a)
agility: agilidade
aging: envelhecimento
ago: atrás (tempo)
agree: concordar
agreement: acordo, contrato
ahead: antes; adiante
ahead of time: com antecedência
air-conditioning: ar-condicionado
aircraft: aeronave, avião
alert: alerta
alike: parecido(a), da mesma forma
alive: vivo(a)
alkaline: alcalina
all: tudo; todo(s), toda(s)
all over: por todo(a), por toda parte
all the time: o tempo todo
alliance: aliança
alligator: jacaré
allow: permitir
ally: aliado(a)
almost: quase
alone: sozinho(a)
along: ao longo de
aloud: em voz alta
already: já
also: também
alternating current (AC): corrente alternada
alternative: alternativa
although: embora
always: sempre
amidst: em meio a
among/amongst: entre, dentre (mais de duas coisas ou pessoas)
amount: quantia, quantidade
anabolic steroid: anabolizante
ancient: antigo(a)
angry: bravo(a), com raiva
annual: anual
anode: ânodo
another: outro(a)
answer: atender (ao telefone, à porta); resposta; responder
anteater: tamanduá
anticipated: antecipado(a)
antonym: antônimo
anxiety: ansiedade
any: algum(a); qualquer; nenhum(a)
anyhow: de qualquer modo
anything: nada
anything else: qualquer outra coisa
appeal: apelar, recorrer

appearance: aparência
apple: maçã
application: aplicação
applied physics: física aplicada
apply: aplicar
appointment: compromisso
approach: abordar; aproximar
appropriate: apropriado(a)
approximately: aproximadamente
apricot: damasco
aquatic: aquático(a)
archery: arte de usar arco e flecha
architect: arquiteto(a)
argument: argumento; discussão
arm: braço
around: à volta de, em volta de, ao redor; por volta de
arrange: arrumar, organizar; combinar de fazer algo
array: agrupamento; conjunto
arrest: prender
arrive: chegar
article: artigo
artisan: artesão(ã)
as: à medida que; quando; tão... quanto; uma vez que; como
as a matter of fact: de fato, efetivamente
as long as: desde que
as well as: bem como, também
aside: de lado
ask: pedir; perguntar
aspect: aspecto
assault: ataque
assistant: assistente
asthma: asma
at any rate: de qualquer modo
at last: finalmente
at least: pelo menos
athlete: atleta
athletic: atlético(a)
athletics: atletismo
atom: átomo
attack: atacar; ataque
attempt: tentar; tentativa
attend: frequentar; comparecer; cursar
attendance: frequência
attended by: com a presença de
attendees: participantes
attention: atenção
attention deficit: déficit de atenção
attentively: atentamente
attic: sótão
attract: atrair
attraction: atração
attractive: atraente; interessante
audience: público (em um espetáculo)
aunt: tia
author: autor(a)
authorship: autoria
available: disponível
avenue: avenida
average: médio(a)
avoid: evitar
avoidable: evitável
awake(n): despertar, acordar
awareness: consciência
away: longe; de distância

Aircraft

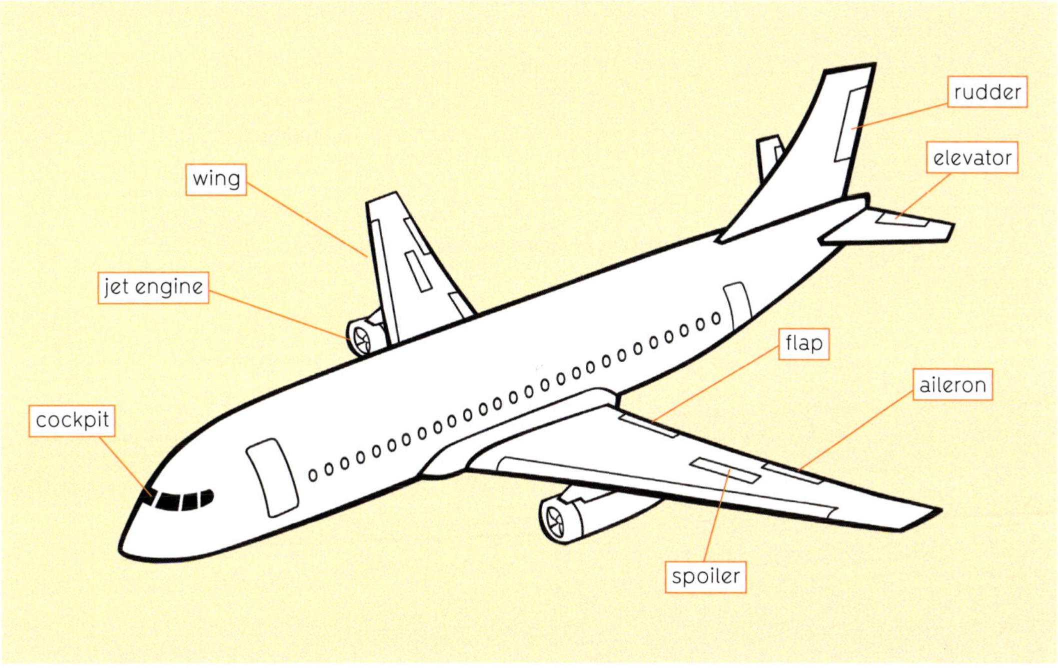

B

back: de volta

background: formação; experiência; origem

bacterial: bacteriano(a)

bad: mau, má; ruim

bad luck: má sorte, azar

bag: bolsa; saco; sacola

balance: equilíbrio

ban: proibir; banir

banana: banana

band: grupo musical, banda

bank: banco; margem de rio

banker: banqueiro(a)

barber: barbeiro

barber shop: barbearia

bare: descoberto

barely: mal

barrel: tonel

based: com base

basement: porão

basic: básico(a)

basketball: basquetebol

bass: baixo (instrumento musical)

bat: morcego

bathroom: banheiro

baton: cassetete

Basketball

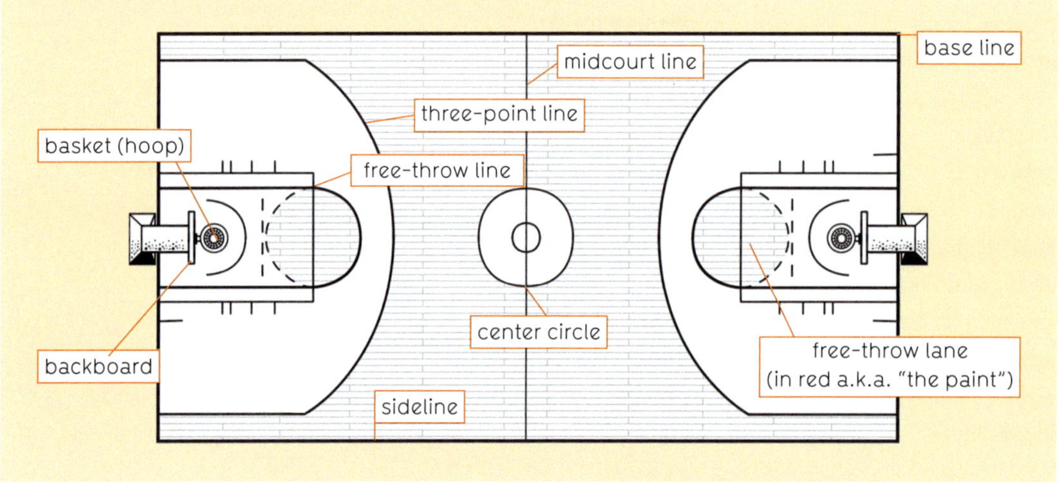

Bathroom

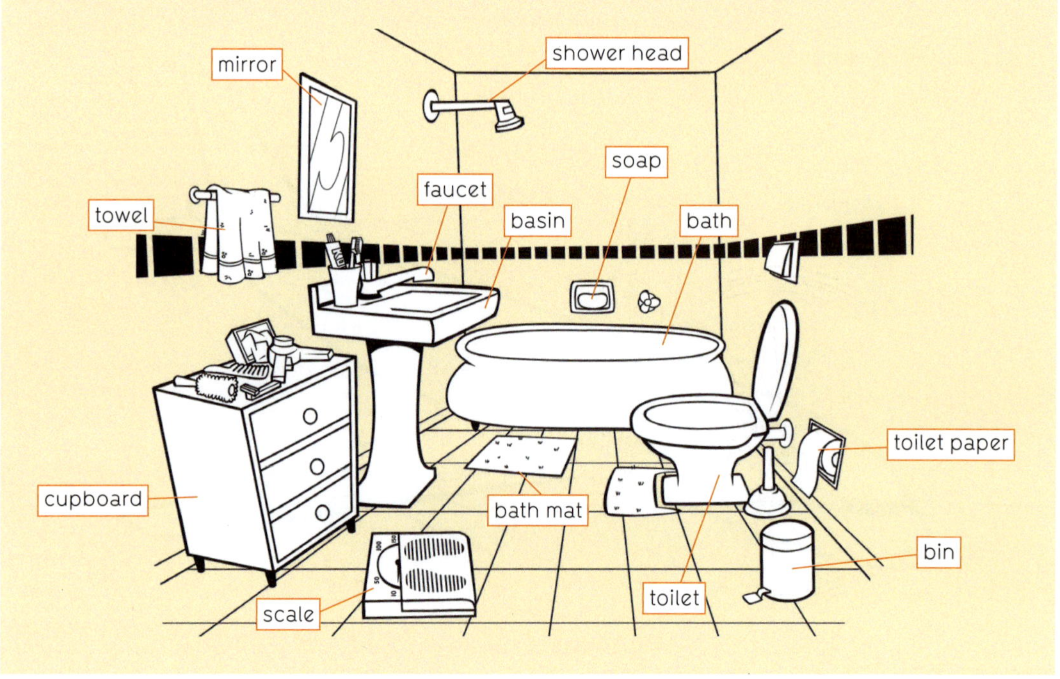

batter: bater; empanar
battery: bateria; pilha
be: ser; estar
be able: conseguir; ser capaz
be aware: saber, estar ciente
be born: nascer
Be careful!: Cuidado!
be down: não estar funcionando
be down with: estar doente
be light: amanhecer
beach: praia
beam: feixe de raio
bean: feijão
beast: besta, fera
beat: bater
beat drums: batucar, tocar tambores
beautiful: bonito(a)
beauty: beleza
because: porque, por causa de
become: tornar-se
beer: cerveja
beet: beterraba
before: antes
beg: implorar
begin: começar, iniciar
behavior: comportamento
behind: atrás
being: ser
believe: acreditar, crer
bell: sino
belong: pertencer
beloved: amado(a)
below: abaixo
bend: curvar
benefactor: benfeitor(a)
benefit: benefício
best: o(a) melhor
bestow: depositar; conceder
better: melhor
between: entre
beverage: bebida
bewildered: perplexo(a)
beyond: além de, do outro lado
bicycle: bicicleta
big: grande
biography: biografia
biological: biológico(a)
bird: pássaro
birth: nascimento
birthday: aniversário
biscuit: biscoito
blame: culpar, colocar a culpa em
blank: espaço em branco
bleeding: sangramento
blind: cego(a)
bliss: alegria
bloat: inchar
block: quarteirão, quadra
blood: sangue; sanguíneo
blow out: estouro de pneu
boat: barco
bodily: corporal
body: corpo
bold: negrito
bondage: cativeiro
bone: osso
book: livro; agendar
bookstore: livraria
boost: aumentar
bored: aborrecido(a); entediado(a)
boring: entediante, chato(a)
born: nascido(a)
borne: suportado; sustentado
boss: chefe
botanist: botânico(a)
both: ambos(as), os dois, as duas
both... and: tanto... quanto

Bicycle

bottom: fundo, parte de baixo
bowel: intestino
bowl: tigela
box: caixa
boy: menino
brain: cérebro
Brazilian: brasileiro(a)
break: quebrar; infringir
break and enter: arrombamento com invasão
break in: invasão
break into: arrombar, invadir
break out: irromper; libertar-se
break room: sala do intervalo
breastfeed: amamentar
brief: breve, curto
brilliant: brilhante
bring: trazer
bring out: mostrar; expressar
bring up: educar
British: britânico(a)
broccoli: brócolis
broke: sem dinheiro
broken: quebrado(a)
brother: irmão
brow: sobrancelha
brown: marrom; castanho
brush: escovar
BSc: Bacharel em Ciências
bucket: balde
build: compleição física; construir
building: construção; prédio
bull: touro
bullet: bala
bulletin: boletim
bunch: monte; maço
bundle: empacotar; unir
burdened: sobrecarregado(a)
buried: enterrado(a)
burn: queimar
burning ache: queimação
bus: ônibus
bus stop: ponto de ônibus
business: negócios
business person: pessoa de negócios
busy: ocupado(a)
but: mas, porém; exceto
butterfly: borboleta
buy: comprar
by: até; de; por
by boat: de barco
by bus: de ônibus
by car: de carro
by plane: de avião

C

cabbage: repolho
cafeteria: lanchonete; cantina (de escola)
cake: bolo
calcium: cálcio
calculate: calcular
calendar: calendário; programação

Buildings

1 airport
2 gas station
3 hospital
4 mosque
5 restaurant
6 art gallery
7 fire station
8 hotel
9 museum
10 school
11 bank
12 cinema
13 church
14 police station
15 synagogue
16 bus station
17 railway station
18 theater

call: chamar; telefonar
call someone names: xingar alguém
calm: calmo(a)
camera: máquina fotográfica
campaign: campanha
camping: acampamento; ato de acampar
can: poder; conseguir
can't help: não conseguir evitar
Canadian: canadense
candle: vela
candy: doce
canoe: canoa
canoeing: canoagem
canopy: cobertura, toldo
cap: boné
capable: capaz
capital letter: letra maiúscula

Cafeteria

Camera

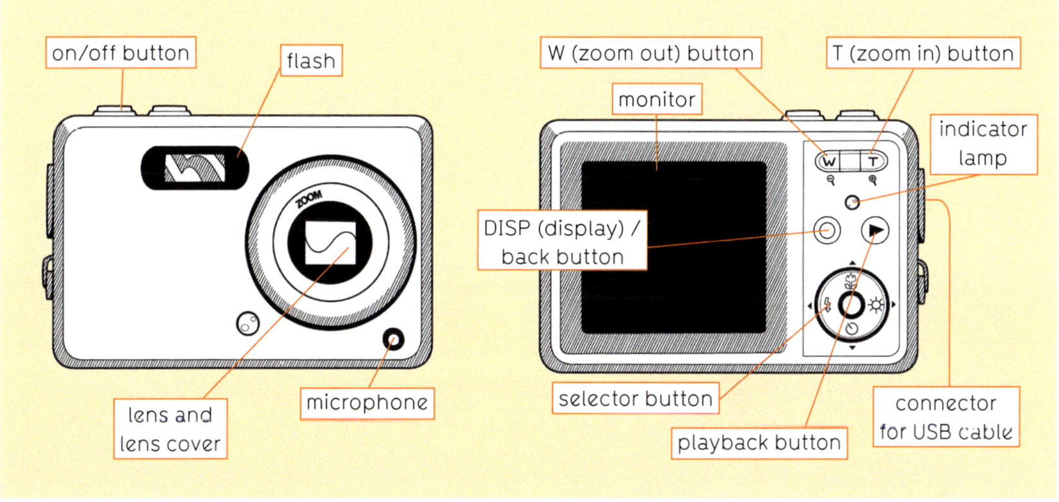

Camping

car: carro
carbohydrate: carboidrato
card: carta (baralho)
care: cuidado
care for: cuidar de
career: carreira
careful: cuidadoso(a)
carefully: cuidadosamente
careless: descuidado(a)
carpenter: carpinteiro(a)
carpentry: carpintaria
carpet man: tapeceiro
carrier: portador(a)
carrot: cenoura
carry: carregar; transportar

Carpentry

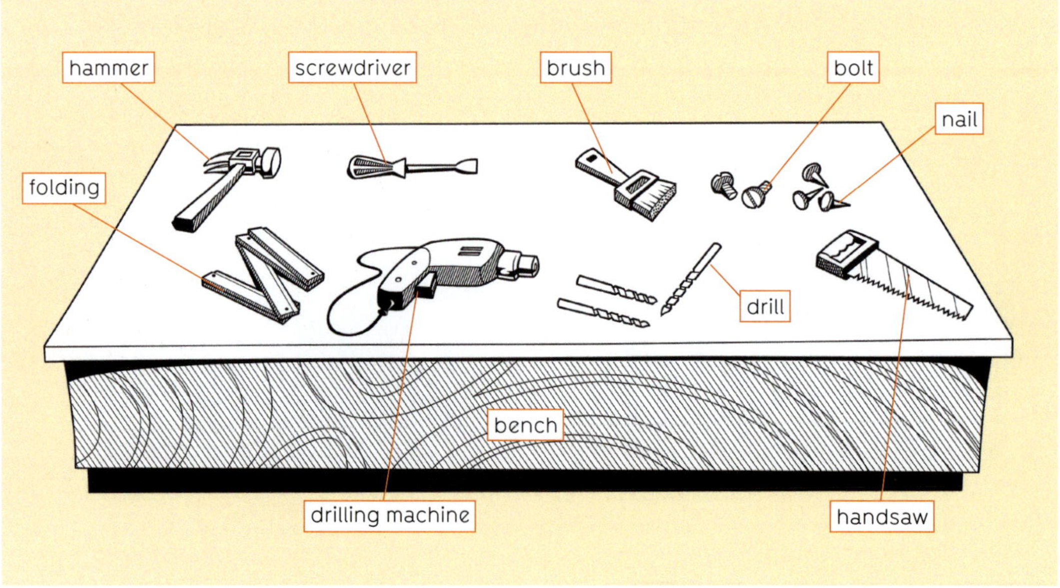

carry forward: seguir adiante
carry on: ir em frente, superar um momento
carry out: realizar
cartoon: história em quadrinhos; desenho animado
case: caso
cast: elenco; lançar; engessar; estabelecer
castle: castelo
cat: gato
catch: pegar, apanhar
catch a cold: resfriar-se
catch my eye: chamar minha atenção
catch on fire: pegar fogo
cathode: cátodo
cattle: gado
cauliflower: couve-flor
cause: causar; causa
caution: advertir
cautiously: cuidadosamente
cave: caverna
cavity: cárie
cease: cessar
celebrate: comemorar
cell: célula
cent: centavo
century: século
cereal: cereal
certainly: certamente
chain: corrente
challenge: desafio
challenged: desafiado(a)
challenging: desafiador(a)
chamber: câmara
Chamber Orchestra: Orquestra de Câmara
champion: campeão(ã)
championship: campeonato
chance: acaso; possibilidade; chance
change: mudar; mudança
chant: canção; cantar, entoar cântico
character: personagem
characterization: caracterização
characterize: caracterizar
characterized: caracterizado(a)
charge: atacar; cobrar
charming: charmoso(a)
chart: quadro
chat: bate-papo
cheap: barato(a)
check: marcar; verificar
cheese: queijo
chemical: produto químico; químico (adj.)
Chemistry: Química
chemistry: química
cherry: cereja
chestnut: castanha
chew: mascar
chicken: frango
chief: chefe; principal (adj.)
child: criança; filho(a)
child labor: trabalho infantil
child rearing: educação da criança
childish: infantil
children (pl. de child): crianças; filhos(as)
choice: escolha
choose: escolher

Cat

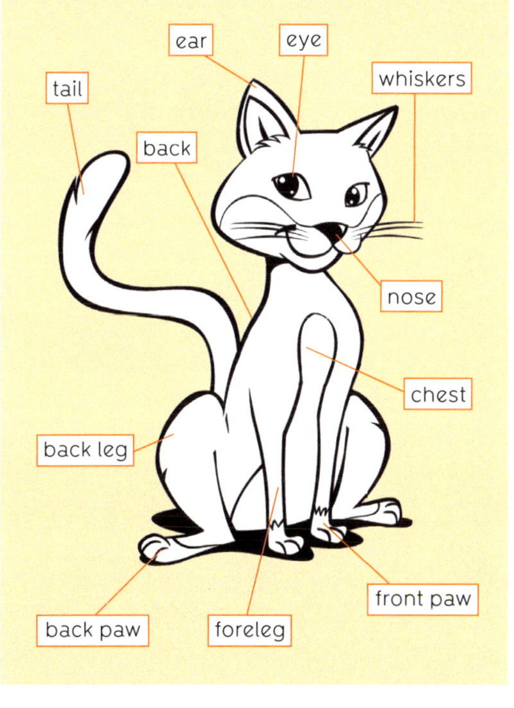

Cell

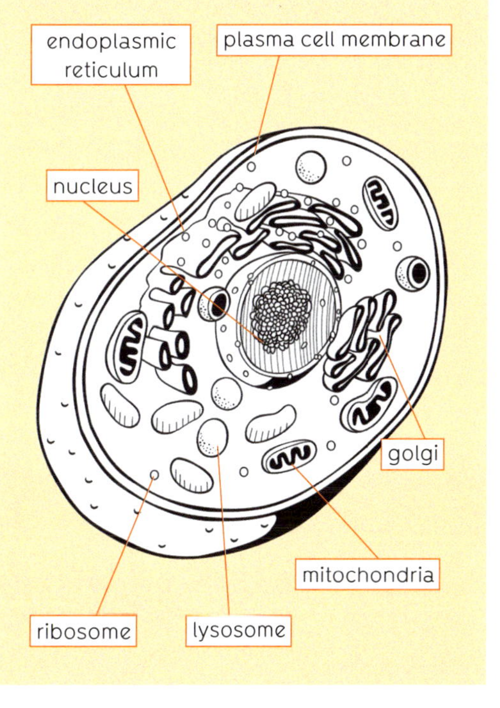

chore: tarefa
Christmas: Natal
chronicle: crônica
church: igreja
circle: circular; círculo
circulation: circulação
citizen: cidadão(ã)
citizenship: cidadania
city: cidade
claimant: autor de um processo judiciário, requerente
class: aula; classe
classify: classificar
classmate: colega de classe
clause: oração (gramatical)
clean: limpar
clear: desmatar
cleverest: o(a) mais sábio(a)
climb: escalar; subir
close: fechar
closet: guarda-roupa, armário
clothes: roupas
clothing: roupa; vestuário
clown: palhaço(a)
coach: instrutor(a)
coal: carvão
coalition: coalizão
code: código
coffee: café
cognitive: cognitivo(a)
coin: moeda
cold: frio(a)
colleague: colega
collect: colher; reunir
college: faculdade
color: cor
colorful: colorido(a)
column: coluna
comb: pente
combat: combater, lutar contra
combination: combinação
combine: combinar, unir
come: vir
come across: encontrar por acaso
come back: voltar
come out: ser publicado
come over as (British): ser visto como
come up: surgir
comeback: retorno
comedian: comediante
comfortable: confortável
commercial: anúncio
committee: comitê; comissão
common: comum
community: comunidade
companionship: companheirismo

Clothes

Coin

compare: comparar
comparison: comparação
compete: competir
competition: competição
competitor: competidor(a); concorrente
complete: completar, terminar; completo(a)
complex: complexo(a)
complexity: complexidade
compose: compor
composer: compositor(a)
compost: adubo
computer programmer: programador(a)
comrade: camarada
conceivable: concebível
concept: conceito
concerning: no que diz respeito a, relativo a, referente a
concert: concerto, *show*
condition: estado
conductor: maestro, maestrina
conference: congresso
confined: confinado(a)
connect: ligar, conectar
consequently: consequentemente
consider: considerar
construct: construir
consultant: consultor(a)
consume: consumir
consumer: consumidor(a)
consumption: consumo
contact: contato
contagion: contágio
contain: conter(-se); reprimir
contemplate: contemplar
content: conteúdo
context: contexto
continue: continuar
continuous: contínuo(a)
contract: contrair
control: controlar; controle
controversial: controverso(a)
controversy: controvérsia
conversational: relativo a conversação
convert: converter
convince: convencer
cook: cozinhar
cool: fresco(a)
cooperate: cooperar
cop: policial, tira
corn: milho
corner: canto; esquina
correct: correto(a); corrigir
correspond: corresponder
cost: custar; custo
costuming: figurino
couch: sofá
could: podia; conseguia
counselor: conselheiro(a)
count: contar
country: país; campo
county: condado
couple: casal
course: curso
course of study: curso (de universidade)
course of treatment: tratamento
court: tribunal
cover: cobrir
cover letter: carta de apresentação
coverage: cobertura
crack: quebrar
crafts: artesanato
cramps: câimbra
crate: engradado (de garrafas)
crazy: louco(a)
create: criar
creator: criador(a)
creature: criatura
cricket: críquete
critic: crítico(a)
criticize: criticar
cross: cruzar, atravessar
crowd: multidão
crowded: cheio de gente, lotado
cry: chorar; gritar
cup: xícara
cure: cura; curar
curious: curioso(a)
current: atual
currently: atualmente
customer: cliente
cut: cortar
cut down: diminuir
cut off: cortar fora
CV: *curriculum vitae*
cycling: ciclismo

D

dad: papai
daily: diário(a)
daily life: vida diária
dairy products: laticínios
damage: danificar, prejudicar; dano, prejuízo
dance: dança; dançar
dancer: dançarino(a)
dandruff: caspa
dangerous: perigoso(a)
dark: escuro(a)
darken: escurecer
darkest: o(a) mais escuro(a)
data: dados, informações
database: banco de dados
date: data; encontro
dating: namorando, saindo (com alguém)
daughter: filha
daunting: desafiante
day: dia
daylight: luz do dia
dead: morto(a)
deal: lidar com
dear: caro(a), prezado(a), querido(a)
death: morte
debt: dívida
decay: deterioração; queda
decide: decidir

decision: decisão
decision-making: tomada de decisão
deck hand: marujo encarregado da limpeza
decline: recusar; baixar
decrease: diminuir
deeply: profundamente
defense: defesa
define: definir
definite: definido(a)
definition: definição
degradation: deterioração; piora
degree: grau
delay: atrasar, retardar; atraso
delivery: entrega
demand: demanda, exigência; exigir
denote: denotar
deny: negar
depression: depressão
derive: derivar
describe: descrever
desert: deserto
deserve: merecer
design: projetar; projeto
designed: projetado
dessert: sobremesa
destroy: destruir
determine: determinar
detox: desintoxicar
develop: desenvolver(-se)
developing country: país em desenvolvimento
development: desenvolvimento
device: dispositivo; aparelho
dialogue: diálogo
dictatorship: ditadura
die: morrer
diet: dieta
dietician: nutricionista
different: diferente
difficulty: dificuldade
diminished: diminuído(a), menor
dining room: sala de jantar
dinner: jantar
dioxide: dióxido
direct current (DC): corrente contínua
directing callers: transferir ligações
disability: deficiência, incapacidade
disabled: deficiente físico ou mental
disagree: discordar
disastrous: desastroso(a)
discover: descobrir
discussion: discussão
disease: doença
disgrace: desgraça; desonra
disguise: disfarçar
dish: louça; prato
dish washer: lavador(a) de pratos
dislike: não gostar
disobey: desobedecer
disorder: desordem
disparity: desigualdade, disparidade
display: expositor(a)
distractibility: distração
distrust: desconfiança
disturb: perturbar
disuse: desuso
diverse: diverso(a)
divert: mudar o curso ou destino, desviar
divide: dividir(-se)
diving: mergulho
do: fazer
do drugs: consumir drogas
do the best: fazer o melhor possível
do the cleaning: fazer faxina
do the cooking: cozinhar
do the dishes: lavar a louça
do the duty: cumprir a obrigação
do the homework: fazer a lição de casa
do well at school: ir bem na escola
dock: doca, estaleiro
doctor: médico(a)
dog: cão
doll: boneca
don: vestir, pôr (roupa)
donation: doação
done: terminado(a)
door: porta
doubt: dúvida; duvidar
down: para baixo
dozen: dúzia
dramatic: dramático(a)
dramatically: dramaticamente
draw: desenhar; delinear
draw from: tirar
draw up: planejar; estabelecer
dream: sonho; sonhar
dress: vestido; vestir(-se)
dressing room: vestiário
dribble: driblar; gotejar
drink: beber
drinking water: água potável
drive: dirigir
driver: motorista
driver's license: carteira de habilitação
drop: deixar cair; diminuir
drop by: visitar sem avisar
drop out: desistir, abandonar
drought: seca
drug: droga; medicamento
drum: tamborilar
drums: bateria, tambores
dry: seco(a)
due to: devido a
dump: jogar fora
during: durante
dweller: morador(a)

E

each: cada, cada um(a)
each other: um(a) com o(a) outro(a)
eagle: águia

ear: ouvido
earliest: o mais cedo
early: cedo; início
earring: brinco
earth: terra
Earth: Terra
easily: com facilidade
east: leste
eastward: em direção ao leste
eat: comer
eatable: comestível
editing: edição
effective: eficiente
efficiency: eficiência
effort: esforço
either: também (em frases negativas)
either... or: ou... ou
elderly: idoso(a)
eldest: o(a) mais velho(a)
elect: eleger
electric fixtures: equipamentos elétricos
electricity: eletricidade
electrolyte: eletrólito
electron: elétron
embarrass: embaraçar, causar desconforto
embryonic: embrionário(a)
emotion: emoção
emphasize: enfatizar
employee: empregado(a)
employment: emprego
empower: delegar poder
empty: vazio(a)
enclosed: anexo(a), incluso(a)
encounter: deparar(-se) com, encontrar
encourage: encorajar, estimular
end: final; terminar, finalizar
ending: fim, final
endocarditis: endocardite
enduring: duradouro(a)
enemy: inimigo(a)
energy: energia
enforce: executar
enforcement: execução
engage: dedicar-se, envolver-se
engaged: envolvido(a); comprometido(a)
engineer: engenheiro(a)
England: Inglaterra
English Channel: Canal da Mancha
enjoy: aproveitar, desfrutar
enjoyment: diversão
enlarge: ampliar; aumentar
enough: suficiente
ensnare: apanhar em uma armadilha
ensure: assegurar, garantir
entail: vincular
enter: entrar
entirely: totalmente, inteiramente
entrance: entrada
environment: ambiente; meio ambiente
environmental: ambiental
environmentally: ambientalmente
epidemic: epidemia; epidêmico(a)
equality: igualdade
escape: escapar
escort: acompanhar
especially: especialmente, principalmente
estimate: estimar
estimated: estimado(a), calculado(a)
ethnicities: etnias
evaluation: avaliação
even: até mesmo, mesmo
event: acontecimento, evento
eventually: finalmente, no fim
ever: alguma vez; jamais
every: todo(a), cada

Eastward

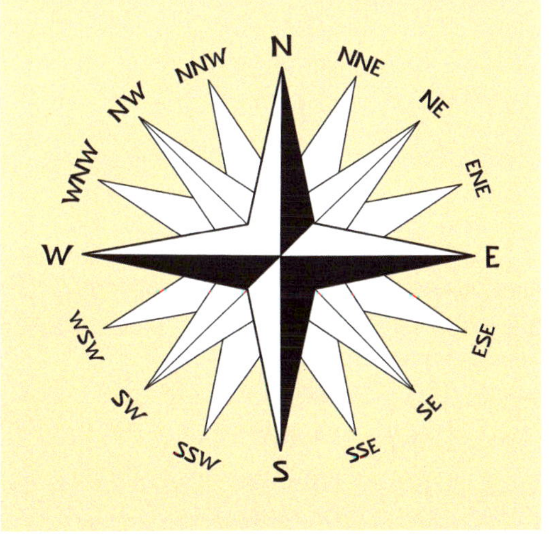

Electric fixtures

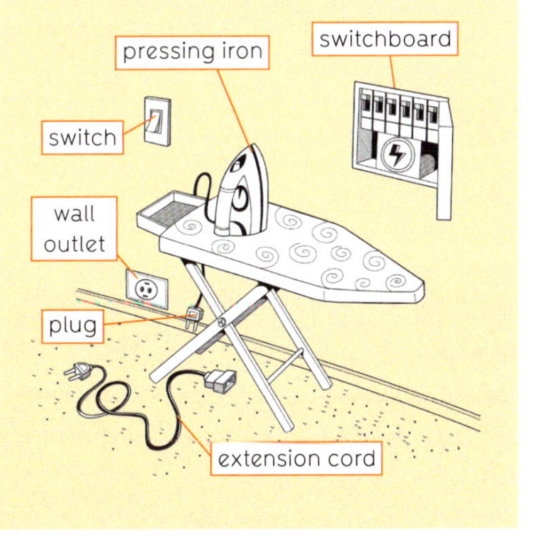

every now and then: de vez em quando
every so often: de tempos em tempos
every time: toda vez
everybody: todo mundo
every day: todo dia
everything: tudo, todas as coisas
everywhere: em todo lugar
evidence: evidência, prova
evil: mau (adj.); mal (subst.)
excellent: excelente
excited: empolgado(a)
exciting: empolgante, excitante, entusiasmante
exclusive: exclusivo(a)
excursion: excursão
exhibit: feira, exposição
exist: existir
expenses: despesas
expensive: caro(a)
experience: experiência; experimentar
expert: perito
explain: explicar
explode: explodir
exploitation: exploração
explosion: explosão
extend: estender; prorrogar
extended family: família que inclui os parentes
extent: extensão
extremist: extremista
eye: olho

F

fabricate: fabricar
face: rosto; enfrentar
facilities: instalações; serviços
facility: facilidade
fact: fato
factory: fábrica
faculty: corpo docente
fail: falhar; não conseguir; ser reprovado(a)
failure: fracasso
fair: feira, exposição; justo(a)
faith: fé
faithful: fiel
fall: cair
false: falso(a)
fame: fama
familiar: conhecido(a)
family: família
fan: fã
fanatic: fanático(a)
far: longe
far from: longe de
far out to sea: para o alto-mar
far upwards: bem para cima
farewell: adeus; despedida
farm: fazenda
farmer: fazendeiro(a)
farther: mais longe
fast: rápido(a)
faster: mais rápido(a)
fat: gordo(a); gordura
fate: destino
father: pai
favorable: favorável
favorably: favoravelmente
fear: medo
feather: pena (animal)
fee: honorários; taxa
feel: sentir(-se)
feel down: sentir-se deprimido
feeling: sensação, sentimento
feet (pl. de *foot*): pés; unidade de medida equivalente a 30,48 cm
feet tall: pés de altura
fellow: companheiro(a), colega; sujeito
female: feminino(a); mulher
fence: cerca
few: poucos(as)
fewer: menos
fiber: fibra
field: campo
fig: figo
fight: combater; luta, briga
fighter: combatente, lutador(a)
figure: figura
figure out: imaginar
figurine: estatueta
fill: encher
fill in: preencher
filled: cheio(a), repleto(a)
film review: crítica de cinema
film run: filmagem
finally: finalmente
finance: financiar
financial: financeiro(a), econômico
find: achar, encontrar
find out: descobrir
finding: achado, descoberta; resultado
fine: fino(a), elegante; legal
finger: dedo
finish: terminar, finalizar
firefighter: bombeiro(a)
fireman: bombeiro
first: primeiro(a); antes
fish: peixe; pescar
fisherman: pescador
fishing: pescaria
fist: punho, mão fechada
fit: preparado(a); adequado(a)
fit muscle: músculo exercitado
fitness center: academia de ginástica
fix: consertar
flare: chama; rojão sinalizador
flash: brilhar
flat: apartamento
flee: escapar, fugir
flight: voo
floor: chão; andar, piso
flotilla: flotilha
flourish: florescer
flow: fluxo
flower: flor
fluently: fluentemente
fly: voar
focus: enfoque
focus point: ponto central
follow: seguir

following: seguinte
food: alimento, comida
fool: bobo; enganar
foot: pé
footsteps: passos
for: para; por; pois
for sure: com certeza
force: forçar
forebearers: antepassados
forecast: prever
forehead: testa
foreign: estrangeiro(a)
forest: floresta
forget: esquecer
form: forma; formulário
formation: formação
former: anterior
foster family: família de criação
found: fundar
fracture: fratura
free: grátis; livre
free radical: radical livre
free time: tempo livre
freedom: liberdade
freestyle: estilo livre (nado)
French: francês(esa)
frequently: frequentemente
Friday: sexta-feira
friend: amigo(a)
friendly: simpático(a), agradável; amigável
friendship: amizade
frightened: assustado(a)
from: de
from now on: de agora em diante
from... to: de... para
front door: porta da frente
fruit: fruta
fuel: combustível
full: cheio(a), completo(a); pleno(a)
full length: comprimento total
fullness: plenitude; abundância
fun: divertimento; divertido
functioning: funcionamento
fund: fundo (dinheiro)
fungi: fungos
furnish: mobiliar
furniture: mobília
further: mais longe; adicional
further out: para mais longe

G

gain: ganhar; adquirir; ganho
game: jogo
gang: gangue
garbage: lixo
garbage bin: lata de lixo
garden: jardim
gardener: jardineiro(a)
gastritis: gastrite
gather: juntar, coletar, reunir(-se)
gathering clouds: nuvens acumuladas
gear: equipamento
gender: gênero, sexo
general: geral
generate: gerar
genius: gênio
geologist: geólogo(a)
German: alemão(ã)
Germany: Alemanha
get: chegar; conseguir, obter
get a rest: descansar
get married: casar(-se)
get out: sair
get ready: aprontar-se
get sucked into: ficar envolvido(a)
get together: reunir(-se)
get up: levantar-se
gift: presente; dom
girl: garota, menina
girlfriend: namorada
give: dar
give away: distribuir
give back: devolver
give in: render-se
give out: emitir
give rise: dar origem
give up: desistir; abandonar
give way: dar passagem; encaminhar
given: dado(a); determinado(a)
glass: vidro; copo
glasses: óculos
glimpse: olhadela
glitter: brilho; brilhar
glorify: glorificar
glossary: glossário
gloves: luvas
glow: brilho; brilhar
go: ir
go about: lidar com
go after: perseguir
go ahead: ir em frente
go along: seguir
go away: sair, ir para longe
go back: voltar
go by: passar (o tempo)
go down: descer; baixar
go fishing: ir pescar
go in: entrar
go on: acontecer
go on a trip: viajar
go out: sair
go over: examinar
go through: passar por
goal: meta, objetivo
gods: deuses
gold: ouro
gonna: going to (expressa ação futura)
good: bom, boa
goods: artigos, produtos
govern: governar
government: governo
grade: nota (avaliação de prova, trabalho); série (escolar)
graduate: formar-se (na escola); formado(a)
graduation: graduação
graln: grão
grandma: vovó
grandparent: avô, avó

Grape Nuts: marca de um cereal matinal
grapes: uvas
graph: gráfico
grass: grama
grateful: agradecido(a)
gratitude: gratidão
great: grandioso(a); ótimo(a)
greatest: o(a) maior
Greek: grego(a)
green: verde
greet: cumprimentar, saudar
grievance: reclamação, queixa; ressentimento
grocery store: armazém, mercearia
grooming: higiene pessoal
group: grupo
grow: crescer
grow old: ficar velho(a)
grow older: envelhecer
grow stronger: fortalecer(-se), ficar forte
grow up: crescer
guarantee: garantia
guava: goiaba
guess: adivinhar
guidance: orientação
guide: guiar
guitar: violão
gypsy: cigano(a)

H

had better: é melhor que
hair: cabelo; pelo
half: metade, meio
hall: saguão; salão
halt: parar, interromper
hand: mão
handle: cabo
happen: acontecer, ocorrer
happiness: felicidade
happy: feliz
hard: difícil; duro(a); árduo(a)
hard work: trabalho duro
hard-pressed: pressionado(a)
harm: fazer mal; prejudicar; dano, machucado
hat: chapéu
hate: odiar
have: ter
have a good time: divertir-se
have a wonderful time: divertir-se muito
have fun: divertir-se
hazardous: perigoso(a)
head: cabeça; dirigir-se
head teacher (British): diretor de escola
head up: subir (as escadas)
headache: dor de cabeça
heal: curar
health: saúde
healthcare: assistência médica; cuidados com a saúde
healthier: mais saudável
healthy: saudável
hear: ouvir; ficar sabendo
hearing: audição
heart: coração
heart attack: ataque cardíaco
heat: aquecer; calor
heat up: aquecer
heavily: pesadamente
heavy: pesado(a)
hectic: muito agitado(a)
helicopter: helicóptero
help: ajudar, socorrer; ajuda
helpful: útil
hepatic: hepático(a)
hepatitis: hepatite
herb: erva
herd: rebanho; bando
here: aqui
hidden: escondido(a)
hide: esconder
high: alto; de altura
high fee: altos honorários
high office: alto escalão
high school: Ensino Médio
highest: o(a) mais alto(a)
highs and lows: altos e baixos
hiking: caminhada
hip-hopper: cantor(a) ou compositor(a) de *hip-hop*
hit: atingir, bater; chocar-se; batida
hitting: bater
hold: segurar; manter; realizar
holiday: feriado
homework: lição de casa
honeymoon: lua de mel
honor: honra
hook: fisgar; gancho
hop: saltitar
hope: esperança; ter expectativa
hopeful: esperançoso(a)
hopeless: sem esperança
horrific: horrível
horse: cavalo
horseback riding: cavalgar
hot: quente
hotline: linha direta
hour: hora
house: casa; alojar
household: lar; família
housewife: dona de casa
how: como; quão
how much: quanto
however: entretanto, porém, no entanto
HRH (Her Royal Highness): Sua Alteza Real
huge: enorme
human: humano(a)
human body: corpo humano
humbled: com humildade
hundred: cem
hunger: fome
hunt: caçar
hunting: caça
hurry: apressar(-se)

hurt: ferir, machucar; machucado

husband: marido

hyperactive: hiperativo(a)

hyperactivity: hiperatividade

I

ice: gelo

ice cream: sorvete

idea: ideia

identify: identificar

idol: ídolo

if: se

House

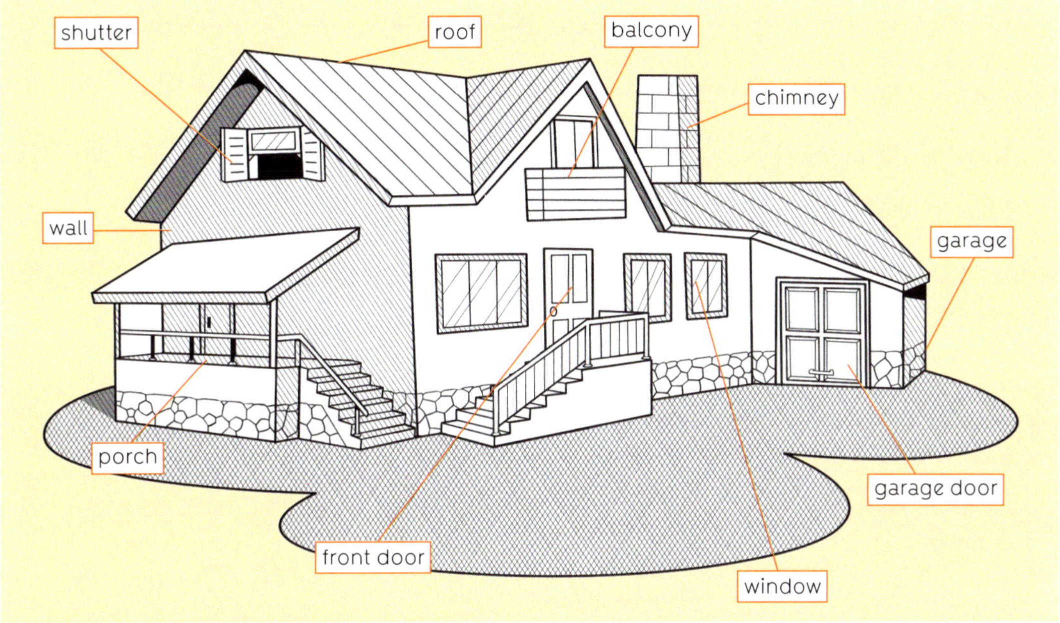

Human body

if applicable: se for o caso
ignore: ignorar
illegible: ilegível
illegitimate: ilegítimo(a)
illicit: ilícito(a)
illiterate: analfabeto(a)
illness: doença
illusion: ilusão
immediate: imediato(a)
immediately: imediatamente
immovable: imóvel
immune: imune
impact: impactar
impede: impedir
impose: impor
impossible: impossível
improbable: improvável
impromptu: improvisado(a)
improve: melhorar
improvement: melhoria
improvisation: improviso
in: em, dentro de
in front of: na frente de
in order to: a fim de, para
in search: à procura
in short: em resumo
in the same way: da mesma maneira
in trouble: com problemas
in turn: por sua vez
inability: incapacidade
inactive: inativo(a)
inapropriate: inadequado(a)
inaugural speech: discurso de posse
incandescent: incandescente
include: incluir
incoherent: incoerente
incompetent: incompetente
inconceivable: inconcebível
incorrect: incorreto(a)
increase: aumento; aumentar
incredible: incrível
indeed: de fato, mesmo
indefinite: indefinido(a)
indifferent: indiferente
infect: infectar
infection: infecção
infiltrate: infiltrar
influence: influência; influenciar
information: informação
infra-red: infravermelho
inherit: herdar
inhibit: inibir
initiate: iniciar
injectable: injetável
injection: injeção
injury: ferimento, lesão
inmate: interno(a), recluso(a)
innate: inato(a)
inner: interior, interno(a)
inoffensive: inofensivo(a)
insane: insano(a)
inside: dentro
insolvable: insolúvel
inspire: inspirar
instead: ao invés de, em vez de
integrity: integridade
intelligence: inteligência
intend: pretender
intention: intenção
interaction: interação
interchangeably: intercambiavelmente
interconnected: interligado(a)
interest: interesse
interested: interessado(a)
interesting: interessante
inter-faith: ecumênico(a)
interpersonal: interpessoal
interpreter: intérprete
interview: entrevista
interviewer: entrevistador(a)
intimate: íntimo(a)
intimidate: intimidar
intimidation: intimidação
into: para dentro
intrapersonal: intrapessoal
introduce: introduzir; apresentar
intruder: intruso(a), invasor(a)
invent: inventar
invention: invenção
inverter: inversor(a)
invest: investir
invite: convidar
involve: envolver
involvement: envolvimento
iron: ferro; ferro de passar; passar roupa a ferro
irritate: irritar
irritation: irritação
island: ilha
isle: ilha
issue: questão, assunto
it takes: leva (tempo para praticar uma ação)
it's no use: não adianta
Italian: italiano(a)
Italy: Itália

J

jacket: jaqueta
jaguar: jaguar
jail: cadeia
jailhouse: prisão
jam: situação difícil ou perigosa
jangle: tilintar, chacoalhar
job: trabalho, emprego
jobless: desempregado(a)
join: unir(-se), juntar(-se)
journalist: jornalista
JSPS (Japan Society for the Promotion of Science): Sociedade Japonesa para a Promoção da Ciência
judge: julgar
jug: jarra
juice: suco
jump: pular, saltar
jungle: floresta, selva
just: apenas, somente; exatamente; acabar de
just as well: do mesmo jeito

K

keep: manter
keep in mind: ter em mente; não esquecer
key: chave
keyboard: teclado
kick: chutar

kid: garoto(a), criança
kids: garotada, crianças
kill: matar
kind: bondoso(a), gentil; tipo
kindness: bondade
kinesthetic: cinestésico(a)
king: rei
kit: equipamento; estojo; *kit*
kitchen: cozinha
knee: joelho
know: conhecer, saber
knowledge: conhecimento
known: conhecido(a)

L

lab: laboratório
labor: trabalho
laborious: laborioso(a); dedicado(a) ao trabalho
lack of: falta de
lady: senhora
lake: lago
land: terra
landfill: aterro
landing: aterrissagem
large: grande
largely: em grande parte
largest: o(a) maior
last: durar; último(a)
lasting: duradouro(a), durável
late: atrasado(a); tarde
lately: ultimamente
later: mais tarde
laugh: rir
law: lei
lawmaker: legislador
lawyer: advogado(a)
lay eggs: botar ovos
layer: camada
lead: levar; liderar
leader: líder
leadership: liderança
learn: aprender; saber
learning: aprendizado
leather: couro
leave: sair; partir; deixar
left: esquerdo(a)
left-handed: canhoto(a)
leg: perna
legend: legenda (em mapa); lenda
legendary: legendário(a), lendário
leisure: recreação, lazer
length: comprimento
leopard: leopardo
leprosy: lepra

Kitchen

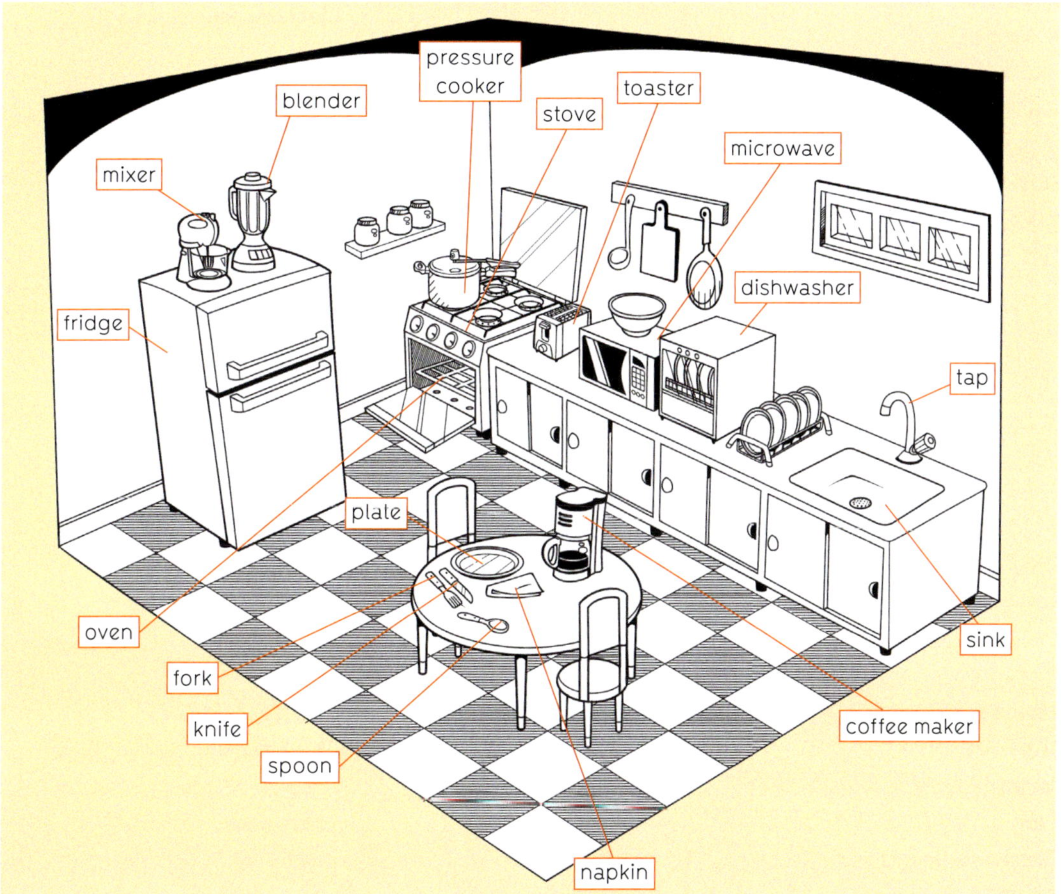

less: menos
letter: carta; letra
lettuce: alface
level: nível
library: biblioteca
lie: mentir; deitar(-se), jazer; encontrar-se
life: vida
life as a whole: vida como um todo
life span: tempo de vida
lifestyle: estilo de vida
light: luz; leve
lighting: iluminação
like: gostar de; como, do mesmo modo
like no other: como nenhum(a) outro(a)
like that: assim
likely: provável
likewise: da mesma maneira
limit: limite
limited: limitado(a)
lining: revestimento
link: enlace; ligação, *link*
listen: ouvir
listener: ouvinte
literally: literalmente
lithography: litografia
little: pequeno(a); pouco(a)
live: viver, morar; ao vivo
live on: continuar a viver
live out: tornar realidade
liver: fígado
lives: vidas
living: vivo
lizard: lagarto
load: carga; um monte de
located: localizado(a)
location: local
lock: trancar
lodging: alojamento
logic: lógica
lonely: sozinho(a), solitário(a)
long: comprido(a)
longest running: apresentado(a), no ar há mais tempo
long-term: a longo prazo
look: olhar; parecer; olhada
look after: cuidar; tomar conta
look at: olhar para
look behind: olhar para trás
look for: procurar
look like: parecer
look up: consultar (uma lista, um dicionário)
looking forward: esperando ansiosamente
lord: senhor
lose: perder
loss: perda; prejuízo
lots of: muito(a), muitos(as)
lottery: loteria
lovable: adorável
love: amor; amar
lover: amante
low: baixo(a)
low income: baixa renda
luck: sorte
lucky: com sorte, sortudo(a)
luggage: bagagem
lunch: almoço
lunch hour: hora do almoço
lured in: atraído(a)
lycopene: licopeno

M

machinery: maquinaria
mad: furioso(a); louco(a)
magazine: revista
magician: mágico(a)
magistrate: juiz, juíza
maid: empregado(a) doméstico(a)
main: principal
maintain: manter
maintenance: manutenção
major: principal
majority: maioria
make: fazer
make a decision: tomar uma decisão
make a mess: bagunçar
make a mistake: cometer um erro; enganar-se
make an experiment: fazer uma experiência
make available: disponibilizar
make fun (of): caçoar; fazer gozação (de)
make it to heaven: alcançar o céu
make love: fazer amor
make money: ganhar dinheiro
make the bed: arrumar a cama
make up: construir
make-up: maquiagem
make up one's mind: decidir(-se)
maker: fabricante
maladjusted: desajustado(a)
maladministration: má administração
male: masculino(a); homem
malformation: má-formação
malnourishment: desnutrição
malnutrition: subnutrição, desnutrição
maltreatment: maus-tratos
man: homem
manganese: manganês
mango: manga (fruta)
manner: maneira
manufacturer: produtor, fabricante
manufacturing: manufatura
many: muitos(as)
march: marcha; marchar
mark: marcar
marketplace: mercado
marriage: casamento
married: casado(a)
masculinized: masculinizado(a)
mask: máscara
mass: massa
masses: massas
master cell: célula principal
Master's Degree: mestrado
mastodon: mastodonte
match: combinar, ligar, relacionar; jogo, partida

material: material
may: poder (verbo modal)
may be: pode ser
maybe: talvez
mean: malvado(a); significar; destinar
meaning: significado
means: meios
measure: medida; medir
meat: carne
mechanic: mecânico(a) (subst.)
mechanical: mecânico(a) (adj.)
medal: medalha
media: mídia
medical drug: medicamento, remédio
medical student: estudante de Medicina
medicine: remédio; medicina
meet: encontrar(-se); conhecer; reunir(-se)
meet the needs: atender às necessidades
meeting: reunião
melt: derreter
member: membro
membership: filiação
memorabilia: recordações, lembranças
menacing: ameaçador(a)
mend: consertar
mentally: mentalmente
mention: mencionar
mere: simples, mísero(a)
mess: bagunça, confusão
message: mensagem, recado
micrometer: micrômetro
microwave: micro-ondas
mid: metade, meio
middle class: classe média
middle income: renda média
middle school: escola de Ensino Fundamental II
might: poderia (verbo modal)
mile: milha (1.609 m ou 1,609 km)
milk: leite
mime: mímica; fazer mímica
mind: importar-se; prestar atenção; mente
mindful: consciente
mine: mina
minimum: mínimo(a)
ministry: ministério
minor: menor (de idade); leve (ferimento)
miracle: milagre
mirror: espelho
miserable: miserável
misery: miséria
misjudge: julgar mal
miss: perder; sentir falta, faltar
missing: que está faltando
mistake: confundir, errar; erro
mithai: docinho indiano
mix: misturar
model: modelo
modern: moderno(a)
modernism: modernismo
module: módulo
mold: molde, parâmetro
mom: mamãe
money: dinheiro
monkey: macaco
more: mais
more than: mais do que
morning: manhã
mortality: mortalidade
most: mais; maioria
most likely: muito provavelmente
mother: mãe
Mother's Day: Dia das Mães
mother-in-law: sogra
mount: monte
mountain: montanha
mousetrap: ratoeira
move: mover, movimentar
movement: movimento
movie: filme
movies: cinema
moving part: parte móvel
MSc: mestre em ciências
much: muito(a)
mud: lama
multiform: multiforme
multiply: multiplicar(-se)
murder: assassinar
muscle: músculo
mushroom: cogumelo
musical instrument: instrumento musical
musician: músico(a)
must: dever

Musical instrument

1 accordion
2 cello
3 clarinet
4 flute
5 banjo
6 saxophone
7 drum
8 electric guitar
9 piano

N

namely: a saber; nomeadamente
narrative: narrativa
national: nacional
nationalism: nacionalismo
nationality: nacionalidade
naturalist: naturalista
naturally: naturalmente
navigator: navegador
near: perto de
nearly: quase
nearsighted: míope
need: precisar; necessidade
neglect: negligenciar; descuidar
neighbor: vizinho(a)
neighborhood: vizinhança, bairro
nerve: nervo
nervous system: sistema nervoso
neuron: neurônio
never: nunca
new: novo(a)
newest: o(a) mais novo(a)
news: notícia; novidade
news show: noticiário
newspaper: jornal
next: próximo(a); em seguida
NGO (non-governmental organization): ONG (organização não governamental)
nice: bom, boa; amável, gentil
night: noite
night school: escola noturna
nightclub: boate
nightmare: pesadelo
nineties: década de 1990
no: nenhum(a); não
no fewer than: exatamente
no longer: não mais
nobody: ninguém
noise: barulho
noisy: barulhento(a)
non-corrosive: não corrosivo(a)
nonsterile: não estéril
nope: não
nor: nem
north: norte
northwest: noroeste
not only... but also: não só... mas também
not really: na verdade não
not at all: nada, nem um pouco; de nada (resposta)
note: anotação; observar
nothing: nada
nothing left: nada resta
novel: romance
novelist: romancista
now: agora
nowadays: atualmente, hoje em dia
nuclear family: família nuclear
nut: castanha; noz

O

oak: carvalho
oatmeal: aveia
obey: obedecer
obscure: obscuro(a)
observation: observação
observe: observar
obsessed: obcecado(a)
obtain: obter
occur: ocorrer
October: outubro
odds: chances, probabilidades
of: de (posse, parte)
off: desconto (em preços)
offer: oferecer; oferta
office: escritório
officer: oficial (exército); funcionário (governo)
official: oficial; funcionário(a) público(a)
offspring: fruto, produto
often: frequentemente; geralmente
oil: petróleo
old: velho(a)
old-fashioned: fora de moda; antiquado
Olympians: atletas das Olimpíadas
Olympic: olímpico
on: sobre, em cima de
on foot: a pé
on the other hand: por outro lado
on the upswing: em ascensão; crescendo
once: uma vez; uma vez que
once again: mais uma vez
one-third: um terço
only: único(a); somente
open: abrir
operate: operar
operation: operação
operationally: operacionalmente
opinion: opinião
opposite: oposto
or so: mais ou menos
orange: laranja
orchestra: orquestra
order: encomendar; encomenda, ordem
ordinary: comum
organism: organismo
other: outro(a)
other than: além de, que não
out: fora
outbreak: surto
outlet: loja de ponta de estoque; saída
outline: contorno, traçado do perfil
output: resultado; produção
outside: do lado de fora
oven: forno
over: sobre, por cima; durante; terminado(a)
over the time: com o passar do tempo
overall: em geral
overcoat: casaco, sobretudo
overcrowded: superlotado
overdress: vestir-se de modo exagerado

overeat: comer demais
overflow: transbordar
overlook: desprezar, não dar importância
overpopulated: superpopuloso
oversleep: perder a hora (dormindo)
overwhelmingly: esmagadoramente
own: possuir, ter; próprio(a)
owner: proprietário(a)
ozone layer: camada de ozônio

P

pack: fazer as malas
package: pacote
page: página
pain reliever: analgésico
paint: pintar; tinta
painter: pintor(a)
painting: pintura
pale: pálido(a)
panel: painel
papaya: mamão
paper: papel; trabalho escolar
paragraph: parágrafo
paralympic: paraolímpico(a)
parasitic: parasitário(a)
parents: pais
parish: paróquia
park: estacionar; parque
partially: parcialmente
partner: parceiro(a)
partnership: parceria
party: festa
pass: ato ou efeito de passar
passer-by: transeunte
passion: paixão
past: passado (subst.); passado(a) (adj.)
pasta: macarrão, massa
pastime: passatempo
pasture: pasto
path: trajetória
pattern: padrão, modelo
pay: pagar
pay a visit: visitar
pay homage: prestar homenagem
peace: paz
peaceful: pacífico(a)
peach: pêssego
pear: pera
peer: fitar, espreitar
pen name: pseudônimo
penny: moeda norte-americana de 1 centavo
people: pessoas; povo
per week: por semana
perceive: perceber
percent: por cento
percentage: porcentagem
perform: desempenhar, executar
performance: apresentação, espetáculo; desempenho
performer: artista
performing arts: artes cênicas
permission: permissão
permitted: permitido(a)
person: pessoa
personal: pessoal
personality: personalidade
Personell Manager: Gerente de Recursos Humanos
persuade: persuadir
pesticide: pesticida
pet: animal de estimação
petty: pequeno(a), sem importância
pharmaceutical drugs: medicamentos
phase: fase
PhD: doutor(a) (título acadêmico)
philosopher: filósofo(a)
phone: telefone
photovoltaic: fotovoltaico
physical: físico(a)
Physical Education: Educação Física
physical fitness: condicionamento físico
Physics: Física
pianist: pianista
pickpocket: batedor de carteira
picture: figura; foto; quadro
pie: torta
piece: pedaço
piece together: montar
pigment: pigmento
pinpoint: localizar com precisão
piracy: pirataria
place: lugar; colocar; situar
plain: claro(a), evidente
plan: planejar
plane: avião
plantation: plantação
planter: plantador(a), agricultor(a)
plastic: plástico
platinum: platina
play: brincar; jogar; tocar (instrumento musical); peça (de teatro)
play the role: desempenhar o papel
player: jogador(a)
pleased: satisfeito(a)
pleasure: prazer
plenty: bastante, em abundância; suficiente
plenty of: muito(a), muitos(as)
plot: trama
plum: ameixa
pluralize: pluralizar
plus: mais
pocket: bolso
poet: poeta(isa)
point of view: ponto de vista
police: polícia
policeman: guarda, policial
policy: política; apólice
political party: partido político
politician: político(a)
pollute: poluir
polygon: polígono
polymerization: polimerização
pool: piscina
poor: pobre; insatisfatório(a), insuficiente
poorer: pior; mais pobre

poorly: pobremente
poorly educated: com pouco estudo
popstar: estrela *pop*
population: população
portray: retratar
pose: apresentar; posar
position: cargo; posição
possess: possuir
possession: posse, possessão
possibility: possibilidade
possible: possível
postcard: cartão-postal
postdoctoral: pós-doutorado
potassium: potássio
potato: batata
pour: despejar
poverty: pobreza
powder: pó
power: força; poder
powerful: poderoso(a)
practical: prático(a)
practice: praticar; prática
practiced: experiente
predicament: apuro
predict: prever
predictable: previsível
prediction: previsão
prefer: preferir
prefix: prefixo
pregnant: grávida
prejudice: preconceito
preposition: preposição
prescribe: prescrever
prescription: receita médica
prescription drug: medicamento sob prescrição médica
present: atual; presente
presently: no momento
press: imprensa
press assistant: assessor de imprensa
pretend: fingir
pretty: bonito(a)
prevent: prevenir, evitar
previous: anterior
price: preço
primary: primário(a)
printed: impresso
printed media: mídia impressa
priority: prioridade
prison: prisão, cadeia
prisoner: prisioneiro(a)
prize: prêmio
probability: probabilidade
probable: provável
problem: problema
process: processo
produce: produzir
profit: lucrar, ganhar dinheiro
prohibited: proibido(a)
promise: promessa; prometer
promote: promover
proper: adequado(a)
property: propriedade
prosecution: acusação; instauração de processo
protect: proteger
protection: proteção
protein: proteína
proud: orgulhoso(a)
prove: provar, mostrar
provide: fornecer; proporcionar
provided that: desde que, contanto que
psychiatrist: psiquiatra
psychiatry: psiquiatria
pub: bar
public speaker: orador(a)
publicity shot: foto de publicidade
publish: publicar
pull: puxar
pull down: puxar para baixo
pump: bomba; bombear
pumpkin: abóbora
punish: punir
puny: fraco, insignificante
purpose: finalidade, propósito, intenção
pursue: perseguir, ir atrás
push: empurrar
put: pôr, colocar
put down: tirar (roupa, óculos, sapatos)
put on weight: engordar
puzzle: confundir
pyramid: pirâmide

Q

quality: qualidade
quarter: quarto; trimestre
queen: rainha
question: questão; questionar
quick: rápido(a)
quickly: rapidamente
quietly: quieto(a), sem barulho
quit: desistir de, parar, abandonar
quite: bastante

R

rabbit: coelho
race: raça; corrida
racer: corredor(a)
racist: racista
radar gun: radar (usado para detectar a velocidade de objetos em movimento)
raging: ruidoso(a), barulhento(a)
rain: chover; chuva
rainfall: chuva; índice pluviométrico
rainforest: floresta tropical
rainy: chuvoso(a)
raise: levantar; aumentar; criar
range: variar
rank: categoria; classificar, ranquear
ransack: vasculhar
rapidly: rapidamente
rare: raro(a); malpassado(a) (carne)
rarely: raramente
rate: índice, taxa
rather: em vez de
ratio: índice, proporção
reach: atingir, chegar

read: ler
read on: continuar lendo
reading: leitura
ready: pronto(a)
real: real, verdadeiro(a)
reality: realidade
realize: perceber, dar-se conta
reason: razão, motivo; raciocinar
reasonable: sensato(a); razoável
receive: receber
recharge: recarregar
rechargeable: recarregável
recipe: receita
recognizable: reconhecível, identificável
record: recorde; relatório
record-breaking: que bate recorde
record labels: gravadoras
recording: gravação
recycle: reciclar
recycling: reciclagem
red: vermelho(a)
redness: vermelhidão
reduce: reduzir
refer: referir-se; referente a
reflex: reflexo
refrain from: abster-se de
refusal: recusa
refuse: recusar(-se)
regard: considerar
regarding: em relação a
regardless: indiferente; descuidado
register: registro
regularly: regularmente
relate: relacionar(-se)
relation: relação
relationship: relação, relacionamento
relatives: parentes
relay: corrida de revezamento
release: divulgar; produzir
release date: data de lançamento
reluctant: relutante
remain: permanecer
remake: nova edição
remark: comentário, observação
remarry: casar(-se) novamente
remember: lembrar(-se)
remind: lembrar
reminder: lembrete; aviso
removal: remoção
renewable: renovável
renown: renome, fama
renowned: renomado(a)
rent: alugar
repair: conserto; consertar
repeat: repetir
repeatedly: repetidamente
replace: substituir
replenish: repor
report: relatório; relatar, informar

Rainforest

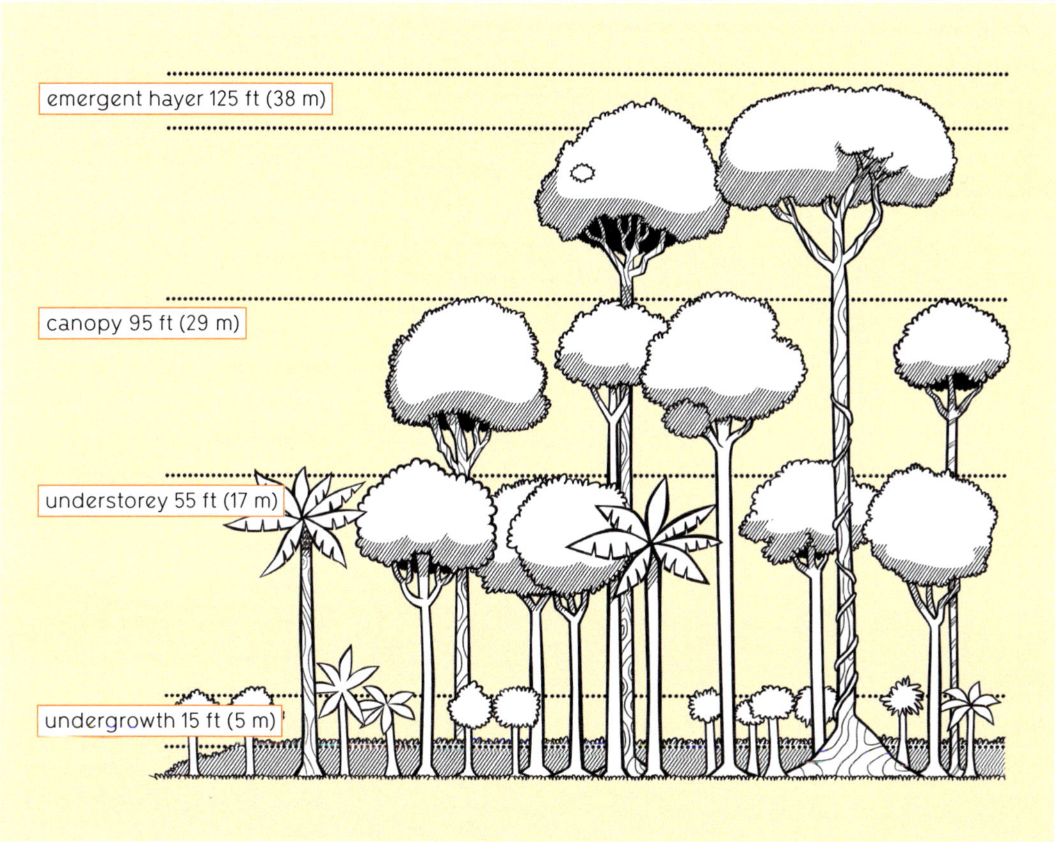

represent: representar
reputation: reputação
request: solicitação
rescue: resgatar; resgate
research: pesquisar; pesquisa
researcher: pesquisador(a)
resin: resina
resource: recurso
respect: respeito
respond: responder, reagir
responsibility: responsabilidade
responsible: responsável
rest: resto; os(as) demais
restoration: restauração
restricted: restrito(a)
restroom: banheiro
result: resultado
résumé: *curriculum vitae*
retail: varejo; comércio
retain: reter
retrieve: recuperar
return: retorno; retornar
reuse: reutilizar
reverse: reverter, inverter
review: rever; revisão; resenha
reward: premiar; recompensar
rewrite: reescrever
rhythm: ritmo
rice: arroz
ride: cavalgar; andar de
right: certo(a); direita; direito
right now: imediatamente, neste momento
right-wing: de direita (partido político)
ring: tocar (telefone)
ringleader: chefe do bando
rise: subir; erguer; levantar-se
rising tide: maré alta
risk: risco
rivalry: rivalidade
river: rio
riverbank: margem de rio
rob: roubar
rock: pedra, rocha

Rice

role: papel
room: quarto (cômodo de uma casa), sala
root: raiz
rubber: borracha
rule: regra
run: correr; temporada
run afoul: ir contra
run after: correr atrás
run away: fugir
run off: fugir
runner: corredor(a) (pessoa)
running: corrida
rush: apressar(-se)
rush out: fugir

S

sack: saco
sacrifice: sacrificar
sadly: infelizmente
safe: seguro(a)
safety: segurança
sail: ir de barco; velejar
sailing: vela (esporte)
sailor: marinheiro(a)
salad: salada
sale: liquidação
sales: vendas
salesperson: vendedor(a)
same: mesmo(a)
sandwich: sanduíche
sanitary: higiênico(a)
sanitation: saneamento
sardine: sardinha
satisfaction: satisfação
save: salvar; economizar
scale: escala
scenario: cenário
scene: cena
scholarship: bolsa de estudos
school yard: pátio da escola
schoolboy: aluno
schoolgirl: aluna
schooling: educação (escolar)
science-based: com base científica

Sailing

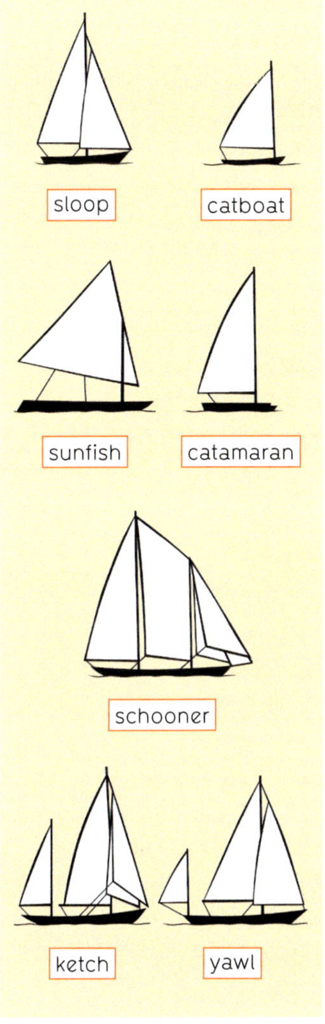

scientist: cientista
scream: gritar
screen: tela
screwdriver: chave de fenda
sculptor: escultor(a)
sculpture: escultura
sea: mar
search: procurar
season: estação
seat: assento
secretary: secretário(a)
secretive: reservado (lugar)
see: ver
seek: procurar
seem: parecer
segment: segmento
select: selecionar
selection: seleção
self-esteem: autoestima
self-medication: automedicação
self-reflect: refletir sobre si mesmo
sell: vender
send: enviar
sense: sentido
sentence: frase
separate: separar
September: setembro
serious: sério(a), grave
servant: empregado(a); serviçal
serve: servir
set: ajustar, acertar; consertar; engessar; estabelecer; conjunto
set aside: pôr de lado
set off: começar
set off a flare: soltar um rojão sinalizador
sever: cortar; romper (relações)
several: vários(as)
severe: sério(a), grave; severo(a)
severely: duramente
sewing: costura
sex: sexo
shake: tremor; sacudir, agitar
shape: forma
share: compartilhar, dividir
sharp: afiado(a)
sheriff: delegado(a)
shine: brilhar; brilho
ship: navio
shipping: frete
shirt: camisa
shirtless: sem camisa
shock: choque
shoe: sapato
shooting: tiroteio
shop: loja
shopping bag: sacola de compras

Sewing

shopping cart: carrinho de supermercado
shore: costa, litoral
short: curto(a)
short stories: contos
shortage: escassez
shorter: mais curto(a)
shortly after: logo depois
short-term: a curto prazo
should: deveria
should be: seria
shoulder: ombro
shout: gritar
show: mostrar, demonstrar; espetáculo
show up: aparecer; comparecer
shower: banho de chuveiro
shrink: encolher
shy: tímido(a)
sick: doente
sickness: doença
side: lado
sideshow: apresentação secundária
sign: sinal
silent: silencioso(a)
silently: silenciosamente
silicon: silicone
silver: prata
simply: simplesmente
since: desde (que)
since then: desde então
sing: cantar
singer: cantor(a)
single: solteiro(a); único(a), só
single-handed: sozinho(a), sem ajuda
sister-in-law: cunhada
sixties: década de sessenta
size: tamanho
ski: esquiar; esqui
skiing: esqui (esporte)
skill: habilidade, destreza
sky: céu
slam: bater algo com violência
slave: escravo(a)
slavery: escravidão

Shape

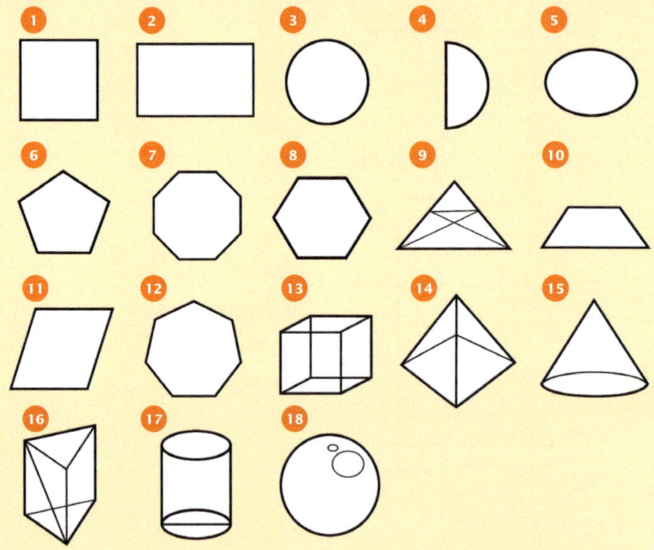

1 square
2 rectangle
3 circle
4 semicircle
5 oval
6 pentagon
7 octagon
8 hexagon
9 isosceles triangle
10 trapezium
11 parallelogram
12 heptagon
13 cube
14 pyramid
15 cone
16 prism
17 cylinder
18 sphere

sledge: trenó
sleep: dormir
sleeping sickness: doença do sono
slew: muitos
slightly: levemente
slim: magro(a)
slow: retardar; lento(a)
slow down: diminuir a velocidade
slowly: lentamente
slum: favela
small: pequeno(a)
smart: inteligente, esperto(a)
smash: esmagar
smile: sorrir
smoke: fumar; fumaça
snail: caracol
snake: cobra
so: assim, então; tão
so far: até agora

so many: tantos
soccer: futebol
soccer-mad nation: país louco por futebol
society: sociedade
sodium: sódio
softly: suavemente
soil: solo
sold: vendido(a)
sole: único(a); exclusivo(a)
solidify: solidificar
solo: desacompanhado(a); solo (música)
solve: resolver, solucionar
some: algum(a), alguns(mas)
someone: alguém
sometimes: às vezes
son: filho
song: música, canção
songwriter: compositor(a) de canção
soon: logo, em breve

Soccer

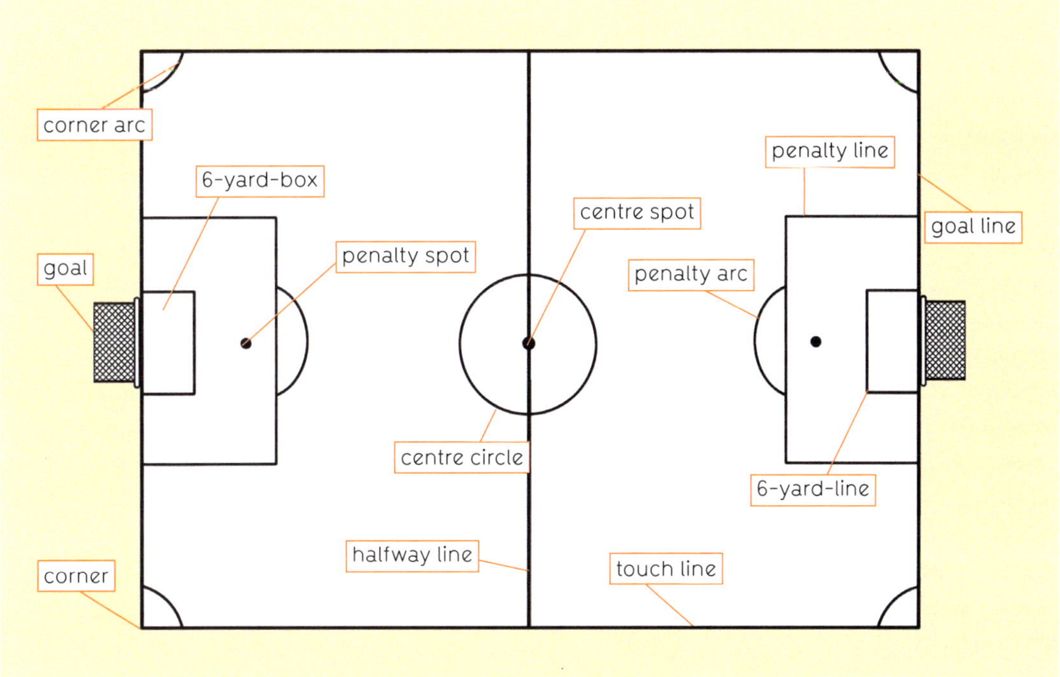

sort: classificar, separar
soul: alma
soundtrack: trilha sonora
soup: sopa
source: fonte
south: sul
southwards: em direção ao sul
Spain: Espanha
span of time: período de tempo
Spanish: espanhol(a); espanhol (língua)
spark: provocar
speak: falar
speaker: palestrante, orador(a); falante
special: especial
specialized: especializado(a)
specific: específico(a)
speech: discurso, fala
speed: velocidade
speed boat: lancha
speed up: acelerar
spend: gastar; passar (tempo)
spilled: derramado(a)
spinal cord: coluna vertebral
spokesperson: porta-voz
sponsor: patrocinar; patrocínio
spotlight: refletor, holofote
spotting tour: turismo de observação
spread: espalhar(-se); disseminação, propagação
spring: primavera
sprint: corrida de velocidade
sprinting potential: potencial para correr
square: praça; quadrado
stable: estábulo
stage: palco; estágio, fase
staggering: surpreendente
stairs: escada
stamp: carimbo
stand: arquibancada; ficar, permanecer
stand for: significar
stand up: levantar-se, ficar de pé
starring: estrelando
start: começar
state: declarar; estado
statement: declaração, afirmação
stay: ficar, permanecer
stay away: ficar longe
steak: bife
steal: roubar
stealing: roubo
steel band: banda de metais
stem cell: célula-tronco
step: passo; etapa
step family: família adotiva
step in: entrar
steroid: esteroide
stigma: estigma, marca
still: ainda; parado(a)
stimulate: estimular
stolen: roubado(a)
stomach: estômago
stomach acid: ácido gástrico
stool: banquinho
stop: parar
stop the newspaper: interromper a entrega do jornal
storage: armazenamento
store: loja; armazenar
storm: tempestade
story: história; conto

story-teller: contador(a) de histórias
story-telling: contação de histórias
straight: direto, reto
stranger: desconhecido(a), estranho(a)
strangle: estrangular; reprimir
strap: tira, alça
straw: palha
strawberry: morango
street: rua
strength: força
strengths: pontos positivos/fortes
stress: enfatizar; estresse, tensão
stretch: esticar
stretching: alongamento
strewn: esparramado(a)
strict: rígido(a), severo(a)
strike: bater, atingir
strive: esforçar-se
stroke: derrame
strong: forte
strongly: fortemente
student: estudante, aluno(a)
studio: estúdio; ateliê
study: estudo; estudar
study hard: estudar muito
stuff: coisas
stuffy: enfadonho(a)
style: estilo
subject: assunto; matéria escolar
subjective: subjetivo(a)
sub-Saharan Africa: África subsaariana
substance: substância
substitute: substituir
succeed: ser bem-sucedido(a)
success: sucesso
successful: bem-sucedido(a)
such: tal
such as: tal/tais como
suck: chupar; aspirar
suck up: absorver, aspirar, sorver
suddenly: de repente
sue: processar
suffer: sofrer
suffix: sufixo
sugar: açúcar
suggest: sugerir
suitable: adequado(a)
summary: resumo
summer: verão
summon: intimar, convocar
sun: sol
Sunday: domingo
sunlight: luz solar
sunrise: amanhecer
supplier: fornecedor(a)
supply: suprir, fornecer
support: apoio; sustentar
suppose: supor, achar
sure: certamente; certo(a), com certeza
surface: superfície
surgeon: cirurgião(ã)
surgery: cirurgia

Street

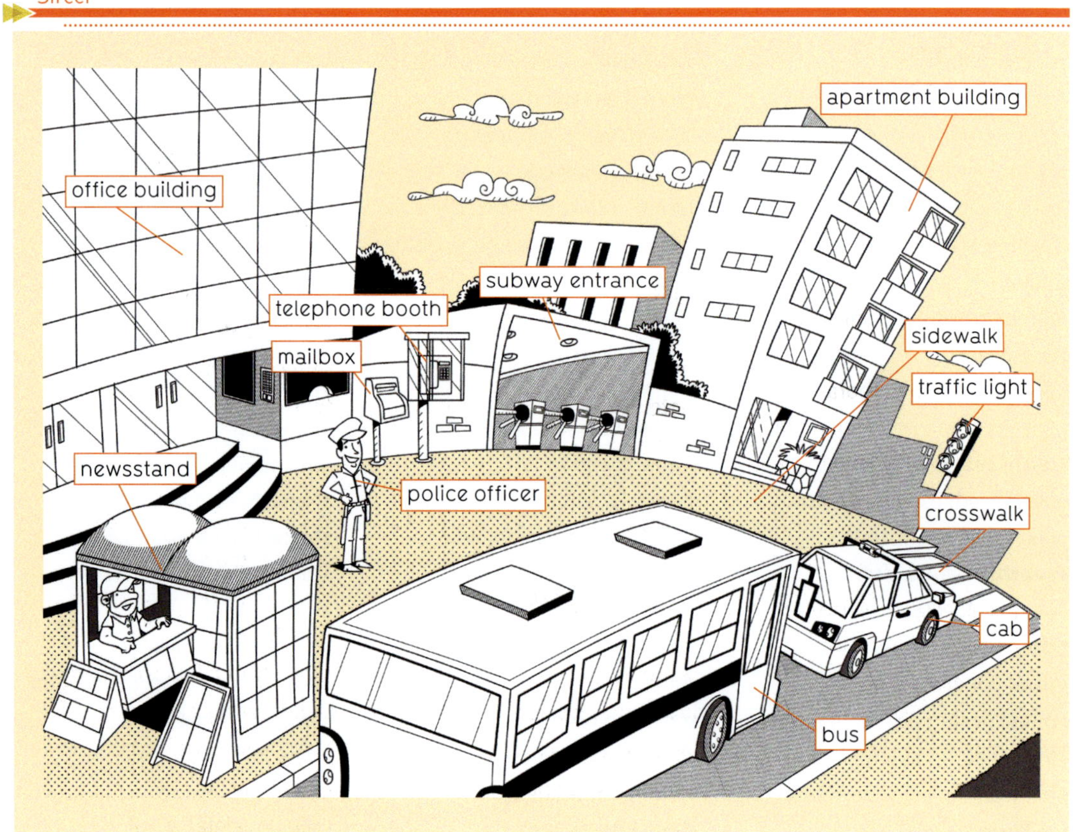

surprise: surpresa
surprised: surpreso(a)
survey: pesquisar; pesquisa
survival: sobrevivência
survive: sobreviver
suspend: suspender
suspicious: suspeito(a)
sustainability: sustentabilidade
sustainable: sustentável
sweat: suar; suor
sweep the floor: varrer o chão
sweet: doce
sweetheart: querido(a)
sweets: doces
swelling: inchaço
swim: nadar
swimmer: nadador(a)
swimming: natação
swimming pool: piscina
swing: girar
switch: trocar, mudar
sworn: juramentado
symbol: símbolo
symptom: sintoma
synonym: sinônimo
synopsis: sinopse
synthetic: sintético(a)
system: sistema

Symbol

1 baggage lockers
2 currency exchange
3 first aid
4 lost and found
5 escalator
6 nursery
7 rail transportation
8 water transportation
9 elevator
10 stairs-up
11 bus
12 ground transportation
13 car rental
14 mail
15 telephone
16 ticket purchase
17 baggage claim
18 immigration
19 no parking
20 no entry
21 litter disposal
22 waiting room
23 information
24 coffee shop

T

table: mesa
table top: tampo de mesa
take: pegar; levar; tomar
take away: levar embora
take care: cuidar, tomar conta
take oath: fazer juramento
take off: tirar (roupa, óculos, sapatos); decolar
take out: tirar, extrair
take place: acontecer, ocorrer
tale: conto
talent: talento
talk: conversar; falar
tall: alto(a)
tap: bater
tape: fita
tapir: anta
target: dirigir-se a; alvo
task: tarefa
taste: experimentar (comida); sabor
tattoo: tatuagem
tea: chá
teach: ensinar
teacher: professor(a)
teaching: ensinamento
team: time
technique: técnica
technology: tecnologia
teddy: urso de pelúcia
teen: adolescente
teenager: adolescente
teeth (pl. de *tooth*): dentes
tell: contar, dizer
tend: cuidar; tender
tenderly: ternamente, com ternura
term: termo
terrible: terrível
terribly: extremamente
text: texto
than: do que (em comparações)
thank: agradecer
thank-you letter: carta de agradecimento
that: aquele(a), aquilo

that way: desse jeito
the day before: no dia anterior, na véspera
the one: aquele(a); único(a)
theater: teatro
theater play: peça de teatro
themselves: eles(as) mesmos(as)
then: então
theoretical: teórico(a)
theoretically: teoricamente
theorist: teórico(a)
theory: teoria
therapist: terapeuta
there: lá, ali
there are: há
therefore: portanto
these: estes(as), esses(as)
thief: ladrão, ladra
thieves: ladrões, ladras
thin: magro(a)
thing: coisa
think: pensar, achar
think up: inventar
third: terço; terceiro(a)
thirsty: com sede
this: este(a), esse(a); isto, isso
those: aqueles(as)
though: embora
thoughtfully: refletidamente
thousand: mil
threat: ameaça
threaten: ameaçar
thrill: encantar
through: através de, por
throughout: durante todo; em todo
throw: atirar
thruway: via expressa; estrada
thug: brigão(ona), encrenqueiro(a)
thumping: com batida
thus: assim, portanto
tick: carrapato
tie: amarrar; dar um nó
tilt: inclinar
time: vez; tempo; hora
tin: lata
tiny: minúsculo(a)
tip: dica
tired: cansado(a)
tissue: tecido
title: título
to: para
to a certain extent: até certo ponto
to date: até esta data
to some extent: até certo ponto
today: hoje
together: junto(a), juntos(as)
toil: trabalhar duro, labutar

Theater

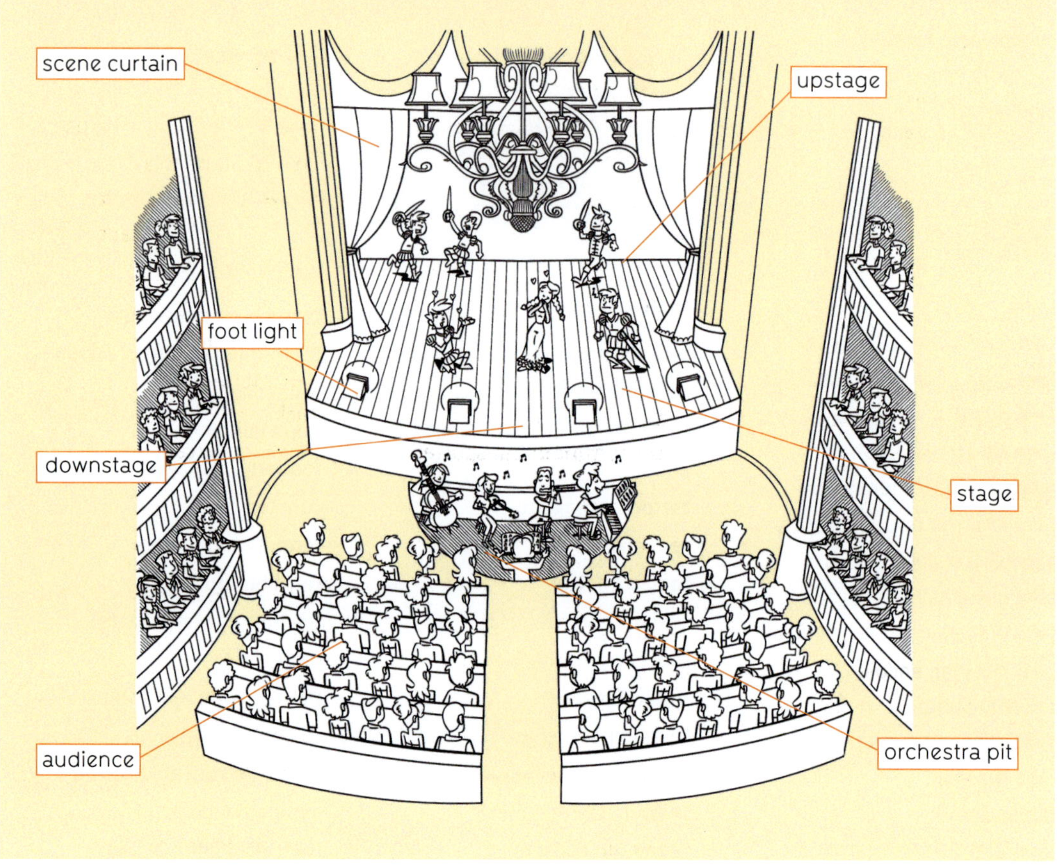

Track and field

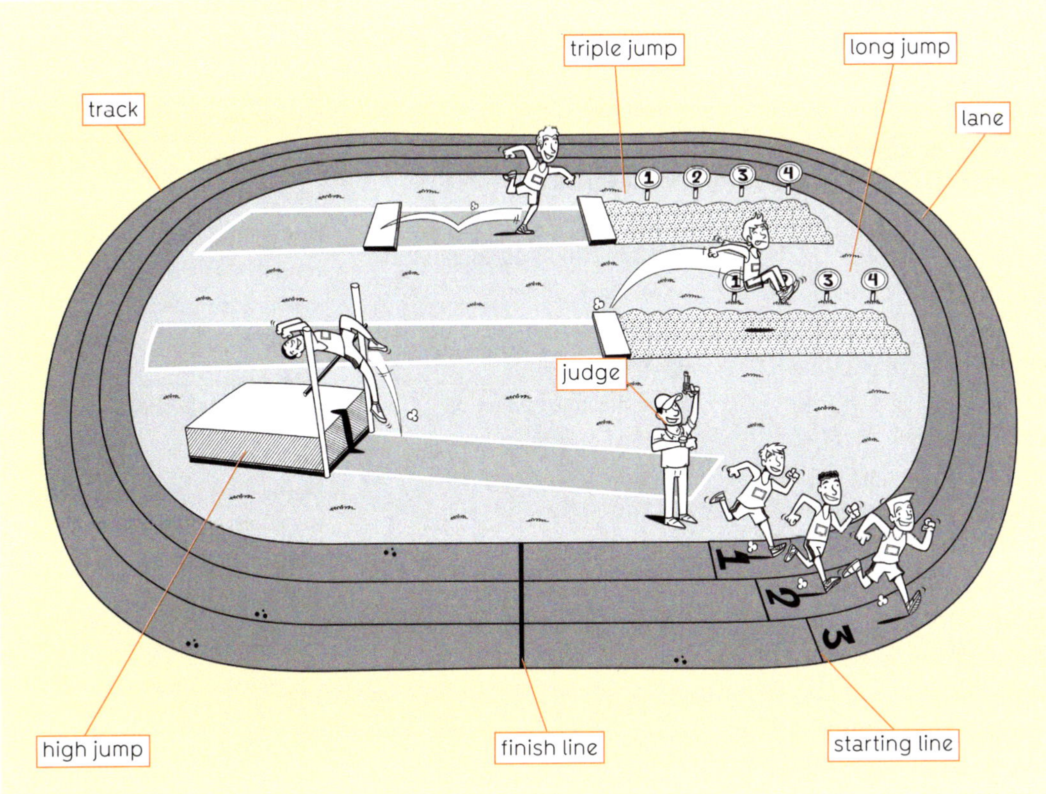

toll: dano
tomato: tomate
tomorrow: amanhã
ton: tonelada
tone: tom
tonight: hoje à noite
too: também (em frases afirmativas); demais
too long: muito tempo
too much: demais
tool: ferramenta, instrumento, equipamento
tooth: dente
top of the hill: topo da colina
tornado: tufão; furacão
torture: tortura
toucan: tucano
touch: tocar, encostar
tour: excursão, passeio
toward: em direção a
tower: torre
town: cidade
toy: brinquedo
trace: seguir; traçar
track and field: atletismo
traffic jam: engarrafamento de trânsito
tragedy: tragédia
trail: trilha
train: trem
trained: treinado(a)
training: treinamento
transfer: transferir
translate: traduzir
transportation: transporte
trap: armadilha
travel: viajar
tray: bandeja
treat: tratar
tree: árvore
treefrog: perereca
trek: caminhar; caminhada
trend: tendência
trial: tentativa; julgamento
trip: viagem
triumph: triunfo
triumphant: triunfante
tropics: trópico
trouble: problema, confusão
true: verdadeiro(a)
truly: verdadeiramente
trust: confiar; confiança
truth: verdade
try: tentar
tsetse fly: mosca-tsé-tsé
T-shirt: camiseta
tuck: guardar; cobrir
Tuesday: terça-feira
tuna: atum
turn: virar(-se); dar a volta; tornar-se
turn against: voltar-se contra
turn away: expulsar; rejeitar
turn back: voltar para
turn down: recusar
turn into: transformar(-se)
turn off: desligar
turn on: ligar

turn out: resultar, acontecer
twist: torcer; girar
two: dois, duas
type: tipo
typical: típico(a)
typically: tipicamente

U

UK (United Kingdom): Reino Unido
ulcer: úlcera
ultimatum: ultimato
umbrella: guarda-chuva
UN (United Nations): ONU (Organização das Nações Unidas)
unabated: sem diminuição
unable: incapaz
unattended: largado(a); desacompanhado(a)
unavoidable: inevitável
unbelievable: inacreditável
uncle: tio
uncomfortable: desconfortável
unconscious: inconsciente
under: sob, embaixo de
undercover: secreto(a)
undergo: passar por; submeter-se a
underline: sublinhar
underneath: embaixo
understand: entender, compreender
understudy: ator (atriz) substituto(a)
undertake: comprometer-se
unemployed: desempregado(a)
unforgettable: inesquecível
unfortunately: infelizmente
unhappy: infeliz
unimportant: sem importância
uninteresting: desinteressante
unknown: desconhecido(a)
unless: a menos que, senão
unlike: diferente; ao contrário de
unnatural: não natural
unsafe: inseguro(a)
unscramble: desembaralhar
until: até (que)
untrained: destreinado(a)
untreated: não tratado(a)
unwanted: indesejado(a)
up to: até
update: atualizar
upper: superior
upper income: alta renda
upset: aborrecido(a)
up-to-date: atualizado(a)
use: usar; uso
used: usado(a)
used to: costumava
usher: conduzir
usually: geralmente
utility: utilidade; serviço de utilidade pública

V

vacations: férias
valley: vale
value: valor
various: vários(as)
vegetable: verdura; legume
venue: local
veranda: varanda
verb: verbo
version: versão
very: muito
very moment: exato instante
vessel: vaso (sanguíneo)
vest: colete
view: olhar, ver, examinar; vista
virtually: virtualmente
visit: visitar; visita
vocabulary: vocabulário
voice: voz
voluntary: voluntário(a) (adj.)
volunteer: voluntário(a) (subst.)
vulnerable: vulnerável

W

wade: andar com dificuldade pela água ou lama
wagon: carroça
wait: esperar
wake up: acordar
walk: andar, caminhar; caminhada
walk away: ir embora
walkway: passarela
wall: muro, parede
wander: perambular
want: querer
war: guerra
warehouse: depósito
warm: morno(a)
warming: aquecimento
warning: alerta; advertência
wash: lavar
washing machine: máquina de lavar roupa
waste: dejeto, lixo, detrito; desperdiçar
watch: assistir a, ver, observar; relógio de pulso
watch out: tomar cuidado
water: regar; água
water body: reservatório
water table: lençol freático
waterfall: cachoeira
watermelon: melancia
way: caminho; jeito, maneira
way of life: modo de vida
weak: fraco(a)
weaken: enfraquecer
weaknesses: pontos negativos/fracos
wear: usar, vestir
wear off: enfraquecer, desgastar
weather: tempo (clima)
weather forecast: previsão do tempo
web: rede, internet
web site: página da internet
wedding: casamento
week: semana
weight: peso

weird: estranho(a), esquisito(a)
welfare: bem-estar, prosperidade
well-being: bem-estar
well-defined: bem definido(a)
well-done: bem passado(a); benfeito(a)
well-exercised: bem exercitado(a)
well-intentioned: bem-intencionado(a)
well-known: bem conhecido(a)
west: oeste
wetland: pântano
what kind: que tipo
whatever: qualquer coisa que, o que quer que seja
wheelchair: cadeira de rodas
when: quando
whenever: sempre que
where: onde
wherever: onde quer que
whether: se
which: que; o(a) qual
while: enquanto; embora
whilst: enquanto
who: quem
whoever: quem quer que
whole: todo(a)
why: por que
wide: amplo(a), largo(a)
widespread: muito espalhado(a), difundido(a)
wife: esposa
win: vencer
window: janela
wine: vinho
wing: asa
winter: inverno
wish: desejar; gostaria; desejo
with: com
withdraw: afastar(-se), retirar(-se)
withdrawal symptoms: síndrome de abstinência
within: dentro de (tempo)
without: sem
witness: testemunha
wolf: lobo
woman: mulher
wonderful: maravilhoso(a)
wood: madeira
word: palavra
work: trabalhar; trabalho, obra
worker: trabalhador(a)
workplace: local de trabalho
workshop: oficina
world: mundo; mundial
World Cup: Copa do Mundo
worldwide: em todo o mundo, mundial
worn-out: desgastado(a)
worry: preocupar-se
worse: pior
worship: adorar, venerar; veneração
worst: o(a) pior
would be: seria
would rather: preferir
wound: ferimento
wrap: embrulhar
write: escrever
writer: escritor(a)
wrong: errado(a)

Y

yard: pátio
year: ano
yellow fever: febre amarela
yesterday: ontem
yet: já; ainda; contudo
You are good for nothing.: Você não serve para nada.
You are not going to make it.: Você não vai conseguir.
young: jovem
youngest: o(a) mais novo(a)
yourself: você mesmo(a)
youth: juventude

Z

zinc: zinco

Infinitivo	Passado simples	Particípio passado	Tradução
to arise	arose	arisen	erguer, levantar
to awake	awoke	awoken	acordar
to be	was/were	been	ser, estar
to bear	bore	born/borne	suportar, aguentar
to beat	beat	beaten	vencer, derrotar
to become	became	become	tornar-se
to begin	began	begun	começar, iniciar
to bend	bent	bent	dobrar, curvar
to bet	bet	bet	apostar
to bite	bit	bitten	morder
to bleed	bled	bled	sangrar
to blow	blew	blown	soprar
to break	broke	broken	quebrar
to bring	brought	brought	trazer
to build	built	built	construir
to burn	burnt/burned	burnt/burned	queimar
to burst	burst	burst	explodir, estourar
to buy	bought	bought	comprar
to cast	cast	cast	lançar
to catch	caught	caught	pegar, apanhar
to choose	chose	chosen	escolher
to cling	clung	clung	agarrar, apegar-se
to come	came	come	vir
to cost	cost	cost	custar
to creep	crept	crept	rastejar
to cut	cut	cut	cortar
to deal	dealt	dealt	lidar, tratar
to dig	dug	dug	cavar
to do	did	done	fazer
to draw	drew	drawn	desenhar; sacar
to drink	drank	drunk	beber
to drive	drove	driven	dirigir, guiar
to eat	ate	eaten	comer

Infinitivo	Passado simples	Particípio passado	Tradução
to fall	fell	fallen	cair
to feed	fed	fed	alimentar
to feel	felt	felt	sentir
to fight	fought	fought	lutar, brigar
to find	found	found	achar, encontrar
to fling	flung	flung	arremessar, lançar
to fly	flew	flown	voar
to forget	forgot	forgotten	esquecer
to forgive	forgave	forgiven	perdoar
to freeze	froze	frozen	congelar
to get	got	got/gotten	obter, conseguir
to give	gave	given	dar
to go	went	gone	ir
to grow	grew	grown	crescer
to hang	hung	hung	pendurar
to have	had	had	ter
to hear	heard	heard	ouvir
to hide	hid	hidden	esconder
to hit	hit	hit	bater, chocar-se
to hold	held	held	segurar; realizar
to hurt	hurt	hurt	ferir
to keep	kept	kept	manter
to know	knew	known	saber, conhecer
to lay	laid	laid	pôr, colocar
to lead	led	led	conduzir; liderar
to learn	learned/learnt	learned/learnt	aprender
to leave	left	left	partir, deixar
to lend	lent	lent	emprestar
to let	let	let	deixar, permitir
to lie	lay	lain	deitar(-se), jazer
to light	lighted/lit	lighted/lit	acender, iluminar
to lose	lost	lost	perder
to make	made	made	fazer

Infinitivo	Passado simples	Particípio passado	Tradução
to mean	meant	meant	significar, querer dizer
to meet	met	met	encontrar(-se), reunir(-se)
to misunderstand	misunderstood	misunderstood	entender mal
to pay	paid	paid	pagar
to put	put	put	pôr, colocar
to quit	quit	quit	desistir, abandonar
to read	read	read	ler
to ride	rode	ridden	cavalgar, andar a/de
to ring	rang	rung	soar, tocar (campainha)
to rise	rose	risen	erguer; levantar-se
to run	ran	run	correr
to saw	sawed	sawed/sawn	serrar
to say	said	said	dizer
to see	saw	seen	ver
to seek	sought	sought	procurar
to sell	sold	sold	vender
to send	sent	sent	enviar
to set	set	set	pôr; dispor
to sew	sewed	sewed/sewn	costurar
to shake	shook	shaken	agitar
to shine	shone	shone	brilhar
to shoot	shot	shot	atirar
to show	showed	showed/shown	mostrar, demonstrar
to shrink	shrank	shrunk	encolher
to shut	shut	shut	fechar
to sing	sang	sung	cantar
to sink	sank	sunk	afundar
to sit	sat	sat	sentar
to sleep	slept	slept	dormir
to slide	slid	slid	escorregar
to slit	slit	slit	fender, cortar
to smell	smelled/smelt	smelled/smelt	cheirar
to sow	sowed	sowed/sown	semear

Infinitivo	Passado simples	Particípio passado	Tradução
to speak	spoke	spoken	falar
to speed	speeded/sped	speeded/sped	acelerar
to spend	spent	spent	gastar; passar (o tempo)
to spin	spun	spun	girar
to split	split	split	dividir, partir
to spread	spread	spread	espalhar
to spring	sprang	sprung	saltar, pular
to stand	stood	stood	ficar, permanecer
to steal	stole	stolen	roubar
to stick	stuck	stuck	grudar
to sting	stung	stung	picar, ferroar
to strike	struck	struck	bater, golpear
to string	strung	strung	amarrar
to swear	swore	sworn	jurar; xingar
to sweat	sweated/sweat	sweated/sweat	suar
to sweep	swept	swept	varrer
to swim	swam	swum	nadar
to swing	swung	swung	balançar
to take	took	taken	pegar; tomar
to teach	taught	taught	ensinar
to tear	tore	torn	rasgar
to tell	told	told	contar; dizer
to think	thought	thought	pensar
to throw	threw	thrown	jogar, atirar
to understand	understood	understood	entender, compreender
to wake	waked/woke	waked/woken	acordar
to wear	wore	worn	vestir, usar
to weave	wove	woven	tecer
to wed	wed	wed	casar
to weep	wept	wept	chorar
to wet	wet	wet	molhar
to win	won	won	vencer
to wind	wound	wound	dar corda; serpentear
to wring	wrung	wrung	retorcer-se; apertar (a mão)
to write	wrote	written	escrever

Roteiro de Utilização do CD